MW00445950

God in
Three
Persons

God in Three Persons

A Contemporary Interpretation of the Trinity

Millard J. Erickson

Baker Books

A Division of Baker Book House Co
Grand Rapids, Michigan 49516

© 1995 by Millard J. Erickson

Published by Baker Books
a division of Baker Book House Company
P.O. Box 6287, Grand Rapids, MI 49516-6287

Second printing, March 1996

Printed in the United States of America

All rights reserved. No part of this publication may be reproduced, stored in a retrieval system, or transmitted in any form or by any means—electronic, mechanical, photocopy, recording, or any other—without the prior written permission of the publisher. The only exception is brief quotations in printed reviews.

Library of Congress Cataloging–in–Publication Data

Erickson, Millard J.
    God in three persons : a contemporary interpretation of the Trinity / Millard J. Erickson.
        p.   cm.
    Includes bibliographical references and indexes.
    ISBN 0-8010-3229-6
    1. Trinity. 2. Trinity—History of doctrines. 3. Trinity—Biblical teaching.
    I. Title.
    BT111.2.E25   1995
    231′.044—dc20   94-46191

Unless otherwise indicated, Scripture taken from the HOLY BIBLE, NEW INTERNATIONAL VERSION®. NIV®. Copyright © 1973, 1978, 1984 by International Bible Society. Used by permission of Zondervan Publishing House. All rights reserved.

To
Karl Isagani Erickson Inoferio
my companion during the writing of a number of these pages
with prayer that he may grow up to
know, love, and serve
the Triune God

Contents

Preface

There are special times when certain doctrines rise to a place of unusual importance and urgency. For reasons that I enumerate in the opening chapter of this book, I believe that at the present time the Trinity is such a doctrine. While certainly one of the most difficult of all doctrines, it deserves close reexamination in our time.

This work grows out of the conviction that the present intellectual and cultural situation calls for restating the traditional doctrine of the Trinity. As with the doctrine of the incarnation, a number of terms and formulas used in the past no longer really suffice to deal with the questions currently being posed. Some persons continue to mouth those expressions, not realizing that they do not relate to the most urgent questions of the present, and perhaps are not even clear in their denotation. Thus, repeating those formulas will not be sufficient, if we are to be responsibly contemporary. Somewhat contrary to my expectation and intention, the outline of this book has taken a form very similar to my earlier work on the person of Christ, *The Word Became Flesh,* although I have consciously shortened somewhat the problems section. The plan of the book involves tracing the process by which the church formulated the classical construction of the doctrine, then describing the major contemporary challenges to that construction, and finally responding to those challenges as well as dealing with some other current issues of both theoretical and practical importance. Readers should note that this work is not intended to serve as a complete history of the doctrine, or to examine every obscure theologian or minute issue that has arisen in that history.

This book represents the first product of my current appointment as research professor of theology at Southwestern Baptist Theological Seminary. I am especially indebted to former Presi-

9

dent Russell Dilday for this appointment, which enables me to give primary investment of my time and energies to theological research and writing, and to Dr. Bruce Corley, dean of the School of Theology, for allowing me to structure my teaching assignment to maximize those efforts. My students in an elective course on this subject at Southwestern Baptist Seminary during the fall of 1992 and the summer of 1993 gave me helpful feedback and raised important questions. Portions of chapters 1, 6, 11, 12, and 14 were given as the Kenneth S. Kantzer lectures in systematic theology at Trinity Evangelical Divinity School, Deerfield, Illinois, February 16 and 17, 1994. Questions and comments by faculty and staff helped me sharpen my thinking at a number of points. Conversations with Dr. Donald Carson, Dr. John Feinberg, and Dr. Paul Feinberg proved especially helpful. Dr. Norman Gulley, professor of theology at Southern College of Seventh-Day Adventists, read the entire manuscript and offered several helpful suggestions, especially regarding chapters 14 and 15. The administration of United Theological Seminary of the Twin Cities, New Brighton, Minnesota, and especially the director of its library, Dr. Arthur L. Merrill, extended me special hospitality and service during a transitional period in my career. Mr. Jim Weaver of Baker Books offered helpful suggestions and encouragement, and Maria denBoer's editing did much to improve the manuscript. In the final analysis, however, all shortcomings of this book are my responsibility.

Introduction

The Importance of the Doctrine of the Trinity for Today

Almost from its inception and throughout its history, the church has faced a variety of theological problems. It solved some in relatively short time. It thought through the issues, using its collective theological knowledge and ability, and came up with answers. Other problems took a longer time to resolve; however, they were then dealt with definitively, so that the church had only to consult what it had said previously, and the questions were answered. Yet other problems were the result of certain cultural situations, so that once that time and situation were past, the issues were no longer pertinent.

The doctrine of the Trinity is virtually unique among doctrines in terms of its perennial pertinence. It was the first major theological issue to which the church turned its attention, and is still of great importance today. Although the church reached its decision regarding the formal statement that it would make on this doctrine quite early, the Trinity has continued to attract attention throughout the history of the church—even to this very time.

This doctrine in many ways presents strange paradoxes. It is very widely held. It is not simply the special view of a particular denomination or sect. It is part of the faith of the universal church. Yet it is a widely disputed doctrine, which has provoked discussion throughout all the centuries of the church's existence. It is held by many with great vehemence and vigor. These advocates are certain they believe the doctrine, and consider it crucial to the Christian faith. Yet many are unsure of the exact meaning of their belief. It was the very first doctrine dealt with systematically by the church, yet it is still one of the most misunderstood and disputed doctrines. Further, it is not clearly or explicitly taught anywhere in Scripture, yet it is widely regarded as a central doctrine, indispensable to the Christian faith. In this regard, it goes contrary to what is virtually an axiom of biblical doctrine, namely, that there is a direct correlation between the scriptural clarity of a doctrine and its cruciality to the faith and life of the church.

In view of the difficulty of the subject and the great amount of effort expended to maintain this doctrine, we may well ask ourselves what might justify all this trouble. What is the special importance of the doctrine of the Trinity, especially for our time?

Historical Priority

The first dimension of the answer to this question is historical or chronological. This was the first doctrine really to captivate the church. Even the disputes about the person of Christ were at least initially a function of this issue. The church considered this issue too important to ignore. It realized that it was dealing with a matter of spiritual life and death. Consequently, a whole series of councils was convened, each of which successively refined the church's position. While some disputed issues eventually simply fade out because the discussants weary of the matter, this one persisted over many decades. The investment of time and effort in this topic was great. As someone has put it, "The roads were filled with traveling bishops." If this doctrine was deemed important enough by the early church to commit such extensive resources to it, then it behooves us to make certain that we give it an appropriate amount of attention as well.

In a very real sense, this was the doctrinal issue on which the church cut its intellectual teeth, so to speak. It was the matter that forced the church to work out its method of correctly defining doctrine. We can therefore learn much about doing theology ourselves by examining the church's effort in this matter. Beyond that, however, this was a discussion that had far-reaching political implications. The Roman emperors realized that with the close connection between the church and the imperial government a doctrinal schism over a matter such as this had the potential for splitting the empire asunder as well.[1] Thus, the doctrine has had significance for the history of our world well beyond merely theological or ecclesiastical bounds.

Current Attention

A second major reason for the importance of the doctrine and thus for our studying it today is the great amount of attention given it in recent years by professional theologians. During the nineteenth century, very little was written on the subject, probably because the doctrine had been pushed to the periphery of theological concern and discussion. Thus, for example, Friedrich Schleiermacher assigned it to the conclusion, virtually an appendix, of his *Christian Faith.*[2] The twentieth century, in contrast, has seen a veritable outburst of interest in the doctrine, indicated by the publication of a large number of book-length treatments. A clue to the changed fortunes of the doctrine is the status that Karl Barth gave it, highlighting it in the very first volume of his *Church Dogmatics.*[3] If Barth was the theologian who opened the twentieth century and was perhaps its greatest theologian, the same could probably be said of Schleiermacher with respect to the nineteenth century. The difference in prominence each of these men gave to the Trinity is noteworthy. In addition to Barth, many major theologians of the twentieth century have given special treatment to the doctrine, among them Wolfhart Pannenberg, Eberhart Jüngel, Jürgen Moltmann, Karl Rahner, and Norman Pittenger. A doctrine that concerns this many theologians of stature certainly calls for our attention, too. For this resurgence of interest is a clue to this doctrine's importance for our time.

Books are not the only vehicle of this renaissance, however. Another way to gauge the currency of a given topic is to observe the number of journal articles treating it. Thus, counting the number of articles on the Trinity indexed in *Religion Index One: Periodicals* at a given time yields a fair indication of the doc-

1. Adolf Harnack, *History of Dogma* (New York: Dover, 1961), 4:60–67.
2. Friedrich Schleiermacher, *The Christian Faith* (New York: Harper & Row, 1963), 2:738–51.
3. Karl Barth, *Church Dogmatics* (Edinburgh: T. & T. Clark, 1975), 1:295–383.

trine's growing importance in recent years. Included in this are a number of symposia dealing with the subject of the Trinity.

Yet this literary output is not evenly distributed over the various segments of the church. There really has been no major scale doctrine of the Trinity produced for some time by persons of distinctly evangelical persuasion, despite the centrality of the doctrine in evangelical theology. Carl F. H. Henry decries this lacuna:

> But American evangelical theology has not on the whole contributed significant literature to the current revival of trinitarian interest. Evangelical publishers meet some of the rising interest by reprinting last-century volumes, and sometimes even without indicating an original publication date. The doctrine of the Trinity is seldom preached in evangelical churches; even its practical values are neglected, except for occasional emphases on the role of the economic Trinity in the church's world missionary mission ("As my Father hath sent me, even so send I you," John 20:21).[4]

Yet Henry's own treatment of this doctrine tends to be a review of the literature produced by others on the subject, rather than the original contribution that he appears to be calling for. Perhaps evangelicalism's preoccupation with its own special doctrines, such as eschatology and biblical inerrancy, has caused its theologians to neglect this crucial doctrine. It is, however, important that evangelicalism not simply allow the rest of the theological population to pass it by in the discussion of this topic. It has much to contribute to the theological enterprise, and surely that should be true with respect to this as with so many other doctrines.

Recently, my wife and I had the privilege of entertaining in our home Wolfhart Pannenberg, certainly one of the leading, if not indeed, the leading, systematic theologian of the last half of the twentieth century. I asked him, in the course of conversation, what he considered the most important doctrine for the present time. Without hesitation, he replied, "The Trinity," and then proceeded to call attention to several major recent treatments. His

4. Carl F. H. Henry, *God, Revelation and Authority: God Who Speaks and Shows* (Waco, Tex.: Word, 1982), 5:212.

judgment constituted a significant confirmation of the estimation I had previously formed.

Importance for Christian Uniqueness

Another major reason for the importance of the doctrine of the Trinity for our present time is its significance for the whole matter of Christian uniqueness. Today the word "globalization" is truly a key word in higher education. This, however, merely reflects a much broader societal phenomenon: all our activity is now being set in a context not simply of our country but of our world. This is a result of several developments that have brought us in contact with persons and cultures from other places. One of these is the increased number of persons who travel abroad, both as tourists and on business. Not only do they come in contact with other persons and cultures, but those of other cultures come in contact with them as well. The media also have contributed to this cultural cross-fertilization by providing exposure to other persons, places, and events. Communications satellites enable us to observe events as they occur half a world away. The special theological import of this phenomenon of globalization is that non-Christian religions are now no longer merely odd or unfamiliar. There also is a general sense of the similarity of other peoples to us, irrespective of cultural differences. Growing out of this is the desire to have closer relationships, to be more nearly united, with these other peoples. One obstacle to this goal has always tended to be the differences among religions. People have strong commitments to their religions, which appear to differ in so many ways that blending them would seem to be impossible.

While there are some common points among religions, some practices and doctrines are problematic. One that causes Christianity to stand out from the others is the doctrine of the Trinity. This doctrine separates Christianity from strongly monotheistic religions, such as Judaism and Islam, as well as from more polytheistic and pantheistic religions such as Buddhism and Hinduism. Increasingly attention therefore focuses on the Trinity and on the incarnation as doctrines that present obstacles to interfaith dialogue or "ecumenical ecumenism," as some have termed it.[5]

Coupled with this is another development of a more general nature: the growing tolerance on the part of Christians for those of other religions. Traditionally, Christians have regarded non-Christians primarily as objects of evangelistic endeavor. The belief of conservative Christians was, for the most part, that those who were not explicit believers in Jesus Christ were lost or outside the realm of God's grace; this naturally included adherents of other religions. More recently, there has been some change with respect to this.[6] Evangelical Christians are becoming increasingly tolerant of non-Christians. This is what James Davison Hunter has referred to as "evangelical civility," the desire not to offend anyone.[7]

One interesting and related phenomenon is the growing missionary effort of non-Christian religions. Missions is no longer a one-way matter of Christian churches sending missionaries to those of other religions. There are now growing evangelistic efforts by those groups, particularly Muslims, relative to Christianity. Some of this is happening rather naturally, through the migration of devotees of those faiths to predominantly Christian countries, especially the United States. The number of Muslims in the United States now exceeds the number of Episcopalians,[8] and their number is increasing. There is vigorous propagation of Islamic teachings throughout the United States. Saudi Arabia and other Muslim countries are spending millions of dollars in community development and other projects in America to help Muslim communities expand.[9] The increasing evangelization of Christians or of religiously uncommitted persons in Christian lands by those of non-trinitarian religions constitutes a challenge and even

5. J. Deotis Roberts, *Black Theology in Dialogue* (Philadelphia: Westminster, 1987), p. 12.

6. E.g., Clark H. Pinnock, *A Wideness in God's Mercy: The Finality of Jesus Christ in a World of Religions* (Grand Rapids: Zondervan, 1992); and John Sanders, *No Other Name: An Investigation into the Destiny of the Unevangelized* (Grand Rapids: Eerdmans, 1992).

7. James Davison Hunter, *Evangelicalism: The Coming Generation* (Chicago: University of Chicago Press, 1987), p. 35.

8. John Naisbitt and Patricia Aburdene, *Megatrends 2000: Ten New Directions for the 1990's* (New York: Avon, 1990), p. 297.

9. Russell Chandler, *Racing Toward 2001: The Forces Shaping America's Religious Future* (Grand Rapids: Zondervan, and San Francisco: Harper San Francisco, 1992), p. 184.

a threat to the doctrine of the Trinity. In addition, the most zealously evangelistic or proselytizing Christian sects, the Jehovah's Witnesses and Mormons, are decidedly non-trinitarian—more correctly, *anti*-trinitarian. All of this activity tends to have an eroding effect on the doctrine of the Trinity.

In the face of this, there is a declining effectiveness of Christian missions on a worldwide scale. This is particularly true with respect to converting people from other major world religions. Most of the success that Christian missions have enjoyed has been in securing converts from tribal religions. While the rate of conversion to Christianity has in some cases been increasing, that rate has not kept pace with world population growth, so that on a relative or comparative basis, the world is becoming progressively less Christian all the time.

Consequently, some Christians are becoming more receptive to "interfaith dialogue," in some sense other than evangelism. There is something of the sentiment that "if you can't beat 'em, join 'em." It is an expectation either that on closer examination we will see that those from other faiths are actually Christians after all (perhaps Rahner's "anonymous Christians")[10] or that all faiths when closely scrutinized turn out to be either the same, or alternate and possibly equal routes to the same goal.

These considerations raise the question of Christianity's relationship to other faiths. How unique is it? There are many areas in which this question must be posed and answered, but one of them is with respect to doctrine. Here the doctrine of the Trinity appears to be one of the most difficult, if not the most difficult, to reconcile with the doctrinal positions of other religions. It presents a major obstacle to assimilation or eclecticism for several reasons.

One of these reasons is the uniqueness of the doctrine. There really is nothing quite like this doctrine in any other religion. Some religions possess multiple deities and others have a single deity, but only Christianity claims both that God is simultaneously in some sense one and in some sense three. More recently, however, growing out of the interfaith dialogue, has come the claim by some such as Raimundo Panikkar, of parallels to the

10. Karl Rahner, *Theological Investigations* (New York: Helicon, 1969), 4:390–98.

doctrine of the Trinity in other religions as well, or, in other words, that Christianity is not totally unique in this regard.[11]

Christianity also has been emphatically monotheistic, creating a barrier to positive relationships with other religions. Here the thrust of the argument is not that its monotheism conflicts with the polytheism of other religions. Rather, its monotheism prevents it from absorbing other religions, since it either must reject their god(s) or accept the other god as being the same as its God (which it does, in the case of Judaism). Christianity cannot, without modifying its basic character, accept gods of other religions as different than its God and yet valid.

Importance to the Issue of the Content of Saving Faith

A further reason for the importance of this doctrine today is that it helps us work through the question of the nature of saving faith. One crucial component of this question is the further issue of minimal belief. To put the issue directly: What doctrinal content must a person know, understand, and believe in order to be savingly related to God? Does someone have to believe the doctrine of the Trinity in order to have eternal life and fellowship with God? This relates emphatically to the concept of "implicit faith" that is being discussed so much these days.[12] Is it possible for someone to believe in the Christian God without fully being aware of what he or she is believing? In extreme cases this leads to something like Rahner's "anonymous Christian." The doctrine of the Trinity is particularly relevant to this question. Because of its unusual character, this doctrine is not likely to be held unconsciously. Further, it is not a belief of natural theology, something that can be arrived at from observation of general revelation alone. Even Thomas Aquinas acknowledged that this doctrine is a product of revealed, not natural, theology.[13] This doctrine takes

11. Raimundo Pannikar, *The Trinity and the Religious Experience of Man* (New York: Orbis, 1973), p. viii.

12. E.g., David K. Clark, "Is Special Revelation Necessary for Salvation," in *Through No Fault of Their Own? The Fate of Those Who Have Never Heard,* ed. William V. Crockett and James G. Sigountos (Grand Rapids: Baker, 1991), pp. 41–43.

13. Thomas Aquinas, *Summa Theologiae,* Ia, 32, 1.

on heightened importance in light of the discussions regarding minimal belief.

The issue is more complex than it may appear at first glance. It is not simply a question of how many persons God is. Rather, the doctrine of the Trinity focuses on the nature of salvation and the means to it. It emphasizes the idea of God himself providing what he requires. This in turn poses the question of the human predicament, which makes this provision necessary. Hence, this doctrine is something of a keystone for a number of other doctrines. Without it, these doctrines collapse, or at least are modified or rendered unnecessary.

Perennial Importance of the Problem

Another reason for the importance of this doctrine is that it poses a continuing problem. Some doctrines, as we noted at the beginning of this chapter, are worked out and thus cease to be major problems. This is not to say that there may not be disagreement and dispute about them, but at least the issues are defined and understood, so that one grasps quite well what he or she is or is not accepting. The nature of the church and its sacramental power would be an instance of this. This state has not been attained with respect to the Trinity, however. There is still confusion about just what the doctrine denotes. The formula was worked out quite definitely in the fourth century. God is one substance or essence, existing in three persons. The difficulty is that we do not know exactly what these terms mean. We know that the doctrine states that God is three in some respect and one in some other respect, but we do not know precisely what those two different respects are.

It is not really clear that we have made significant progress in understanding the problem. We may not be much closer to being able to articulate just what we mean by this doctrine than were the delegates to the Councils of Nicea and Constantinople in A.D. 325 and 381, respectively. The doctrine of the Trinity is a perennial problem, like the problem of evil. It therefore needs our continued attention.

Another difficulty stems from the categories used by those who worked out the doctrine of the Trinity that the church adopted. They used Greek categories such as substance, essence, and person, which had corresponding Latin concepts when translated into the forms of thinking that characterized the Eastern church. Over the years, questions have been raised regarding those concepts. One contention is that the Trinity is simply a product of those ancient Greek categories. It is not present in biblical thought, but arose when biblical thought was pressed into this foreign mold.[14] Thus, the doctrine of the Trinity goes beyond and even distorts what the Bible says about God. It is a Greek philosophical, not a Hebraic biblical, concept.

Some contend that these ways of thinking may have been appropriate for that day. It made sense to those ancient people to express their belief in these terms. That way of dealing with things is not adequate for our time, however. For one thing, those concepts simply do not make sense to people today. The reference of these terms is not understood. Moreover, these are not only confusing or obscure concepts; they are untenable. Contemporary philosophy and physics have rendered the concepts of substance and essence unacceptable. They are not adequate to current understanding of the reality of this world. The very terminology is confusing and misleading, because of the change of denotation from that day. For example, the term "person" conveys a meaning quite different today from what the Latin *persona* meant in the fourth century. Whether holding that the early trinitarians were misguided or that their thought simply is no longer adequate for today, the critics of the Greek metaphysical way of expressing the Trinity are convinced that perpetuation of that language is counterproductive.[15]

There are more moderate and more radical versions of this position. More moderate persons would say that the ancient expressions are inadequate. Yet the basic meaning of these expressions can be retained and presented by using other, more adequate terminology and concepts. The more radical persons, on the other hand, insist that the idea of the Trinity is inextricably tied up with that metaphysic. It is not an essential element in

14. Cyril C. Richardson, *The Doctrine of the Trinity* (Nashville: Abingdon, 1958), pp. 32–35.

15. Maurice Wiles, *The Making of Christian Doctrine: A Study in the Principles of Early Doctrinal Development* (Cambridge: Cambridge University Press, 1967), p. 9.

Christianity. It is simply a form of expression that Christianity took at one point in time; it may be abandoned without any inherent loss to Christianity.

A Test of Religious Language

The study of the doctrine of the Trinity is also important because it presents us with an excellent case of the issue of religious language. The problem here is that of the meaningfulness of the terminology used, namely, that we do not seem to know what we are referring to. Basically, we can identify rather clearly what this form of the doctrine of God is not. It rejects both monotheism and polytheism, but just what it affirms is not as clear. Because God is not an object of our experience, it is difficult for us to describe what the doctrine of the Trinity is referring to. It appears to be without any real analogies.

On the surface, the doctrine seems to present an outright contradiction. The contention is that God is both one and three. If, however, he is one, how can he also be three? The usual response is that God is not one and three at the same time and in the same respect. If that is the case, however, what is the respect in which he is one and the respect in which he is three? That is where the vagueness becomes really serious. Distinguishing or defining just what these two dimensions of God's nature are seems at best to be quite difficult. Again, the formula appears quite vacuous.

The neoorthodox maintained that God could not really be conceptualized. He could not be thought of, or grasped, in logical categories; he could only be encountered. This is of course tied closely to a view of special revelation in which there is not communication of information, but an encounter with a person, whose presence is revelation. The difficulty here, however, comes from asking how we know, on these grounds, that God is triune. What does it mean to encounter God as triune rather than as simply one? How would a Christian's encounter with God differ from a Jew's? The usual response here is to say that we encounter, not one, but three, as God. Here again, however, how do we know that it is the Son or the Spirit, rather than the Father that we encounter? How do we know them to be one, rather than letting the doctrine slip into tritheism? This is a major problem that neoorthodoxy never fully solved. Thus, this route to the meaningfulness of language fails us as well. The thrust of this whole issue is that the doctrine of the Trinity needs attention if we are to be able to maintain the meaningfulness of religious language in general.

The Challenge of Twentieth-Century Philosophies

The study of the doctrine of the Trinity is also important because major twentieth-century philosophies threaten it. Actually, not just the doctrine of the Trinity but basically all metaphysics is undermined by these philosophies. The Trinity is especially problematic, however, because it is so strongly metaphysical. Interestingly, it is not just one philosophy or family of philosophies that presents the challenge, but most philosophies of this century. In general, the twentieth century has been hostile or averse to metaphysics and to substantives, preferring adjectives or verbs.

The first major philosophy of this century to present problems was logical positivism. This philosophy focused its attention on the issue of meaning. It basically classified all cognitively meaningful sentences into two types: mathematical-type sentences, in which the meaning of the predicate is included analytically in the subject; and scientific-type sentences, in which the predicate adds something not present in the subject. The meaning of this latter type of sentence is the set of sense data that would verify (or falsify) it. Thus, all sentences that go beyond sense experience are literally non-sense and, thus, meaningless. This was eventually seen to be too severe a truncation of the concept of meaning, however, for this principle (known as the verification principle) could be seen to be meaningless on its own terms. Thus, this type of philosophy (sometimes known as ideal-language philosophy) gave way to a more versatile and flexible type of philosophy, known as ordinary-language philosophy, or simply analytic or linguistic philosophy. This philosophy did not insist that all language must meet some preset criteria in order to be considered meaningful, but rather that there were various types of language games, and that the meaningfulness of a given type of sentence would be seen in its fulfilling the criteria of that type of sentence.

And here theological propositions, at least those of such complexity as those explicating the Trinity, seemed unduly obscure.

Pragmatism was another philosophy hostile to speculative philosophy. It insisted that the meaning of a sentence was the consequences that this sentence had for practical action. Two sentences that possessed no practical difference were not meaningfully different.[16] They were distinct but not different. Consequently, the test for theological propositions was what difference for behavior they might imply. Such doctrines as the Trinity seemed to be meaningless, abstract, far removed from practical life.

Finally, existentialism, as a uniquely twentieth-century philosophy, also posed objections to the Trinity as well as all doctrines like it. For existentialism, ideas are not for reflecting on; they are for acting on. The issue of reality is to choose, to decide, not to cogitate. Most doctrinal issues, insofar as they bog persons down in endless and fruitless speculation, deflect them from decision. They are therefore merely another form of "inauthenticity," just as excusing oneself on the basis of some causal factor or going along with the crowd.[17] The doctrine is irrelevant to life, and maybe worse, even detracts from it in the fullest sense.

The Challenge of Certain Contemporary Theologies

The study of the doctrine of the Trinity is important because it is challenged by certain twentieth-century theologies. One of these is liberation theology. In its more radical forms, liberation theology redefines theology so that it becomes critical reflection on praxis.[18] This means, however, that abstract doctrines do not furnish much basis for theologizing. In fact, history suggests that the doctrine of the Trinity has been part of a great doctrinal system that has been used to justify oppression and exploitation. Whether this doctrine was actually correlated with oppression, it has certainly accompanied such oppression.

16. William James, "What Pragmatism Means," in *Pragmatism* (New York: Meridian, 1955), pp. 42–43.

17. Martin Heidegger, *Being and Time* (New York: Harper & Row, 1962), pp. 211–19.

18. Gustavo Gutiérrez, *A Theology of Liberation: History, Politics and Salvation* (Maryknoll, N.Y.: Orbis, 1973), pp. 7–15.

Feminism has been even more outspoken and pointed in its objection to the doctrine of the Trinity. This objection comes in several different forms and at several different points. One objection is that the doctrine has fostered hierarchicalism. Just as God is Father, so the male has somehow come to be regarded with greater respect and dignity. The qualities of masculinity have been exalted. Further, the fact that Jesus was a man makes a male the object of worship. For the most part, the church, taking its lead from these doctrines, has insisted that its leadership, both lay and clergy, is to be restricted to men. This is considered fitting, since some believe the leadership is to emulate the Godhead. Thus, both the "Father" and "Son" concepts are considered by some to be inherently sexist. Some feminists are advocating the elimination of such terminology in favor of more generic role titles, such as "God the Creator, God the Redeemer, and God the Sanctifier." This, however, reduces the Trinity to a functional Trinity, thus eliminating any real distinction of persons and tending toward modalism.

The Challenge of Current Forms of Religion

There are other doctrinal challenges coming from less formal or traditional types of Christianity. The challenge, in other words, is more generically religious, although not in the sense of the world religions mentioned above. One of these is the New Age religion, which has a generally pantheizing effect. It does not so much challenge the validity of the Christian understanding of God as it does its uniqueness. Humans are to be channels of divine power. Some may conceive of the source of this power under the nomenclature of the Christian God, even the Trinity. Others, from a different background, may work with different concepts and terminology. Yet any attempt to make the Trinity exclusive or normative, as orthodox Christianity has done, must be rejected.

The other major source is the Christian sects, especially Jehovah's Witnesses, who vehemently reject the biblical doctrine of the Trinity. Frequently, Jehovah's Witnesses especially target relatively new converts of orthodox Christianity as their prospects, initially stressing those points of agreement that the two groups hold. When combined with the zealous approach generally characterizing the outreach efforts of this group, the movement constitutes a genuine challenge and threat to orthodoxy.

The Decline of Doctrine in the Church

A further reason for studying this important doctrine is the general decline of doctrine in the church, or at least in some parts of it, today. There are a number of dimensions of and reasons for this decline. One is that doctrine is not being widely taught. Generally the teaching of doctrine has been part of the process of disciplining, which follows evangelism. There appears to be a decline in this dimension of the church's traditional ministry, partly due to a change in the strategy of evangelism. Instead of church being a place where persons come to be instructed, built up in the faith, and prepared to go out into "the world" to do evangelism, it has increasingly become the place where evangelism is done. In a number of churches, Sunday morning services are geared to "seekers," persons who have not yet made a commitment to Jesus Christ and who may lack some of the essential background to do so. Instruction and edification are left to another service, often on a midweek evening. As a consequence, the Sunday morning fare is rather thin. Unfortunately, however, Sunday morning is when most people attend church, and so the level of teaching never becomes very deep.

There also is a decline in teaching because of clergy pragmatism. Increasingly the criterion of a course of action is, "if it works, do it." In a success-oriented culture like ours, there is strong pressure on a pastor to produce numerical results. Numbers are the most important consideration. People do not come to church to hear a discourse on a dry subject like the Trinity. If anything, treatises on such subjects will tend to drive people away. Consequently, any involved theory is viewed as both unnecessary and detrimental. Why introduce a subject that has been the occasion of considerable controversy in the past? And why stifle the free expression of faith with the "paralysis of analysis"?

This aversion to doctrine in turn both reflects and is reflected in the popular piety of the day. There is a great deal of romanticism in the general culture, and a consequent considerable amount of pietism in the church. There is a decided preference for feeling over against reflection or cogitation. One has only to observe the type of music currently popular in many churches to note this trend. A significant number of people want to come to church to feel good. Doctrine is not conducive to this, however. The study of doctrine is hard work, and hard work is not necessarily pleasant.

A further factor in the decline of doctrine is Hunter's concept of the civility of evangelicals. The church strives to avoid making an issue of anything that might be divisive. Certainly the doctrine of the Trinity, with its hair-splitting tendencies, fits this description. There is a need for tolerance, and that includes not only differing interpretations of the Trinity, but also different levels or stages of understanding of this subject.

Interrelatedness with Other Doctrines

The doctrine of the Trinity is also important because of its interrelatedness with other doctrines. Theology is organic, so that the view held of one doctrine also affects other doctrines. Because the Trinity is such a fundamental doctrine, alterations in it have far-reaching effects in the formulation of other doctrines. So, for example, the way one understands the Trinity has considerable implications for one's view of the atonement. The atonement may be understood as a rather unfair or unethical treatment of Jesus by God, who punished his Son unfairly for something he did not do. Conversely, the atonement may be viewed as God's own self-sacrificial action to meet his own demands. The understanding of humanity and its essential character may be illumined by the doctrine of the Trinity. Humanity as we see it, sinful and corrupt, is evidently not the way humanity is in its essence, because Jesus, the second person of the Godhead, became united with humanity. It is encouraging to realize that humanity need not forever be as we now find it empirically.

Another place where the doctrine of the Trinity comes clearly into play is in the attitude and action relative to the Holy Spirit. If we have a subordinationist view of the Trinity, the Holy Spirit may in practice be treated with less than the full respect given the other members of the Trinity. Or, conversely, we may be inclined to give the Holy Spirit more prominence than we give the other members of the Trinity, at least in practice.

If the organic character of theology means that the doctrine of the Trinity affects other doctrines, the reverse is also true. Our formulation of other doctrines will affect the conclusions we come to regarding the doctrine of the Trinity. So, for example, the recent signs and wonders movement tends to emphasize Jesus' humanity, thereby underscoring our ability to perform the same wondrous works that he did.[19] Similarly, a doctrine of the church that splits it too sharply from Old Testament Israel might tend to divide the body of Christ from the people of Jehovah, thereby fragmenting the Trinity and leading to a more tritheistic than a trinitarian view.

Effect on Practical Christian Experience

The study of the Trinity is also important because our belief in this area affects our practical Christian experience. While the correlation is not always complete or perfect, there is a relationship between these two areas. Thus, the conception of the nature of the God in whom we believe and whom we love and serve affects considerably our practice of piety. One of these areas is that of worship. If all persons of the Trinity are equally God in their being, power, and holiness, then we properly should worship all three. Our worship services should reflect that. While we will sometimes tend to emphasize one person of the Trinity more than the others, this emphasis should not be totally one-sided. For example, when we are emphasizing the atonement, a greater prominence will naturally be given to Jesus Christ, God the Son. We should, however, also include some reference to the Father, to whom the sacrifice is offered, and to the Spirit, through whom Christ offered himself up. A proper understanding of the nature of the Trinity, and the mutual relationship and equality of the members, will prevent us from falling into any sort of "Jesus only" worship.

The other major area the doctrine of the Trinity can influence is prayer. Frequently prayer seems to be engaged in without any

19. Charles H. Kraft, *Christianity with Power: Your Worldview and Your Experience of the Supernatural* (Ann Arbor, Mich.: Vine, 1989), p. 174.

conscious or explicit attention to the one to whom the prayer is offered. Prayer may be indiscriminately offered to the Father, or to Jesus, or simply to "God," without any real focusing of the object of the prayer in terms of the subject of the prayer. Sometimes the prayer is directed exclusively to one person of the Godhead. We may never pray to the Holy Spirit. Yet a correct understanding of the Trinity will and should inform our thinking so that our prayers are directed to the Godhead as a whole or to a specific person as appropriate. This is an area about which relatively little thinking has been done. Yet if all three persons are indeed deity and if each has distinctive roles to perform, then we should ask about the impact of these truths on the very practical matter of how and to whom we pray.

Lack of Authoritative Rulings for Evangelicals

Finally, studying the doctrine of the Trinity is important particularly for those of us in the free church movement because the decision of a council at some point in church history carries little significance for us. There are groups for which a magisterium decides doctrinal matters. The church possesses an authority vested in certain offices that enables the occupants of those offices to rule correctly and definitively on doctrinal and other matters. For those persons, particularly for those who hold that the history of the church carries revelatory significance, the actions of the church councils such as Nicea are authoritative. At least the correct formal understanding of the Trinity is settled by the pronouncement of those councils. Interpretation of those pronouncements is all that is now necessary.

For those in the more informal tradition, however, this does not solve the problem. Placing trust in the Bible supremely and in each Christian's ability to interpret it under the illumination of the Holy Spirit, such persons do not automatically concede the correctness of the council's conclusion. Thus, the declarations of the councils must be scrutinized and evaluated. A heavier responsibility is placed on members of this stream of Christianity than on those of other traditions.

Yet the problem is not as narrowly restricted as might seem to be the case. The number of those who would accord authority to bishops and to official councils is greatly reduced from former times. Previously the Roman Catholic Church most closely adhered to the declarations of the ecumenical councils. Yet even many members of that church have since Vatican II come to have serious questions about the binding character of councils. Thus, the issue is much more open than was once the case. Perhaps the councils did not come to correct and final conclusions. Since some councils overruled and contradicted earlier ones, in principle not all of them could have been correct. It therefore becomes incumbent on us to scrutinize carefully the creeds formulated by the councils, to make certain they embody most fully the truth about the deity.

Part 1

The Formulation of the Doctrine of the Trinity

1

Formulating the Doctrine
in the First and Second Centuries

The doctrine of the Trinity as we know it today did not simply spring full blown onto the scene of Christian thought at the beginning of the church's life. It went through a long process in which the church weighed varying interpretations of the biblical data and selected those it judged to be more adequate. At the same time, the church was progressively dealing with different and more refined issues, and in so doing was sharpening the focus of its thinking. It was defining virtually all of the issues that we face today, albeit in differing form at different periods. To trace the history of that progressive development will constitute the task of the next three chapters. We will see the doctrine of the Trinity being developed, layer by layer.

The Earliest Period

Christianity, from its very beginning, was strongly monotheistic. This was in part attributable to its origin in Judaism, with its strong monotheism, enunciated in passages such as the Shema of Deuteronomy 6. That emphasis was necessary as a protection against the inclusivism and pluralism of many Hebrews. The people of Israel tended to adopt or assimilate into their worship the deities of other peoples around them.

This same danger was also potentially present for Christianity. Whereas the Jews lived among other peoples who had their own deities (henotheism), Christianity sprang to life within the context of the Roman Empire, with its numerous deities (polytheism). Under increasing attack for the exclusiveness of their belief, Christians were in danger of purchasing peace at the price of the uniqueness and exclusiveness of their own commitment to Jehovah and to Jesus Christ. Consequently, the restriction of belief to one god was an indispensable factor in the preservation of Christianity's essence.

So strong was this emphasis that Hermas could write that the first commandment is to "believe that God is one, Who created and established all things, bringing them into existence out of non-existence."[1] This view of the oneness of God was to prove to be Christianity's bulwark against a wide variety of competitive beliefs, including pagan polytheism, the emanationist views of Gnosticism, and Marcionite dualism.[2]

The problem, however, was how to combine with this strong monotheism the new content of the Christian revelation, or what we would call the New Testament. To some adherents of Judaism, the new ideas of Christianity appeared to be some sort of polytheism, since its followers apparently worshiped more than one god. This content has been summarized by Kelly: "Reduced to their simplest, these were the convictions that God had made Himself known in the Person of Jesus, the Messiah, raising Him from the dead and offering salvation to men through Him, and that He had poured out His Holy Spirit upon the Church."[3] There was a strong belief in the special status of Jesus Christ. He was the one in whom (or through whom) they had salvation. He had more fully revealed the truth of God than had any of the prophets. And he was to be worshiped, just as the Jews had worshiped Jehovah.

In addition a unique place was given to the Holy Spirit. In the Old Testament, there had been belief in the "Spirit of God." The Spirit was not necessarily differentiated as a separate person from Jehovah; rather, the focus was on his manifestation, activity, and power. In the New Testament he was the one who had

---

1. Hermas, *Mandates* 1.1.
2. J. N. D. Kelly, *Early Christian Doctrines* (New York: Harper & Row, 1960), p. 87.
3. Ibid.

been promised by Jesus as "another comforter" (ἄλλος—another of the same kind). He was seen as the empowerer promised by Jesus (Acts 1:8), who had come upon the Christians powerfully at Pentecost as well as on later occasions. He had spoken in the past through prophets and through David. He was the source of their Scriptures.

Even before its canonization the New Testament already exerted a powerful influence, revealing both dyadic and triadic patterns. Within the liturgical and catechetical practices of the early church these patterns were beginning to emerge rather clearly. In the writings of Ignatius[4] and Justin[5] we find suggestions that these patterns had rather early begun to settle into semifixed formulas. Later in the second century there are more detailed citations of "the rule of faith," which represented the teachings passed down from the apostles and expounded in freely worded summaries.[6] Some of these formulas are dyadic in nature, while others are triadic; the latter type gradually became normative. Irenaeus gives one of these statements of the rule of faith, in which God the Father; the Word of God or Son of God, Christ Jesus our Lord; and the Holy Spirit are grouped together.[7]

This triadic pattern is also clearly present in the baptismal formula. Whether one concludes that the threefold pattern found at the conclusion of Matthew's Gospel is an authentic word of Jesus, it is apparent that the church used this formula from quite an early period. The *Didache* specifies baptism in the threefold name.[8] Justin says that "In the name of God the Father and master of all things, and of our Savior Jesus Christ, they are washed in the water."[9] In the same writing he says that baptism is "in the name of God the Father and master of all things," of "Jesus Christ, Who was crucified under Pontius Pilate," and "of the Holy Spirit, Who foretold by the prophets the whole story of Jesus."[10] Irenaeus, similarly, states, "We received baptism for the

4. Ignatius, *Epistle to the Ephesians* 18.2; *Epistle to the Trallians* 9; *Epistle to the Smyrneans* 1.1–2.
5. Justin Martyr, *First Apology* 21.1; 31.7; *Dialogue with Trypho* 63.1; 126.2.
6. Tertullian, *Prescription of Heretics* 13; *On the Veiling of Virgins* 1; *Against Praxeus* 2.
7. Irenaeus, *Proof of the Apostolic Preaching* 6.
8. *Didache* 7.1–3.
9. Justin Martyr, *First Apology* 61.3.
10. Ibid., 61.10–13.

remission of sins in the name of God the Father, and in the name of Jesus Christ, the Son of God, Who was incarnate and died and rose again, and in the Holy Spirit of God."[11]

The doxology displays a similar pattern. Justin assumed that the doxology ("Glory to the Father of all things, in the name of the Son and of the Holy Spirit") was included in the eucharistic prayer.[12] The same is true of the doxology with which Polycarp is reported to have ended his prayer before his martyrdom: "I glorify Thee through the everlasting and heavenly high-priest Jesus Christ, Thy beloved Son, through Whom be glory to Thee together with Him, and the Holy Spirit."[13]

It should be noted that the instances we have cited are from a prereflective or pretheological stage of the church's development. They represent doctrine implicitly rather than explicitly held. These constitute four levels of doctrinal activity.

1. The level of piety includes worship, evangelism, prayer, and similar practices. Beliefs here are at least implicit, but have not yet become explicit.
2. The level of doctrine involves a more conscious thinking out of what is believed, a more self-conscious form of doctrine. Also, there is more explicit teaching, indoctrination, and catechizing.
3. The level of theology encompasses the more disciplined and extensive examination of the issues of theology, often occasioned by discovery of diversity of belief within the Christian community. Awareness of the possibility of alternative positions requires more analysis and debate. The form that this activity often took was in the pattern of ecumenical councils, convened to discuss crucial doctrines and the deviations from traditional interpretations of them.
4. The level of metatheology deals not merely with the content of theology, but with its very basis and method. The question, "What is the correct doctrine?" must eventually be followed by, "How do we decide between interpreta-

11. Irenaeus, *Proof of the Apostolic Preaching* 3.
12. *First Apology* 65.
13. *Martyrdom of Polycarp* 14.3.

tions of a doctrine?" and "How do we arrive at doctrinal understandings?" Here we find the really critical examination of the discipline of theology.

The Apostolic Fathers

The next major period in the history of the church is the period frequently referred to as the apostolic fathers. These writers of the ancient church were purported to be pupils of the apostles. They included Barnabas, Hermas, Clement of Rome, Ignatius, Polycarp, Papias, and the author of the epistle to Diognetus.[14] The title "apostolic," as designating those who studied with the apostles, is problematic in the case of each of these men, but is applied most appropriately to Clement, Ignatius, and Polycarp. The designation, taken as conventional rather than descriptive, designates the earliest noncanonical writings of the late first and early second centuries.[15]

The problems the church was facing are reflected in the nature of the fathers' writings. Earlier, the primary problem had been conflict with the Jews. That conflict, however, was now largely in the past.[16] This allowed more attention to be given to the positive witness to the traditional faith. This witness was still at the second stage of doctrinal development—self-consciously doctrinal, but in the form of proclamation rather than analysis. It was, therefore, not expressed in especially systematic fashion. The materials are often fragmentary and give a variety of perspectives, rather than being homogeneous.[17]

It is helpful to compare the endeavors of these writers to what Paul was attempting to accomplish in his writings. At Corinth Paul encountered problems with the "spirit people." Consequently he found it necessary to lay down some clearer definitions of the faith, which encompassed what had been said in the original Spirit-utterances. The pastoral epistles, in particular, lay

14. "Apostolic Fathers," in *The New Schaff-Herzog Encyclopedia of Religious Knowledge*, ed. Samuel Macauley Jackson (Grand Rapids: Baker, 1960), 1:248.

15. "Apostolic Fathers," in *The New International Dictionary of the Christian Church*, ed. J. D. Douglas (Grand Rapids: Zondervan, 1974), p. 59.

16. Paul Tillich, *A History of Christian Thought: From Its Judaic and Hellenistic Origins to Existentialism* (New York: Simon and Schuster, 1967), p. 17.

17. Kelly, *Early Christian Doctrine*, p. 90.

down certain patterns of ecclesiastical order. By the time of the apostolic fathers, there was a considerable decline of reliance on the charismatic utterances. Indeed, there was a tendency to regard these utterances as relatively unnecessary. It was believed that everything the Spirit had to say had already been expressed and preserved in Scripture and the tradition. Norms and authorities were arising in the Christian congregations.[18] Relatively little place was given to inspired speeches.

When we turn to the thought of specific writers from this group, we may first note Clement of Rome, who offers relatively little direct discussion of the question of the Trinity. He does coordinate the three persons in a question, "Have we not [all] one God, and one Christ? Is there not one Spirit of grace poured out upon us?"[19] With respect to Christ, Clement assumes his preexistence, since he spoke through the Spirit in the Psalms, and is the means by which God has always ruled.[20] He is the "way in which we find our Savior, even Jesus Christ, the High Priest of all our offerings."[21] Clement understands the Holy Spirit in terms of his inspiring God's prophets in all ages, the Old Testament writers as well as himself.[22] What is notable about Clement's writing is the absence of any treatment or even any apparent awareness of the problem of the relation of the three persons to each other. Clement's thought reflects the second stage of development, doctrine, rather than that of theology, or the critical wrestling with the problems arising within one's statement of doctrine.

The second letter of Clement to the Corinthians is actually a sermon rather than an epistle. It is, indeed, the oldest surviving sermon of the Christian church after the New Testament.[23] It begins with the exhortation: "Brethren, we ought so to think of Jesus Christ as of God, as of the judge of living and dead."[24] He is the savior and revealer of the Father,[25] and, "being first of all

18. Tillich, *History of Christian Thought*, p. 18.

19. Clement of Rome, *First Epistle to the Corinthians* 46.6.

20. Ibid., 16.2; 22.1.

21. Ibid., 36.1–2.

22. Ibid., 8.1; 13.1; 16.2.

23. Jaroslav Pelikan, *The Christian Tradition: A History of the Development of Doctrine* (Chicago: University of Chicago Press, 1971), 1:173.

24. Clement of Rome, *Second Epistle* 1.1.

25. Ibid., 3.1.

spirit, Christ the Lord, who saved us, became flesh and so called us."[26] From this, one might infer that Clement has confused Christ with the Holy Spirit, but that inference is refuted by his statement later in the document that the Spirit is to be identified with the preexistent spiritual church, which is evidently distinct, in his understanding, from the preexistent Christ. It appears, therefore, from this particular writing, that Clement holds to three persons: God the Father; Christ, who was spirit and became flesh; and the Holy Spirit, the heavenly church and mother of the faithful.[27]

A similar dual use of the term "spirit" is found in the writing of Barnabas. On the one hand, he refers to the Spirit as inspiring prophets and preparing in advance those whom God calls.[28] On the other hand, he refers to the spiritual nature of the divine element in Christ's body, speaking of it as "the vessel of spirit."[29] Probably the most significant part of his theology, however, is his emphasis on the preexistence of Christ. Christ was present and cooperated with God the Father at creation; in fact, the words, "Let us make man in our image," were spoken to him.[30]

Ignatius's references to issues related to the Trinity are more extensive. Most of his statements are dyadic in nature. He says that "there is one God, Who has revealed Himself through His Son Jesus Christ, Who is His Word emerging from silence."[31] He speaks of Christ as "the Invisible, who for our sake became visible, the Impassible, who became subject to suffering on our account and for our sake endured everything."[32] He describes him as the Father's "thought" and "the underlying mouth by which the Father spoke truly."[33] He even refers to him as "our God,"[34] and describes him as "God incarnate" and "God manifested as man."[35] Although this dyadic pattern dominates Ignatius's thought, there are also a few references that are more clearly trinitarian or at

---

26. Ibid., 9.5.
27. Kelly, *Early Christian Doctrines*, p. 91.
28. *Epistle of Barnabas* 6.14; 12.2; 19.7.
29. Ibid., 7.3; 11.9.
30. Ibid., 5.5.
31. Ignatius, *Epistle to the Magnesians* 8.2.
32. Ignatius, *Epistle to Polycarp* 3.2.
33. *Epistle to the Ephesians* 3.2; *Epistle to the Romans* 8.2.
34. *Ephesians* 18.2; *Epistle to the Trallians* 7.1.
35. *Ephesians* 7.2; 19.3.

least triadic in nature. The Holy Spirit is the basis of Jesus' virginal conception,[36] the one by whom Christ established and confirmed the church's officers,[37] and the gift sent by Christ, who even spoke through Ignatius.[38] Ignatius uses triadic references at least three times in his writings,[39] the most picturesque being a figure of the church as a temple formed by Christians as the stones. God the Father is the builder; the cross of Jesus Christ is the crane by which they are hoisted up; the Holy Spirit is the howser.

There has been some dispute about the exact nature of Ignatius's thought. Based on his language, some have thought that he was actually an economic trinitarian or a modalist. This would make the Son and the Spirit merely modes of the Father's self-revelation, not real distinctions within God's essential being. Kelly, however, maintains that this view is incorrect.[40] Ignatius depends heavily on John's Gospel, and reflects its emphasis on the unity of the Son and the Father. Further, Ignatius's references to the Son deriving his sonship from the conception in Mary's womb should be thought of as simply a common usage in theology prior to Origen; they do not carry any idea of denial of the Son's preexistence. On the contrary, Ignatius says of the Son that he "existed with the Father before the ages," and that he "came forth from the unique Father, was with Him and has returned to Him."[41] This view of the Son is also reflected in Ignatius's practice, as well as in his overt teaching, his use of formulas of greeting and farewell in his letters,[42] and his entreaty to his readers to address their prayers to Jesus Christ.[43] While there is no officially developed doctrine of the Trinity, there is more evidence of consciousness of the issues than in prior writers.

In Hermas, we find something quite different. There is no reference to Jesus by name, possibly because of the author's preoccupation with the sovereignty of the Father and with repentance. The Son is only discussed in two of his *Similitudes*. The first is a

36. Ibid., 18.2
37. *Epistle to the Philadelphians* inscription.
38. Ibid., 7.1; *Ephesians* 17.2.
39. *Ephesians* 9.1; *Magnesians* 13.1; 13.2.
40. *Early Christian Doctrines*, p. 93.
41. *Magnesians* 6.1; 7.1.
42. *Ephesians* 21.2; *Magnesians* inscription; *Trallians* 13.2; *Romans* inscription.
43. *Ephesians* 20.1; *Romans* 4.2.

parable that obviously is patterned on the biblical parable of the owner of the vineyard. The owner goes away, entrusting his vineyard to a servant. Upon returning, he is so pleased with the way that servant has cared for the vineyard that, after consulting with his "well-beloved son and heir," he makes the servant "joint-heir" with the son.[44] Hermas explains that the owner is the Creator, the estate is the world, the servant is the Son of God, and the "beloved son" is evidently the Holy Spirit.[45] Later, he amends the interpretation to make clear that the servant is not to be thought of as a mere man. It was because of the cooperation of his flesh with the spirit that God promoted the servant in this fashion.[46] In a second image Hermas pictures the church as a tower built on an unshakable rock. The Son of God is again identified with the Holy Spirit, born before the world.

Clearly Hermas understands the Godhead to involve three persons, distinct from one another. The distinction, however, derives from the incarnation. Prior to that, the preexistent Son of God was identified with the Holy Spirit, so that there were only two persons, the Father and the Holy Spirit, not three. The third person became deity through adoption, as it were. He was elevated to a position of equality with the other two persons as a reward for his merits—specifically, for having cooperated fully with the preexistent indwelling Spirit. Thus we have a blend of binitarianism and adoptionism, which at least formally fits the pattern of the triadic formula that was being accepted in the church.

There is yet another idea attached to this scheme, however. It is found in several passages that refer to an angel who is superior to the six angels who form God's inner council.[47] This angel, named Michael,[48] is spoken of as "most venerable," "holy," and "glorious." Kelly believes that Hermas saw this angel as the Son of God and equated him with the archangel Michael.[49] He bases this on the several parallels between the two: both have supreme power over the people of God;[50] both pass judgment on the

44. *Similitudes* 5.2.
45. Ibid., 5.5.
46. Ibid., 5.6.
47. *Visions* 5.2; *Mandates* 5.1.7; *Similitudes* 5.4.4; 7.1.5; 8.1.2.
48. *Similitudes* 8.3.3.
49. Kelly, *Early Christian Doctrines*, p. 95.
50. Ibid., 5.6.4; 8.3.3.

faithful;[51] both hand sinners over to the angel of repentance to be reformed.[52]

To summarize the material found in the writings of the apostolic fathers, then, we find rather sparse and inconclusive data. There is clear evidence of belief in the preexistence of Christ, and of his role in both creation and redemption. When we attempt to go beyond this in our interpretation the way becomes increasingly obscure. The idea that the divine element in Christ was preexisting spirit took various forms. Sometimes it was in the form of belief that the man Jesus had been adopted into the Godhead because of his responsiveness to divine working in his life. Some of the fathers, such as Ignatius, asserted his equality with the Father, even referring to the Son as ingenerate, as was the typical designation of the Father, and giving instructions to direct prayers to the Son. In *The Shepherd of Hermas*, Christ is occasionally identified as a sort of supreme angel. It probably would be an overstatement to say that we find here a fully worked out doctrine of the Trinity, in the strict sense. The use of triadic expressions and conceptions is profuse, however. It is probably correct to say that we have here a movement from the stage of piety to that of doctrine, self-consciously held and taught. There even is the beginning of truly theological reflection on the Trinity, especially in the thought of Ignatius.

The Apologists

The apologists were the first group of Christian thinkers to attempt to relate the teachings of Christianity to the broader world of thought. They desired to show the rationality of the Christian faith. Whereas the first Christian thinkers and writers were working within an atmosphere in which the Jewish background provided the major challenge, the apologists saw the rivalry as coming more from paganism, and a rather sophisticated paganism at that. In particular, they were the first theologians to attempt to offer a rational explanation of the relationship of Christ to God the Father. Because they were convinced monotheists, this required some intensive work.

51. Ibid., 8.3.3; 9.5.2–7; 9.6.3–6; 9.10.4.
52. Ibid., 8.2.5; 8.4.3; 9.7.1–2.

Basically, their solution was to treat the preexistent Son as the Father's thought or mind. He was the expression of the Father's thought in creation and revelation. In this explanation, they drew heavily on the concept of the divine Logos or Word. This concept, of course, was at least formally found in John's Gospel. It had much wider currency, however. It was found in later Judaism and in Stoicism, and through the influence of Philo it had become a fashionable cliché. John had stated that the Logos was with God in the beginning, and Ignatius had spoken of Christ as the Father's Word spoken forth from him. The apologists' unique contribution was in drawing out the further implications of the concept. Thus, they sought to explicate the twofold fact of Christ's pretemporal presence and unity with the Father and his coming into space and time in the incarnation. While explicating Old Testament texts such as Psalm 33:6 ("By the word of the LORD were the heavens made") they also drew on the technical distinction in Stoicism between the immanent word and the uttered or expressed word. Having seen this general characterization of the thought of the apologists, let us now note the ideas of four specific representatives.

Justin Martyr is probably the clearest example of the thought of the apologists. He develops the idea of the Logos as the principle of reason in all things; the Logos is thus the unifying principle between humans and God, which gives them knowledge of him. Since all humans possess this inner reason, this Logos enabled even persons living before Christ to gain some fragmentary elements of truth.[53] Thus, even pagans who lived by reason were in a sense "Christians before Christ."[54] The Logos took definite form and in its entirety became incarnate in the person of Jesus.[55] The thought behind this is that the Logos is the intelligence or rational thought of the Father, expressed in the person of the Son.[56] Justin, however, maintained that the Word was not only distinguished from the Father in name, as the light is from

53. *Second Apology* 8.1; 10.2; 13.3.
54. *First Apology* 46.3.
55. Ibid., 5.4; *Second Apology* 10.1.
56. It should be noted that in his dialogue with the Jew, Trypho, Justin ceased to employ the idea of the seed of the Logos being implanted in every person. Harnack concludes from this that Justin did not consider this a conception of fundamental importance (Adolf Harnack, *History of Dogma* [New York: Dover, 1961], 2:187).

the sun, but was also numerically distinct.[57] He argued for this point from three considerations: (1) the alleged appearances of God in the Old Testament;[58] (2) the passages in the Old Testament that represent God as conversing with another, who presumably is a rational person like himself;[59] and (3) the Wisdom texts, such as Proverbs 8:22–31, since the offspring must be other than the begetter.[60]

In addition to the incarnation, the two other functions of the Logos are, according to Justin, to be the Father's agent in the creation and ordering of the universe[61] and to reveal truth to men.[62] The Logos is definitely not a creature. While creatures have been "made," he is God's "offspring,"[63] his "child,"[64] his "unique Son."[65] This generation or emission of the Logos does not, nevertheless, involve any diminution of himself by the Father. Justin uses the analogy of lighting one fire from another. The fire giving the light is no less for having kindled the latter.[66] So it is with the Father begetting the Logos. There really is no cutting away of part of the Father in order to bring the Son into being.

It is important to distinguish Justin's view from some later ones. The generation of the Son is not his origination but the hypostatization of the Logos. The Logos was the same in essence before and after the generation.[67] What actually happened was that this was the point of beginning of his relationship with the world as the incarnate person.

Justin's disciple, Tatian, followed much the same line of thought, even using the same imagery. The issuing forth of the Word from the Father does not cause any decline in or subtraction from what the Father is. Tatian offered an analogy: when you and I converse, you listen to my words, but I am not deprived

57. *Dialogue with Trypho* 128.4.
58. Ibid., 56.4; 60.2.
59. Ibid., 62.2.
60. Ibid., 129.3–4.
61. *First Apology* 59; 64.5; *Second Apology* 6.3.
62. *First Apology* 5.4; 46; 63.10; *Second Apology* 10.1–2.
63. *First Apology* 21.1; *Dialogue with Trypho* 62.4.
64. *Dialogue with Trypho* 125.3.
65. Ibid., 105.1.
66. Ibid., 61.2.
67. Ibid.

of them for having spoken them to you.[68] Tatian, however, contrasted more sharply than had Justin the two states of the Logos. Before creation God was alone; the Logos was immanent within him as his potentiality for creation. At the moment of creation he leaped forth from the Father as his "primordial work." Once born, "spirit derived from spirit, rationality from rational power," he served as the Father's agent in creating and governing, particularly in making humans in the divine image.[69] There was, however, no severance of the divine nature, but only the distribution of it.[70]

Theophilus of Antioch taught a similar doctrine. What was distinctive about his writings was his rather open use of Stoic terminology. He also emphasized the immanent presence of the Word within the "bowels" of God. God emitted him before creating the universe, then had him as his counselor, his intelligence and thought, his assistant in the creation of all things.[71] By begetting the Logos, the Father did not empty himself of his Word, but provided himself with an always available consort.[72] Like Justin, Theophilus held that the Old Testament theophanies were preincarnate appearances of the Word.[73] God cannot be contained in space and time, but the function of the Word whom he generated was to manifest his mind and will in the created order. Like Tatian, Theophilus did not identify by name the Word with the historical person Jesus of Nazareth; however, he did apply the Logos passage in John to his own understanding of the Logos.[74]

Athenagoras gave a somewhat more complete view of the Godhead. He insisted that Christians were not atheists, as over against those who criticized them because they had no visible objects of worship. Rather, he said, this God "is apprehended by the understanding only and the reason," and "as the eternal mind, had the Reason within himself, being from eternity endowed with reason."[75] This Word, whom he identifies as the Son of

---

68. Tatian, *Oration to the Greeks* 5.1.
69. Ibid., 7.1–2.
70. Ibid., 5.14.
71. Theophilus of Antioch, *To Autolychus* 2.10.
72. Ibid., 2.22.
73. Ibid.
74. Ibid.
75. Athenagoras of Athens, *A Plea for the Christians* 10.1.

God,[76] is the principle of rationality, both in God and in the created universe. Although the Word is God's offspring, he never actually came into being. Rather, having been with God and in God eternally, he issued forth at a point in time.[77]

We may now sum up what the apologists said about the Father, the Son, and the relationship between them. For them, the name "God the Father" meant not merely the first person of the Trinity, but the entire Godhead. Further, the inner essence of the Logos is identical with the essence of God himself. Having been immanently present within the Father from eternity, he has been generated as the product of God's self-separation, sent forth from him. Yet there has been no stripping of reason or rationality from God, even though the Word is the fullest embodiment and expression of this. From the point of his being begotten, the Word is distinct from the Father. He had always been, as the reason within the Father, but only at the point of his generation did he come to have personality. And, because of his finite origin, the Word is able to enter into the world, which the Father cannot.

Finally, we must examine briefly the apologists' understanding of the Holy Spirit and of his relationship to the Father and the Son. The treatment here is relatively sparse, which probably should not be a surprise to us, since the major point under dispute was the status of the Son or Logos. Justin several times coordinates references to the three persons, primarily citing or drawing on baptismal or eucharistic formulas, or official catechetical teaching.[78] There are numerous references to "the Holy Spirit" or "the prophetic Spirit" in his writings. While he is often rather unclear regarding the relationship of these to the Logos, he attempts to find testimony regarding the Spirit's existence as a third divine being in Plato's writings.[79] Kelly regards this as evidence that Justin distinguished between the Logos and the Spirit.[80] Tatian said that the Spirit of God is not present in all, but comes down to some who live justly and unites himself with their souls, announcing to them the future that is hidden to oth-

76. Ibid., 10.1ff.
77. Ibid., 12.2.
78. *First Apology* 61.3–12; 65.3.
79. Ibid., 60.6–7.
80. Kelly, *Early Christian Doctrines,* p. 102.

ers.[81] Athenagoras emphasized the role of the Spirit in inspiring the prophets, and was apparently familiar with the threefold formula.[82] He defined the Spirit as an effluence from God, which flows from him and returns to him like a beam of the sun.[83] Theophilus identified the Spirit with Wisdom, which God used along with his Word in creation (Ps. 33:6).[84] He was the first to use the term "triad" with respect to the Godhead, stating that the three days that preceded the creation of the sun and the moon "were types of the Triad, that is, of God and of His Word and of His Wisdom."[85]

What we have here appear to be statements that are not only less extensive than the apologists' view of the Logos, but also less coherent, doubtless because of having received less intensive and extensive thought. The major role assigned to the Spirit by these theologians seems to be the inspiring of the prophets. Justin felt, based on Isaiah 11:2, that with the coming of Christ prophecy would cease among the Jews. The Spirit, from this point, would be Christ's Spirit, and would bestow his gifts on Christians.[86] He actually suggests in some places that it was the Logos who inspired the prophets,[87] a sentiment shared by Theophilus.[88] Justin even interpreted the divine Spirit and the power of the Most High mentioned in Luke 1:35 as coming on Mary as being, not the Holy Spirit, but the Logos, who entered the womb of Mary, serving as the agent of his own incarnation.[89]

Yet for all this lack of clarity and coherence, it appears that the apologists held the basics of a trinitarian view. Their understanding of the Spirit is that he is the Spirit of God, just as the Word is the Word of God. He shared the divine nature, being an effluence from God. The parallel of their understanding of the Spirit to their doctrine of the Son or Word is clear. The Father has from all eternity had his Word and his Spirit or Wisdom immanent

81. Tatian, *Oration to the Greeks* 13.3.
82. Athenagoras of Athens, *A Plea for the Christians* 7.2; 9.1; 10.3.
83. Ibid., 10.3.
84. Theophilus, *To Autolychus* 1.7; 2.18.
85. Ibid., 2.15.
86. *Dialogue with Trypho* 87.2ff.
87. *First Apology* 33.9; 36.1.
88. Theophilus, *To Autolychus* 2.10.
89. *First Apology* 33.4ff.

within him, and at some point they issued from him. Justin
stated that Christians venerated Christ and the Spirit in the second and third ranks, respectively.[90] Athenagoras expresses a similar sentiment when he speaks of Christians as "men who
acknowledge God the Father, God the Son and the Holy Spirit
and declare both Their power in union and Their distinction in
order."[91] The subordination pertains to the "economic Trinity,"
although the use of that terminology here is actually anachronis-
tic. In putting forth the Word and the Spirit, God did not empty
himself of them.

The apologists, we may note, were responding to a specific
situation and at a specific time in the life of the church. Their
desire to show that Christianity was the true philosophy may at
times have led them to adapt their theology to the prevailing
culture more than some might be inclined to do. Yet they did so
because they wanted to relate the doctrines that they held to the
broader streams of thought. In so doing, it is apparent that
what we would today call the Trinity was included in what they
felt needed to be preserved. They drew out the implications of
the implicit beliefs, thus forwarding to some degree the understanding of these revealed truths. At the same time, they passed
on to the immediately succeeding generations of Christians and
theologians categories and partially developed thoughts that
would both need and would lend themselves to additional
development.

Irenaeus

The final theologian of the second century to be considered
here is Irenaeus, thought by many to be the major theologian
prior to Origen. Zahn says that he was the first writer of the post-
apostolic period who deserves to be called a theologian.[92] Irenaeus was in many ways strongly influenced by the apologists.
He was, however, more primarily a churchman than they were,
and consequently more concerned to preserve the church's

90. Ibid., 13.3.
91. *A Plea for the Christians* 10.3.
92. T. Zahn, "Irenaeus," in *The New Schaff-Herzog Encyclopedia of Religious Knowledge*, ed. Samuel Macauley Jackson (Grand Rapids: Baker, 1959), 6:30.

teaching than to show its harmony with secular philosophers. Consequently, one of his major differences from the apologists is the absence in his writings of indications of knowledge of the secular philosophers.

Relatively little is known about the exact biographical details of Irenaeus's life. He was born somewhere in Asia Minor, probably about A.D. 130. This is surmised from the fact that he remembers being taught by Polycarp, who died in 155, as indicated in his letter to Florinus, preserved by Eusebius.[93] Irenaeus became a priest and went as a missionary to Lugdunum, in the south of France, which is now Lyons. We know relatively little of him before the year 177, when the imprisoned believers in Lyons sent him to Rome to Bishop Eleutherus with a letter in which they pled for the peace of the church in the face of the Montanist issue.[94] Upon his return to Lyons he was elected bishop, succeeding the martyred Pothinus; he apparently remained in that office until his death at the end of the century. His greatest extant work consists of the five books commonly known as *Against Heresies*, which were probably written over a period of time during the early years of his service as bishop.[95] His writing reflects the life of a busy missionary bishop, rather than that of a cloistered scholar. His concern is practical, rather than academic. But while he writes as a pastor rather than as a professional theologian, it is as a pastor who realizes that theological controversy is sometimes necessary to guard his flock against the ill effects of erroneous thinking.

Irenaeus's writing about the person and nature of God was, to a large extent, developed in reaction to Gnosticism. There were, of course, several varieties of Gnosticism, but the common theme in the form to which Irenaeus was relating was the absoluteness of God and the consequent impossibility of bridging the huge gulf between him and the world. Irenaeus's first point is to emphasize that the supreme God is the Creator. The Gnostics would have no difficulty acknowledging the greatness of the supreme God, but would find the idea of this God creating mate-

---

93. Eusebius, *Ecclesiastical History* 5.10.4–7.
94. Ibid., 4.1.2; 5.3.4.
95. John Lawson, *The Biblical Theology of Saint Irenaeus* (London: Epworth, 1948), p. 4.

rial unacceptable. Irenaeus frequently repeats this concept: "This God, the Creator, who formed the world, is the only God, and there is no other God besides Him."[96] God is the only Creator, and he has created everything that is. He conceived the plan of creation himself, rather than receiving it from anyone else.[97] Nor was he dependent on any other source, having created all things from nothing, not employing any preexisting matter.[98]

Irenaeus then responds to the view of the Gnostics. They maintained that God had bridged the gap between himself and the creation by a series of emanations. Irenaeus denies this, and then goes on to argue for the connection of God with the creation through his doctrine of the two hands of God. He cites Isaiah 40:12: God creates and cares for the whole creation, in the palm of his hand. He then goes on to make more explicit how God does this: "It was not angels, therefore, who made us, nor who formed us. . . . For God did not stand in need of these, in order to the accomplishing of what He had Himself determined with Himself beforehand should be done, as if He did not possess His own hands. For with Him were always present the Word and Wisdom, the Son and the Spirit, by whom and in whom, freely and spontaneously, He made all things."[99]

This statement might appear to be parallel to the Gnostic conception of the supreme being creating through a series of emanations. It should be noted, however, that in Irenaeus's thought the direct action of God is involved. The identification of the Spirit of God with the hand or finger of God is underscored by the Evangelists' use of these terms in parallel passages in the Synoptic Gospels. Thus, in Luke 11:20, Jesus is reported as saying, "But if I drive out demons by the finger of God, then the kingdom of God has come to you." In Matthew 12:28, however, Matthew reports the words of Jesus as being, "But if I drive out demons by the Spirit of God, then the kingdom of God has come upon you." Irenaeus makes clear that the Son is fully divine: "the Father is God, and the Son is God, for whatever is begotten of

96. Irenaeus, *Against Heresies* 2.16.3.
97. Ibid.
98. Ibid., 4.38.3.
99. Ibid., 4.20.1.

God is God."[100] There is also the famous statement: "What is invisible in the Son is the Father, and what is visible in the Father is the Son."[101] The parallelism between the Word and Wisdom, the Son and the Spirit, certainly seems to establish the divinity of the Spirit as well. Irenaeus says that we "should know that He who made, and formed . . . and nourishes us by means of the creation, establishing all things by His Word, and binding them together by His Wisdom—this is He who is the only true God."[102] It appears that Lawson is correct in his assessment of this problem: "*'The Two Hands of God'* is an expression of the immediacy of creation, not of its mediacy. It is an unfolding of the implications of the phrase 'One Creator God.' It justifies the claim that S. Irenaeus taught the doctrine of creation 'by the whole Trinity.'"[103]

It is not only creation that is the work of the Triune God, however. Revelation and inspiration are also to be understood in this way. So Irenaeus writes, "The Son reveals the knowledge of the Father through His own manifestation, for the Son's manifestation is the making known of the Father."[104] And the Son and Spirit are both involved in the inspiration of the prophets: "The Word of God . . . who was manifested to the prophets according to the form of their prophesying . . . and the Holy Spirit, through whom the prophets prophesied."[105]

Some of the expressions Irenaeus used have occasioned considerable debate about whether he actually was a modalist, although before his time, as it were. To be sure, he has certainly stressed the economic Trinity, being virtually the originator of that concept. It should be noted, however, that there are some significant differences between his view and that of the modalists whose thought we will examine in the next chapter. Although the separate functioning of the Son and the Spirit, or the Word and Wisdom, began with the creation, they had always been immanent within the Father, and were present and operative simul-

---

100. *Proof of the Apostolic Preaching* 47.
101. *Against Heresies* 4.6.6.
102. *Against Heresies* 3.24.2.
103. Lawson, *Biblical Theology*, p. 125.
104. Irenaeus, *Against Heresies* 4.6.3, 6.
105. *Proof of the Apostolic Preaching* 6.

taneously in the works that were executed. They are not successive forms that he took. Thus, it appears that what we have here
is an expansion of and advance on the thought of the apologists.
There is also here a preparation for the greater refinement that
would necessarily come.

2

Formulating the Doctrine in the Third Century

As the church reflected further on the amazing claims that Scripture seemed to make, it found itself in a strange situation. There were a number of different strands of witness in the Old Testament which, when combined with various New Testament passages, shed somewhat varying light on the status of the Son and his relationship to the Father. Pelikan identifies at least four of these.[1] First, passages of adoption indicate a time at which the Son became divine, implying that there was a time at which deity was conferred on him, such as at his baptism or resurrection (Ps. 2:7; Heb. 1:5). Second, passages of identity, by speaking of Yahweh as "the Lord," set forth an identity between Christ and the Father (Isa. 63:9; Ps. 96:10; LXX). Third, passages of distinction speak of one Lord and another Lord, thus drawing some distinction between them (Ps. 110:1; Acts 2:34). Fourth, passages of derivation refer to the Father as "the greater" or use titles such as angel, Spirit, Logos, and Son, and suggest that he "came from" God and was in some sense less than God (Gen. 22:15; John 14:28). Depending on which of these one chose to emphasize, very different views of the Trinity might emerge from biblical theology.

1. Jaroslav Pelikan, *The Christian Tradition: A History of the Development of Doctrine* (Chicago: University of Chicago Press, 1971), 1:175.

53

Denial of the Real Personal Deity of Christ: Dynamic Monarchianism

It was this first group of passages that was highlighted by an early school of theologians in their attempt to deal with the puzzling status of the Son. This is the movement generically known as adoptionism, whose Christology has been defined by Harnack as follows: "Jesus was . . . regarded as the man whom God hath chosen, in whom the Deity or the Spirit of God dwelt, and who, after being tested, was adopted by God and invested with dominion."[2] In this period, however, the major view of this basic orientation is linked with another view with which it has many differences, under the generic name of Monarchianism. This grouping, which goes back at least as far as Novatian,[3] seems to be based on the assumption that the primary objective of each group was to preserve the monotheism that had been inherited from Judaism. While this may well have been the attitude and motive of the successors of these persons in Novatian's day, it seems not to have been the primary concern of the originators of the movement that we now know as "dynamic Monarchianism" or "rationalistic Monarchianism." Rather, it appears that for them, philosophical considerations were of greatest importance.[4]

Harnack observes that by the end of the second century, through the work of Irenaeus and the anti-Gnostic writing of Tertullian, the doctrine of the Logos—the idea of the preexistence of Christ as a distinct person—would seem to have been firmly established as a part of orthodoxy and universally recognized as part of the rule of faith. He contends, however, that this view was not at least initially, universally accepted and was more slowly incorporated into the creed than were such doctrines as God as Creator, the real body of Christ, and the bodily resurrection. What was really significant, however, from his perspective, is that the doctrine of the Logos legitimized the incorporation of philosophical speculation, specifically, Neo-Platonic philosophy within the creed of the church.[5]

2. Adolf Harnack, *History of Dogma* (New York: Dover, 1961), 1:191.
3. Novatian, *On the Trinity* 30.
4. J. N. D. Kelly, *Early Christian Doctrines* (New York: Harper & Row, 1960), pp. 115–16.
5. Harnack, *History of Dogma*, 3:1–2.

A group given the nickname of the "Alogi" by Epiphanius and Philastrius is sometimes regarded as a precursor of dynamic Monarchianism. Our knowledge of them and their views is derived primarily from Hippolytus and Epiphanius. They were strongly opposed to the practice of prophecy in the churches, and rejected the teachings of Jesus about the coming and ministry of the Holy Spirit. In particular, they rejected the Johannine writings, including the Gospel of John's teaching about the coming of the Paraclete.[6] They recognized the Synoptic Gospels and accepted the miraculous virgin birth, but maintained that primary emphasis should be placed on the human life of Jesus, and on his birth, baptism, and temptation. They rejected the Logos formula and the idea of the eternal generation of Christ, making God's empowerment of him at his baptism of crucial importance.[7] Harnack's assessment of their view is that, although they did not use the expression "a mere man," they did really highlight the concept that Christ was at his baptism ordained to be the Son of God.[8]

The real onset of dynamic Monarchianism, however, was through the thought of two men named Theodotus. The first, a learned leather merchant, had probably had contact with the Alogi in Asia Minor; he brought some of their ideas to Rome about 190.[9] In many areas of his doctrinal teachings, such as divine omnipotence, creation, and the virgin birth, he was apparently quite orthodox.[10] Jesus was not to be thought of, however, on the model of a heavenly divine being who had taken on humanity. Instead, after a thorough testing of his piety, at his baptism the Holy Spirit descended on him. He thus became Christ and was empowered and equipped for his special ministry. As a result, his righteousness exceeded that of all other humans; that means that he therefore can be considered their authority. Yet even this and his working of miracles still should not be thought of as making him divine, although some of Theodotus's followers held that at the resurrection Jesus was made truly God.[11] It ap-

6. Epiphanius of Salamis, *Against Eighty Heresies* 51.35.4.
7. Ibid., 51.6.
8. Harnack, *History of Dogma*, 3:17–18.
9. Ibid., 3:21.
10. Hippolytus, *On Heresies* 7.23.
11. Ibid.

pears that, unlike the Alogi, Theodotus and his followers accepted the Johannine literature but followed their type of exegesis and appealed to such texts as Deuteronomy 18:15 and Luke 1:35 (the latter amended to read, "Spirit of the Lord").[12] They used the former of these passages to argue that even the risen Christ was not God, and considered Matthew 12:42 evidence that the Holy Spirit was superior to the Son of Man.[13] Philaster complained that they were selective in their use of Scripture, relying heavily on the passages that referred to Jesus as human, but avoiding those that identified him as divine.[14] They also were very interested in logic and geometry and in the writings of Aristotle, Euclid, and Galen. Theodotus was excommunicated by Pope Victor, on the charge that he taught that Jesus was mere man (which necessarily places the date before 199). We do not know how large his following was at this point, but it could not have been too substantial, or the pope would not have dared excommunicate him.[15]

The second Theodotus, a banker, was one of those who continued the teaching of the leather merchant, along with Asclepiodotus. Relatively little is known about the views of this younger Theodotus. Based on one passage in Theodotus's discussion of Hebrews, Hippolytus found a major heresy—belief in and worship of Melchizedek.[16] It appears that Theodotus and his colleagues held that besides the Father, the only divine being was the Spirit, who was identical with the Son; that the Holy Spirit had appeared to Abraham in the person of Melchizedek; and that Jesus was a person on whom the Spirit had come in a remarkable way.[17] From this it may well have been an easy move to worshiping Melchizedek.

As noted above, this movement was apparently not of very large magnitude in Rome. It was, however, sufficiently large so that an attempt was made to form a separate church there. The Confessor Natalius was persuaded to become its bishop at a sal-

12. Epiphanius, *Against Eighty Heresies* 54.3.1–6.

13. Adolf Harnack, "Monarchianism," in *The New Schaff-Herzog Encyclopedia of Religious Knowledge,* ed. Samuel Macauley Jackson (Grand Rapids: Baker, 1959), 7:455.

14. Philaster, *Book of Heresies* 54.

15. Harnack, *History of Dogma,* 3:22–23.

16. Although Harnack considers this an overstatement. Ibid., p. 26.

17. Epiphanius, *Against Eighty Heresies* 55.9.

ary of 150 denarii per month. The attempt soon failed, however, and Natalius returned to the mother church. He testified that he was persuaded by visions of "holy angels," who pursued and beat him during the night.[18]

Against the views of the Theodotians several objections were registered, which Eusebius has extracted from *The Little Labyrinth*. The first was one that we would probably not consider a valid objection today: the use of grammatical and formal exegesis, rather than allegorization, "to prove their 'godless tenets.'" The second was the use of textual criticism, seeking to correct the manuscripts of the Bible—in itself a commendable concern, but biased by the theological presuppositions of these persons. Finally there was the study of logic, mathematics, and empirical sciences, "in order by the science of unbelievers to support their heretical conception."[19] While we would like to know more about their exact views, it appears that they may have understood orthodoxy to be committed to ditheism, for Novatian puts in their mouths the argument, "If the Father is one and the Son another, but the Father is God and Christ is God, then there is not one God but two Gods are at once brought forward, the Father and the Son."[20]

One more movement in the West may have been related to this type of Monarchianism. Shortly after the two Theodotuses, some disciples gathered around the teaching of a man named Artemis. We know relatively little about the exact views of this group, except that they appealed to the historical justification of the teaching of their view in Rome. They maintained that Zephyrinus, bishop at the time of the attempted formation of a separate church, had falsified the true doctrine that they defended.[21] Beyond that we know relatively little of their views, except that they apparently refused to call Christ "God." We do know that Artemis was still alive in 270. This movement faded in significance in the West. In the East, however, Artemis apparently continued to exert considerable influence, so that Eusebius calls him the "father" of Paul of Samosata. He had attained considerable notori-

18. Harnack, *History of Dogma*, 3:23.
19. Eusebius, *Ecclesiastical History* 5.28.
20. Novatian, *On the Trinity* 30.
21. Eusebius, *Ecclesiastical History* 5.28.3.

ety and had even apparently surpassed Theodotus in the church's memory. In the subsequent age the formula, "Ebion, Artemis, Paulus (or Photinus)" became stereotyped, and when later supplemented by the addition of the name of Nestorius, the phrase became a constant feature of Byzantine dogmatics and polemics.[22]

If dynamic Monarchianism faded rather quickly in the West, this was not its fate in the East, at least in part because of a more favorable political environment. Some Eastern thinkers rejected the Logos Christology.[23] Origen did not treat these persons as heretics. Rather, they were misled or "simple" Christian brethren, who required friendly teaching. Beryll of Bostra, an Arabian bishop, taught Monarchianism, which aroused opposition from the bishops of the province. Origen was drawn into the controversy and apparently amicably convinced the bishop of his error.[24]

It was Paul of Samosata who made the strongest case for dynamic Monarchianism in the East. Paul was bishop of Antioch, the most important see in the East.[25] Beginning about the year 260, he began opposing the idea of the essential divinity of Christ. According to one sixth-century writer, Paul did not apply the title "Word" to Christ, but said that the Word was God's commandment and ordinance—what God ordered through men and thus accomplished.[26] God was simply to be thought of as one person. In God both a Logos (Son) and Sophia (Spirit) can be distinguished, but they are qualities rather than separate persons.[27] While Paul's views are difficult both to reconstruct and to interpret, it appears that the church was not wrong in understanding him to have called Jesus "Christ" only after the baptism, when the Logos entered into him through means of the Holy Spirit. Paul also forbade addressing psalms to Jesus.[28] He seems to be denying that the Logos became a distinct personal presence. The church's understanding of his view was that "Christ . . . was in

22. Harnack, *History of Dogma*, 3:32.
23. Origen, *Commentary on the Gospel of John* 2.2.
24. Eusebius, *Ecclesiastical History* 6.33.
25. Harnack, "Monarchianism," p. 456.
26. *On Sects* 3.3.
27. Harnack, *History of Dogma*, 3:40.
28. Eusebius, *Ecclesiastical History* 7.30.10.

his nature an ordinary man"[29] and that "Jesus Christ is from below."[30] While it is difficult to apply contemporary categories to the thought of Paul, it does appear that the union between the Logos and Jesus was not ontological but moral, and that, as Pelikan puts it, the union was "analogous to the union between the Christian and the 'inner man' or between the prophets of the Old Testament and the inspiring Spirit."[31] He differed from the two Theodotuses by incorporating into his thought the orthodox terminology of the Logos; however, he gave the language a different meaning than the orthodox.

There were, as there frequently are in theological disputes, considerable political dimensions to this discussion. This view was expounded, not in the Roman Empire, but in Antioch, which then belonged to Palmyra. Paul held a high political office in the kingdom of Zenobia and was on good terms with the queen. Harnack says that because the fall of Paul would have meant the triumph of the Roman party in Antioch, we may assume that a political party lay behind the theological issues, and that his opponents were of the Roman party in Syria. This may be assuming more than the evidence justifies. It is clear, however, that it would have been difficult to obtain condemnation of Paul's views, since he presided over the provincial synod. Since an Oriental general council had been successfully undertaken in 252 to deal with the views of Novatian, which had threatened to split up the East, this was again attempted in Paul's case. One council was held at Antioch in 264, which did not arrive at a decision, allegedly because the accused cleverly concealed his false doctrines.[32] At a second council, even Bishop Fermilian of Caesarea gave up the idea of a condemnation because Paul promised to change his opinions. At a third council, held between 266 and 269 (probably in 268), on the way to which Fermilian died at Tarsus, Paul was condemned and excommunicated and Domnus was appointed as his successor. Paul, protected by Zenobia, retained his position for another four years; the church in Antioch split. In 272 Antioch was taken by Aurelian; the emperor, to

29. Ibid., 7.27.2.
30. Ibid., 7.30.11.
31. Pelikan, *Christian Tradition,* 1:176.
32. Eusebius, *Ecclesiastical History* 7.28.2.

whom an appeal was made, decreed that the church building was to be given to the person with whom the Christian bishops of Italy and Rome corresponded by letter. This in effect proved to be the end of Paul's party in Antioch.[33]

This does not mean, however, that all influence of Paul's thought also ceased. Harnack suggests that a number of traces can be found. He believes that Lucian and his academy, which was the alma mater of Arianism, were inspired by Paul's thought, and that the thought of Photinus in the fourth century approximated that of Paul. Theodore of Mopsuestia was accused of teaching the views of Paul; not only was he condemned, but so was Paul once again. The Acta Archelai expresses a Christology that was basically that of Paul, which leads Harnack to conclude that even at the beginning of the fourth century there were clergy on the extreme eastern boundary of Christendom who still held a basically adoptionist Christology.[34]

Denial of the Distinctness of the Persons: Modalistic Monarchianism

It appears that dynamic Monarchianism was never very widely held. The same cannot be said for modalistic Monarchianism. Like the former movement, it appears to have had its beginnings in Asia Minor and then spread to Rome. There are several indications of how widespread this movement was. Hippolytus tells us that at that time the Monarchian controversy agitated the entire church.[35] Tertullian[36] and Origen[37] indicate that in their time the economic Trinity and the technical application of the conception of the Logos to Christ were regarded with suspicion by the mass of Christians. Harnack goes so far as to say that, "Modalism . . . was for almost a generation the official theory in Rome."[38] The primary theological motivation behind this doctrinal view was concern to preserve monotheism and the full

33. Harnack, *History of Dogma*, 3:38-39.
34. Ibid., 3:48–50.
35. Hippolytus, *On Heresies* 9.6
36. Tertullian, *Against Praxeus* 3.
37. Origen, *Commentary on the Gospel of John* 2.3.
38. Harnack, *History of Dogma*, 3:53.

deity of Jesus Christ. To persons adhering to modalistic Monarchianism, the Logos theology, which suggested that the Logos or the Son was a distinct person from the Father, appeared to jeopardize this unique oneness of God. Even as early as Justin's time we read of objections to his teaching that the Logos was "something numerically other" than the Father, his opponents contending that the Power issuing from the Godhead was distinct only verbally or in name, being a projection of the Father.[39] It was, however, Noetus of Smyrna who first attracted attention for teaching along this line. Whether in his native Smyrna[40] or in Ephesus,[41] this seems to have occurred sometime in the final twenty years of the second century, although his condemnation may not have taken place until 230, when most of the controversy in Rome had subsided.[42]

Although our knowledge of Noetus's views comes to us almost exclusively through the writings of Hippolytus and the fourth-century Epiphanius, we are able to reconstruct fairly well his relatively uncomplicated teachings. Noetus maintained that there is one God, the Father. If, after all, there was only one God and if Christ was God, as seemed to be taken for granted, then Christ must be identical with the Father. How else could he be God? Noetus replied to his accusers, "What wrong have I done, glorifying the one only God, Christ, Who was born, suffered and died?"[43] The second major tenet, deduced from the first, is also mentioned in this statement: patripassianism, or the view that the Father suffered in the Son. Noetus reasoned as follows: "I am under necessity, since one [God] is acknowledged, to make this One the subject of suffering. For Christ was God, and suffered on account of us, being himself the Father, that he might be able to save us."[44] To support these contentions, his followers appealed to such biblical texts as Exodus 3:6 (taken together with Exod. 20:3) and Isaiah 44:6, which emphasize the uniqueness of God; Isaiah 45:14–15 and Baruch 3:32–36, which suggest that this unique God was present in Jesus Christ; and John 10:30, 14:8–10, and

39. Justin Martyr, *Dialogue with Trypho* 128.3–4.
40. Hippolytus, *Against Noetus* 1.
41. Epiphanius, *Against Eighty Heresies* 1.
42. Harnack, *History of Dogma*, 3:57.
43. Hippolytus, *Against Noetus* 1.
44. Ibid., 2.

Romans 9:5, which seemed to identify the Father and the Son.[45] They rejected the Logos doctrine by arguing that the prologue of John's Gospel was to be taken allegorically.[46]

A pupil of Noetus, Epigonus, came to Rome during the reign of Zephyrinus, possibly about the year 200, and began teaching his doctrines there. He found a responsive pupil, Cleomenes, who was regarded as the head of the modalist party in the early years, with that distinction later falling on Sabellius. According to Hippolytus, they believed in one identical Godhead, which could be referred to indifferently as Father or as Son. These names did not stand for real distinctions, but were mere names applicable at different times.[47] It may even be that this Godhead was believed to be like Heraclitus's universal monad, which comprised mutually contradictory qualities.

There was, as we noted earlier, rather widespread sympathy for this view. In fact, Bishop Zephyrinus, like his predecessor Victor, seems to have been attracted to this view. He was primarily attempting to keep peace within the catholic church. Relatively unsophisticated in theological matters, Zephyrinus was advised by Callistus, who upon his death in 217 became his successor and served until 222. Callistus continued Zephyrinus's policies, and even determined to excommunicate both Sabellius and Hippolytus. Callistus constructed a formula designed to satisfy the less extreme members of both parties, which it succeeded in doing. His formulation thus became the means by which some of these modalists were able to accept the Logos doctrine.[48]

Tertullian also gives us insight into this party in his writing against a person named Praxeus. There has been much speculation and debate about who Praxeus was, some thinking that this was a nickname meaning "busybody" or "tradesman," and identifying him with Noetus, Epigonus, or even Callistus. Harnack believes the correct view to be that of Döllinger and Lipsius— that Praxeus was a confessor of Asia Minor who came to Rome some twenty years before the height of the controversy there.

45. Ibid., 2, 6–7.
46. Ibid., 15.
47. Hippolytus, *On Heresies* 9.5.
48. Harnack, *History of Dogma*, 3:57–58.

Tertullian laid hold of this name because Praxeus had been the first to teach this doctrine in Carthage, and was an ardent anti-Montanist against whom Tertullian had a strong antipathy.[49] What is important is not his identity, however, but his teachings, which can be quite clearly delineated from Tertullian's writing.

According to Tertullian, Praxeus taught that the Father and the Son were one identical person,[50] the Word having no independent subsistence.[51] It was the Father who entered the virgin's womb, thus becoming, as it were, his own Son.[52] The Father, therefore, suffered, died, and rose again.[53] In one person were united the mutually contradictory attributes of being invisible and then visible, impassible and then passible.[54] Praxeus and his followers ended up having to recognize, however, a duality in the person of the Lord, the man Jesus being the Son and the divine element being the Father.[55] From this followed the formula that "while it is the Son who suffers, the Father co-suffers."[56]

Considerably more sophisticated was the thought of Sabellius, who attempted to respond to and blunt the criticisms leveled against the earlier versions of modalism. His central proposition was that Father, Son, and Holy Spirit are the same, the three names being attached to one and the same being. His major concern was the maintenance of monotheism. According to Epiphanius, his followers asked, "What shall we say, have we one God or three Gods?"[57] It is also alleged that he used the analogy of the sun; its one essence radiates both warmth and light and also possesses an astrological form (τὸ σχῆμα).[58] On this model, the Father is the form or essence; the Son and the Spirit are his modes of self-expression. He put forth his activity in three successive "energies": first, in the Father as Creator and Lawgiver; then in the Son as Redeemer, beginning with the incarnation and ending at the ascension; finally, in the Spirit as giver and sustainer of

49. Ibid., 3:59–60.
50. Tertullian, *Against Praxeus* 5.
51. Ibid., 7.
52. Ibid., 10.
53. Ibid., 1; 2.
54. Ibid., 14.
55. Ibid., 27.
56. Ibid., 29.
57. Epiphanius, *Against Eighty Heresies* 62.2.
58. Ibid.

life.[59] While it is difficult to construct with absolute certainty all of the details of Sabellius's thought, it seems that we have at least correctly apprehended the general contour here.

Hippolytus and Tertullian

We now proceed to examine the thought of Hippolytus and Tertullian. We might well have considered them before Monarchianism, but since they wrote largely in response to modalism, this seems the most logical way to proceed. It is not always desirable to derive one's understanding of the beliefs of a theologian from what he says about the thought of others, but such reflection does compel a thorough delineation of a number of significant issues. One can only speculate how the thought of the person under examination might have developed differently, had it not been for the stimulus of such polemics. There is much in common between Hippolytus's and Tertullian's thought, since both were reacting, during this period of their development, to the same heresy; there are also points of difference. Hippolytus's thought was less extensive than that of Tertullian, and more oriented to past issues; Tertullian was the more creative of the two.[60] Indeed, in many ways, Tertullian's formulation of the relationship of the one and the three was that which the church was to take as its basic formula for many years. It was he who coined the term "Trinity" (*trinitas*).[61]

The preservation of the Logos doctrine that had been expounded by the apologists was a major goal of both these men. It is perhaps in employment of this concept, together with their strong desire to preserve monotheism, that the first major pole of their thought can be observed. They emphasized the concept of God existing alone from all eternity, yet having within him and indivisible from him, his reason or Word. This is the concept of *Logos endiathetos,* which was familiar since the apologists; Hippolytus actually employed the term.[62] Although God was alone, yet in a sense he was not alone, for *ratio* and *sermo* existed within

59. Ibid., 62.1.
60. Kelly, *Early Christian Doctrines*, p. 110.
61. Tertullian, *Against Praxeas* 3, 11, 12.
62. Hippolytus, *On Heresies* 10.29.

him. He thought and spoke inwardly. If, after all, even humans can converse with themselves and make themselves the object of their thoughts, then how much more must this be possible for God?[63] Hippolytus distinguished between God's Word and his Wisdom, as did Tatian and Irenaeus, naming them separately, as when he says, "Though alone, he was multiple, for he was not without his Word and his Wisdom, his Power and his Counsel."[64] Tertullian tended to equate them with one another.[65] Yet he makes the complementary truths of the aloneness of God and the presence of this reason even more explicit: "before all things God was alone, being his own universe, location, everything. He was alone, however, in the sense that there was nothing external to himself. But even then he was not really alone, for he had with him that Reason which he possessed within himself, that is to say, his own Reason."[66] Tertullian also makes clearer than any of his predecessors the otherness or individuality of this immanent reason or Word. We have noted already the comparison that he makes of God to a human person interacting with and reflecting on himself. He says that the rationality by which one cogitates and plans is somehow "another," or "a second" in himself. So it is with the Word, with which God has been reasoning and reflecting from all eternity. It constitutes "a second in addition to himself."[67] Yet it is correct to say that prior to choosing to reveal himself and to create the world, God was the only person.[68]

The other major point of the trinitarian thought of these two men lies in their understanding of what happened when God did act to reveal himself. Hippolytus taught that when God willed, he engendered his Word, using him to create the universe, and his Wisdom, to adorn or to order it.[69] In other words, that which was internal to him became in some sense external to him and distinguishable from him. Further, when redemption of the world was the goal of God's action, he made the Word, who had previously been invisible, visible through the incarnation. Thus, alongside

---

63. Tertullian, *Against Praxeas* 5.
64. Hippolytus, *Against Noetus* 10.
65. Tertullian, *Against Praxeas* 6.
66. Ibid., 5.
67. Ibid.
68. Tertullian, *Against Hermogenes* 3.
69. *Against Noetus* 10–11.

the Father (that is, the Godhead itself), there was "another," a second "person" (πρόσωπον). The Spirit completed the triad.[70] If, however, there are three revealed in this economy, this does not detract from the unity. There is only one God. Hippolytus says, "When I speak of 'another,' I do not mean two Gods, but as it were light from light, water from its source, a ray from the sun. For there is only one Power, that which issues from the All. The All is the Father, and the Power issuing from the All is the Word. He is the Father's mind. . . . Thus all things are through Him, but He alone is from the Father."[71] Neither Hippolytus nor Tertullian really held that it could properly be said that there was a Son prior to the incarnation. Hippolytus was hesitant to refer to the Word as Son in any other sense than proleptically until the incarnation.[72] Tertullian, like the apologists, dated his "perfect generation" from his issuing forth from the Godhead for the purpose of creation.[73]

Tertullian was the one who concocted the formula, "one substance, three persons." For although there was only person prior to the decision to create, when the Father chose to send forth his Son, the Logos came into existence as a real being.[74] There was a unity of Father and Son, but the unity was a oneness of substance. The Father is one person and the Son is another person; they are different persons, not different things. Thus, the Son also has the same power as the Father, with relationship to the world,[75] and has had it from the very beginning of time.[76] Tertullian sought to show by argument that the three persons were actually manifestations of a single indivisible power, noting that in imperial government one and the same power can be exercised by coordinate agencies.[77] He insisted, as had the apologists, that this distinction between persons did not involve any real separation or division.[78] It was a *distinctio* or *dispositio* (that is, a dis-

---

70. Ibid., 7; 11; 14.
71. Ibid., 10.
72. Ibid., 15.
73. *Against Praxeus* 7.
74. Ibid., 5.
75. Ibid., 2.
76. Ibid., 16–19.
77. Ibid., 3.
78. Ibid., 8; *Apology* 21.11–13.

tribution), not a *separatio*. He illustrated this point with the unity between the root and its shoot, the source and the river, and the sun and its light. The Father and the Son are one identical substance, which has not been "divided" but "extended."[79] He examines carefully Jesus' statement, "I and the Father are one." He notes that in the Latin text with which he was working, the word "one" is *unum* (neuter), rather than *unus*. He renders this as "one reality" rather than "one person." What Jesus was asserting here was unity of substance rather than numerical unity.[80] What, of course, should follow is to say that this was the affirmation of the translators of the Latin Vulgate, since the text was in Greek, and the words of Jesus that they report were probably spoken in Aramaic.

Tertullian's use of the term "person" deserves special examination. We have seen that in his view, the three are all one indivisible substance. These three, however, were represented as three πρόσωπον or *persona*. The term πρόσωπον originally meant "face" or "expression," and then "role"; it eventually came to signify "individual," usually emphasizing the external aspect or objective presentation. The primary meaning of *persona* was "mask," from which the transition was easily made to the actor who wore it and the character he or she played. In legal usage, it could mean the holder of the title to a property, but Tertullian was using it to connote the concrete presentation of an individual. It should be noted, for the sake of our later discussion, that neither the Greek nor the Latin word carried with it prominently the idea of self-consciousness that today is so much associated with the terms "person" and "personal."[81]

Tertullian's discussion of this issue is expressed in rather crude, materialistic language. Kelly claims that, due to his background in Stoic thought, Tertullian regarded the divine substance as a highly rarified species of matter.[82] Tertullian says, "The Father is the whole substance; the Son is truly derived from and part of the whole."[83] This might be taken as implying that the

79. *Apology* 21.12.
80. *Against Praxeus* 25.
81. Kelly, *Early Christian Doctrine*, p. 115.
82. Ibid., p. 114.
83. *Against Praxeus* 9.

Son is separated or divided from the Father, but must be understood in light of Tertullian's statements about distinction, rather than division, as well as the specific context here, which makes clear that no such severance is intended. Underlying this is his basic conception about the Godhead. The whole fullness of the Godhead, that is, the Father, is not capable of entering into the finite. Indeed, Tertullian goes to great lengths to argue that the Father is by nature impassible, but that the Son is capable of suffering.[84] The divine being that enters into the world must merely be a part of the deity, or as we have described it above, the substance of the deity "extended" into the world.[85] Thus, when Tertullian considers the idea that there may be differences among the persons with respect to status (that is, fundamental quality), substance, or power, he insists that the Godhead is indivisibly one. The threeness must be understood as pertaining to the "grade" (*gradus* = Greek τάξις), "aspect" (*forma*), or "manifestation" (*species*) in which the persons are presented. They are one in what they are, although there is an order among them in the revelation of the persons. It appears that what he is saying is not simply that the Father, the Son, and the Spirit divide the substance among them, or that they hold title to the common substance jointly (a notion reflective of Tertullian's legal training), but rather that they share the same substance or are the same substance. The Godhead being indivisible, they are one identical being.

We have observed that there was some alternation in earlier Christian thought between dyadic or binitarian and triadic or trinitarian language. Tertullian was clearly trinitarian, as we can see from his statements about the Spirit. He spoke of the Son as a second person in addition to the Father. In the third place, he says, is the Spirit. This Spirit is the "representative" or "deputy" of the Son.[86] He issues from the Father by way of the Son.[87] He is "third from the Father and the Son, just as the fruit derived from the shoot is third from the root, and as the channel drawn off from the river is third from the spring and as the light-point

---

84. Ibid., 29.
85. Ibid., 14.
86. *Prescription of Heretics* 13.
87. *Against Praxeus* 4.

in the beam is third from the sun."[88] This one is a person,[89] also, so that Tertullian can speak of the Godhead as a Trinity.[90] Indeed, Tertullian was the first person to use the term *trinitas*. The three are really three persons, numerically distinct, although they are one substance. They are "capable of being counted."[91] Thus, he can say, "We believe in one only God, yet subject to this dispensation, which is our word for economy, that the one only God has also a Son, His Word, Who has issued out of Himself . . . which Son then sent, according to His promise, the Holy Spirit, the Paraclete, out of the Father." Later in this same context Tertullian speaks of "the mystery of the economy, which distributes the unity into Trinity, setting forth the Father, Son and Spirit as three."[92]

There is, of course, much here that is still not clear. One might wish for a clearer indication of the relationship of these three persons to the one substance. We shall see later, in the discussion of logical problems, the difficulty of making sense of the statement that the three persons are one substance, that they are three persons, but one thing. There is some lack of clarity about the nature of the relationships of one person to another (in what sense there is or is not subordination of the Son to the Father, for instance). One also sees here the difficulty faced by those working with a translation of the Bible, in which a crucial theological distinction is derived from terminology in the receiving language of the translation. Yet when one thinks how great an advance this thought is on that which had preceded it, one cannot help but be impressed. This was not the final solution of the problems, but it was a real breakthrough in the way in which the problems were approached.

Hippolytus and Tertullian make several contributions to the doctrine of the Trinity. One was simply the coining of the term, *trinitas*, which by its very use served as a constant reminder of the fact that God is both one and three. A second was in more explicitly relating the Spirit to the Godhead. Third, a set of catego-

88. Ibid., 8.
89. Ibid., 11.
90. Ibid., 3; 11; 12; *On Modesty* 21.
91. *Against Praxeus* 2.
92. Ibid.

ries is introduced for distinguishing the threeness from the oneness, namely, three persons and one substance. Fourth, the adaptation of the concept of person to this discussion, when properly understood, advanced the discussion considerably. Yet, as so often is the case, the very suggestions implicit within this theology were taken and developed in both conservative and more liberal directions by differing theologians.

Origen

Certainly on any measure Origen was one of the most significant theologians of the early church and of any era in its history. Some have even argued that he was the outstanding theologian of the early church. He attempted to bring together two major disciplines, theology and philosophy, for he was steeped in the dominant philosophy of this time, generally referred to as middle Platonism. As a churchman, he was committed to the triadic rule of faith that the church held. Thus, one of his greatest contributions was to express that triadic faith using the categories of Platonism.

The starting point of Origen's theology is the great God, the Father. Everything must derive from something unchanged and unchanging, and this is God, the Creator of all. Origen refers to him as "altogether Monad, and indeed, if I may so express it, Henad."[93] He alone is God in the proper sense, being alone ungenerated; it is significant that Jesus spoke of him in John 17:3 as "the only true God."[94] This God is perfectly good and powerful, and must always have had objects on which to exercise these attributes. Because of his goodness he reveals or communicates himself, and because of his immutability he always communicates thus. Consequently, he has brought into existence a world of spiritual beings or souls, coeternal with himself.[95]

This perfect, ungenerated God cannot, however, really relate to this multiplicity. Consequently, his Son is his mediator. This is the presence of the Logos in the person of Jesus. The Logos, as can be seen from John 1:1 and Hebrews 1:1, is the express image

93. Origen, *On First Principles* 1.1.6; *Against Celsus* 7.38.
94. *Commentary on the Gospel of John* 1.20.119.
95. *On First Principles* 1.2.10; 2.9.1.

of the Father.[96] His Son is the meetingplace of a plurality of "aspects," which appear to represent the Platonic ideas.[97] These "aspects" represent the manifold characters that the Word presents either in his eternal being (such as Wisdom, Truth, Life) or as incarnate (for example, Healer, Door, Resurrection). He is of the very same nature as the Father, having been eternally begotten by the Father. He was always with the Father; it cannot be said that "there was when He was not."[98] This begetting is an indescribable occurrence. It cannot be properly called an emanation, but rather is an act of the will, arising from an inner necessity.[99] The Logos thus produced is not an impersonal force of the Father, but is really a personally existing being.[100] He is another person,[101] namely, the second person in number.[102] He is a God, but his deity being derivative, he is said to be a "secondary God."[103] There also is, thirdly, the Holy Spirit, "the most honorable of all the beings brought into existence through the Word, the chief in rank of all the beings originated by the Father through Christ."[104]

The Father, Son, and Spirit are three ὑπόστασεις, according to Origen.[105] Origen is not simply saying, as had Tertullian, that God manifests himself as three in the economy, but the concept stems from his doctrine of eternal generation. Whereas *hypostasis* and *ousia* were originally synonyms, Origen gives *hypostasis* here the meaning of an individual subsistence. He objects to modalism, whose error he feels consisted in treating the Three as numerically indistinguishable, separable only in thought. Rather, he insists, the Son is "other in subsistence than the Father," and the Father and the Son "are two things in respect of Their Persons, but one in unanimity, harmony and identity of will."[106]

---

96. Ibid., 1.2.13.
97. *Against Celsus* 2.64; *Commentary on John* 1.20.119.
98. *On First Principles* 1.2.4, 9.
99. Ibid., 1.2.2; 4.28.
100. Ibid., 1.2.2.
101. *On Prayer* 15.
102. *Against Celsus* 8.2.
103. Ibid., 5.39; *Commentary on John* 6.39.202.
104. *Commentary on John* 2.10.75.
105. Ibid.
106. *On Prayer* 15.1; *Against Celsus* 8.12.

The issue of the unity of these three persons is an important one, and is best seen with respect to the Father and the Son, to which Origen gives the greatest attention. In the passage quoted above, it is largely a moral union, with the wills of the two being virtually identical.[107] The Son, it should be recalled, is eternally begotten by the Father, poured out from his being and so participates in his Godhead.[108] Both share the same essential nature, and if it is said that in the strict sense the Father alone is God, it is because the Son possesses the substance of deity by participation or derivation from the Father.[109]

Origen's special contribution to the discussion of the Trinity is his emphasis on the eternal uniqueness and personality of the three members of the Godhead. There also is here, together with the insistence on the full deity of each of the three, a type of subordinationism. This is due to the fact that the Father alone is αὐτόθεος, the other two persons having their divinity by way of derivation from the Father. Each of these characteristics was destined to have its own special development and defense in coming years.

There is another somewhat unusual tenet of Origen's view, which most clearly reveals his dependence on Platonism. In Plato's thought, the ideas or forms are the most real. These qualities, such as honor, humanness, and whiteness, are sometimes thought of as universals or abstract qualities, but are better thought of as formulas for the qualities. Specific or concrete things display these qualities by participating in the appropriate form. Thus, a horse is a horse because it participates in the form of "horseness." Horseness is not a horse, however, nor is the form or idea of whiteness white, as I believe Plato was trying to show in the *Parmenides*.[110] There is, finally, the idea of the Good, which illumines all. It is that which, in the myth of the cave in the *Republic*, causes the forms to cast shadows on the wall.[111] In

---

107. *Commentary on John* 13.36.228f.

108. Ibid., 2.2.16.

109. Ibid.

110. Millard J. Erickson, *Platonic Forms and Self-Predication; A Critical Examination of Gregory Vlastos' Interpretation of the "Third Man Argument" in the Parmenides* (unpublished M.A. thesis, Department of Philosophy, University of Chicago, 1958). See also, A. E. Taylor, "I—On the First Part of Plato's *Parmenides*," *Mind*, n.s., 12 (January 1903): 1–20.

111. Plato, *The Republic*, Book 7; cf. Book 6.

some understandings of Plato, the idea of the Good is thought to play much the same role as does God in theistic worldviews. If that view is a correct interpretation of Origen's view, then God the Father is the idea of the Good, and the Son contains within himself, as it were, the ideas. What is problematic for Christian theology in this view, however, is the world of spiritual beings or souls, which are coeternal with God, since he has always had to have such as objects of his goodness and power. This element of his thought remains to be worked out, but it is not an integral part of the doctrine of the Trinity, except insofar as it is required by the Platonic philosophy he is employing.

3

Formulating the Doctrine
in the Fourth Century

We come now to perhaps the most significant doctrinal dispute in the history of the church, the Arian dispute. This was at once an issue involving both Christology and the Trinity. It concerned the nature and deity of Jesus Christ. We will here, however, be considering it not as a christological issue, that is, as an issue of the relationship of the deity to the humanity of Christ. Rather, we will be considering it as a trinitarian issue, that is, of the relationship of Christ's deity to that of the Father.

Arianism: The Equality and
Identical Natures of the Persons

The background to the Arian dispute is important to our understanding of it. During this period political issues, not only of the church but also of the empire, were of great importance. There had been a significant debate, centered especially on the modalistic Monarchianism associated with Sabellius. What emerged from this debate was two parties: one emphasizing the divine trias, and the other emphasizing monotheism or monarchy. The pope, Dionysius, declared that two things must be preserved: the divine trias and the "holy message of monarchy."[1] By

1. Paul Tillich, *A History of Christian Thought: From Its Judaic and Hellenistic Origins to Existentialism*, ed. Carl E. Braaten (New York: Simon & Schuster, 1968), p. 68.

taking key expressions of both groups and insisting on their retention, he had guaranteed the political unity of the church, saying that both held something indispensable and in effect insisting that each party also hold the distinctive of the other party. And, whether he realized it or not, the pope had also determined, at least for a time, that the course of orthodox theology would continue along trinitarian lines.

Unfortunately, however, he did not say how this was to be done. One thinks here of the story of how during World War II German submarines were sinking U.S. merchant ships, bound for Europe with war supplies. The U.S. government was becoming desperate trying to find ways to stop this loss. They solicited suggestions from government employees and from the public. One man proposed an interesting solution. "Just heat the water in the Atlantic Ocean to 212 degrees Fahrenheit," he said, "and when the submarines surface, you can just pick them off with the surface ships' guns or bomb them." "That is a great solution," a government official commented, "but how will we heat so much water that much?" "Don't ask me," said the man. "I just make policy; I don't carry it out." That was much the sort of predicament that Dionysius left to the church.

The church was forced to continue its struggle, but with the parameters quite clearly defined. Because there was an apparent internal inconsistency, numerous efforts were made to determine how the divine trias and monarchy could be held simultaneously. Previously, it had been possible to emphasize one to the virtual exclusion of the other, but at least during the reign of Dionysius, this course of action would no longer be acceptable.

It is also important that we see the ideological background of the debate. The titles "Logos" and "Son of God" had been used to stress adoption, identity, distinction, and derivation in such a way as to combat successfully the Monarchianism that threatened the belief in the separate identity of the Father and the Son. Among those who had thus successfully engaged in the battle were Tertullian and Novatian in the West and Origen in the East; Origen especially had a strong influence on the future shape of theology.[2]

2. Ibid.

An ambiguity in Origen's thought, however, was to cause certain difficulties. Origen taught both the indwelling of Christ in the believer's heart, derived from Scripture, and the speculative interpretation of this idea, stemming from the Greek doctrine of the Logos. The alternation between these two ideas resulted in Christ the Logos being thought of as both personal and impersonal. Another ambiguity is found in Origen's thought, as well as that of a number of other theologians of the time. In pressing the case against the Sabellians, Origen had insisted that the Son was distinct from the Father and yet eternal, so that no one was to claim a beginning for the Son, before which he did not exist. However, at the same time Origen interpreted passages of distinction and especially passages of derivation in such a way as to make the Logos a creature, subordinate to God, "the firstborn of all creation, a thing created, wisdom."[3] His primary proof text in support of this latter conception was Proverbs 8:22–31.

It was this biblical text that was to lead to considerable debate. An extended treatment of this passage distinguished the preexistent Logos from the creatures. Athenagoras contended that God, being eternally "endowed with reason," had the Logos within himself eternally.[4] The Son as Logos, therefore, "did not come into existence" but was eternal. Theophilus attributed the inspiration of the Old Testament prophets to the Logos, whom he identified as the Spirit of God, who had existed before the world began.[5]

The Proverbs 8 passage had been a major weapon used by the church to repel the heresy perceived as coming from the Sabellian emphasis on the identity of the Son with the Father, rather than their distinction. Now, however, as the threat shifted to become the identity of essence and the equality of the Son with the Father, the same passage was used against the orthodox view. As Hilary put it regarding the Arian use of the passage, "the weapons, granted to the church in its battle against the synagogue," came to be used "against the faith set forth in the church's proclamation."[6] Used as a passage of distinction, Proverbs 8:22–23 easily was made into a passage of subordination.

3. Origen, *On First Principles* 1.2.1.
4. Athenagoras of Athens, *A Plea for the Christians* 10.2.
5. Theophilus of Antioch, *To Autolycus* 2.10.
6. Hilary of Poitiers, *On the Trinity* 12.36.

When the great Oriental council that met at Antioch in 268 ruled in favor of the Logos doctrine and against the views of Paul of Samosata, Paul was deposed and excommunicated. His work was taken up by the most learned man in the East at that time, Lucian of Samosata. Trained in the thought and method of Paul, he established an exegetical-theological school in Antioch, which for a time was out of communion with the church there, but later, shortly before Lucian's martyrdom, made its peace with the church. Although beginning with Paul's Christology, Lucian came to unite it with the Logos doctrine. Harnack regards Lucian's thought as a blend of that of Paul and that of Origen,[7] noting that Epiphanius classified Lucian and Origen together as teachers of the Arians.[8] It was in this matrix that Arius, a pupil of Lucian's, developed his view.

It appears, from what we can reconstruct, that the Arian controversy broke out over the exegesis of Proverbs 8:22–31. Alexander, the bishop of Alexandria, called on several presbyters, especially Arius, to give an account of their understanding of a passage of Scripture, presumably Proverbs 8:22–31. In his letter to Eusebius, Arius quoted verses 22–23, to the effect that "Before he was begotten or created or ordained or established, he did not exist."[9] In a confession addressed by Arius and several colleagues to Alexander, he quoted the same verbs in asserting that the Son had been "begotten timelessly by the Father and created before ages and established."[10]

Emperor Constantine, in his analysis of the origins of Arianism, referred to an "unprofitable question" raised by Arius that had led him to speculations that were better left alone.[11] Thus, suggests Pelikan, we must look at the presuppositions or the fundamental theological conceptions of Arius that led him to his particular interpretation of the Proverbs passage.[12] The first of these was a strong emphasis on monotheism, in the form of the conception of the absoluteness of God. God was the "one and

    7. Adolf Harnack, *History of Dogma* (New York: Dover, 1961), 4:3.
    8. Epiphanius of Salamis, *Against Eighty Heresies* 76.3.
    9. Arius, *Epistle to Eusebius* 5.
    10. Arius, *Epistle to Alexander* 4.
    11. Eusebius of Caesarea, *Life of Constantine* 2.69.1.
    12. Jaroslav Pelikan, *The Christian Tradition: A History of the Development of Doctrine* (Chicago: University of Chicago Press, 1971), 1:194.

only."[13] He was "the only unbegotten, the only eternal, the only one without beginning, the only true, the only one who has immortality, the only wise, the only good, the only potentate."[14] God was said to be "without beginning and utterly one [ἀναρχὸς μονώτατος]" and "a monad [μόνας]."[15] There had always been a divine monad, but a dyad had come into being with the generation of the Son and a triad with the production of the Spirit or wisdom.[16] "The triad is not eternal, but there was a monad first."[17]

Given this absolute conception of God's uniqueness, it is not surprising that Arius also held to a strongly transcendent view of God. God is not capable of sharing his substance with anything or anyone else. If he did, this would make the Father "composite and divisible and mutable and a body."[18] He had to be understood in such a fashion that he would not undergo any of the changes that affect a body. He had to be kept separate from any involvement with the world of becoming. He so transcended the realm of created and changeable things that there was not, and ontologically could not be, any direct contact with them. This was required by two considerations. It was necessary because of the nature of God, and also because of the fragile character of the creatures, which "could not endure to be made by the absolute hand of the Unoriginate."[19]

What, then, was the understanding of the Son in this theology? It simply was not possible, given this understanding of the Father, to speak of the divine in Christ as being God in some unequivocal sense. The Arians cited such clearly monotheistic passages as Deuteronomy 6:4 and posed this question to their opponents: "Behold, God is said to be one and only and the first. How then can you say that the Son is God? If he were God [God] would not have said, 'I alone' or 'God is one.'"[20] The Arians in-

13. Didymus of Alexandria, *On the Trinity* 3.16.
14. Arius of Alexandria, *Epistle to Alexander* 2.
15. Ibid., 4
16. Athanasius, *On the Synods of Ariminum and Seleucia* 15.3.
17. Athanasius, *Orations Against the Arians* 1.17.
18. Arius, *Epistle to Alexander* 5.
19. Athanasius, *Orations Against the Arians* 2.24; *On the Decrees of the Synod of Nicea* 8.1.
20. Athanasius, *Orations Against the Arians* 3.7.

stead declared, "God has not always been a Father," and "Once God was alone, and not yet a Father, but afterwards he became a Father."[21] For if there was a point at which the Son came into being, then prior to that, God was not a Father; more seriously, if God has always been Father, then the Son has always been, and this coeternity of the Son with the Father would mean blasphemy against God.[22]

The issue of the person of Jesus Christ, or of the relationship between the divine and human natures, arose out of the question of the relationship of the divine in the Son to the divine in the Father. In other words, the Christology grew out of the doctrine of the Trinity, rather than vice versa, although even using the term "Trinity" in such a context is something of a misnomer. The desire to preserve the Father's uniqueness and absoluteness required this view of the Son. The Arian understanding of the person of Christ can be summarized in four major propositions.

First, the Son is a creature, whom the Father has formed out of nothing by his fiat. The term "beget" was to be understood in this context in the figurative sense of "make."[23] He is not to be understood as an emanation from the Father, or a portion of the substance of the Father. That would be to treat the Godhead in physical categories.[24] Although he is a perfect creature, and therefore not to be compared to the rest of the creation, he is a creature, created by the Father.

Second, as a creature the Word must have had a beginning. He came into existence before the times and the ages. He was born outside of time, and prior to his generation he did not exist.[25] This produced the monotonously repeated Arian litany, "There was when he was not." While they did not say that there was "a time when he was not," they did say that there was "a then when he was not." To hold, as did the orthodox, that the Son was coeternal with the Father seemed to Arius to involve "two self-existent principles," which would contradict monotheism.

Third, the Son cannot really have communion with the Father,

21. Ibid., 1.5; 9.
22. Ibid., 1.14.
23. Athanasius, *Orations Against the Arians* 1.5, 9.
24. Arius, *Epistle to Alexander* (in Athanasius, *On the Synods of Ariminum and Seleucia* 16).
25. Ibid.

or any direct knowledge of the Father. Although he is God's Word and Wisdom, he is distinct from that Word and Wisdom that belong to God's very essence.[26] He is a creature, and his substance is not that of God. He does not have by nature the divine attributes. Since he is not eternal, his knowledge is not perfect either. It is only a relative knowledge. He cannot even know or comprehend the Father perfectly and accurately.[27]

Finally, the Son must be liable to change and even to sin. The Arians' official position was that while this was true, God foresaw that by his own choice the Son would remain free from committing sin, and so he bestowed this grace on him in advance.[28]

We should note that the Arians used the term "angel" to refer to the relation of the Son of God as creature to God the Creator. They used their interpretation of Proverbs 8:22–31 to show that this preexistent one was one of the angels, although of course preeminent among them.

The effect of this Arian view was to make Christ or the Word something more than any other creature, but also something less than the Father. He was, in other words, a semi-God. He was the first and highest of the creatures, and the only one directly created by God. He was the agent through whom the Father created and relates to the rest of the creation. He is not eternal, but was brought into being at some point before time began.

The real implications of this view fell in the area of soteriology. The orthodox view, as Athanasius was to argue, held that the gap between God and man, both ontologically and morally/spiritually, was successfully bridged by the one who was fully God and fully human. The Arian view, however, with its emphasis on the extreme transcendence of God, created a gap that could only partially be bridged by a demigod. This Logos was the pioneer of salvation by first attaining the glory of God by his own effort and then enabling those who followed him to do the same. In this regard, Arius's understanding of salvation was quite similar to that of Paul of Samosata.[29]

---

26. Athanasius, *Orations Against the Arians* 1.5; 2.37.
27. Athanasius, *Epistle to the Bishops of Egypt and Libya* 12; *On the Synods of Ariminium and Seleucia* 15; *Orations Against the Arians* 1.6.
28. Athanasius, *Orations Against the Arians* 1.5.
29. Athanasius, *On the Synods of Iriminium and Seleucia* 26.4.2.

The Nicene Solution

In June 325 a general council met at Nicea. The number of bishops was apparently somewhere between 250 and 300. The most important of the Eastern bishops were present, but the West was poorly represented; the bishop of Rome did not attend but sent two presbyters in his place. The emperor at first gave the council a free hand, but was prepared to step in if necessary to enforce the formula that his advisor Hosius had agreed on with Alexander of Alexandria.[30] Apparently a fairly large percentage of the delegates were not theologically trained, but among those who were, three basic "parties" were discernible: Arius and the Lucianists, led by Eusebius of Nicomedia; the Origenists, led by Eusebius of Caesarea, already highly reputed; and Alexander of Alexandria, with his following. The Lucianists, who fully expected to prevail, without previously conferring with the Origenists, put forth a rather blunt statement of their beliefs. To their considerable surprise, this was summarily rejected. It was then their hope that the Eusebian position, which was something of a midpoint between the Arian and the Alexandrian parties, would prevail. Indeed, Eusebius put forth a creed, which was unanimously pronounced to be orthodox by those present. Those of the party of Alexander, however, were not fully satisfied. They were favored by the emperor, and followed the strategy of accepting the Creed of Caesarea while demanding a more precise definition of some of its key terms.[31]

The emperor favored the inclusion of the word *homoousios*, as suggested to him by Hosius. The Alexandrian party then presented a carefully worked out statement, which they said was a revised form of the Creed of Caesarea, with certain steps taken to close loopholes that could be interpreted in Arian fashion. The Origenists had considerable reservation about some elements of the creed, fearing that phrases such as "out of the Father's substance" and "of the same substance as the Father" could be interpreted in a material sense, could be understood as Sabellian, and were not of biblical origin.[32] The emperor exerted considerable

---

30. Theodoret of Cyrrhus, *Ecclesiastical History* 1.11.
31. Ibid.
32. Eusebius, *Epistle to the People of Caesarea* 5; 7.

influence, saying that there was a desire to preserve the spirituality of the Godhead. Consequently, the statement was approved by all except three members of the council. Even most of Arius's allies abandoned him, and as Pelikan says, "saluted the emperor, signed the formula, and went right on teaching as they always had."[33]

The creed read as follows:

> We believe in one God, the FATHER Almighty, Maker of all things, visible and invisible;
>
> And in one Lord JESUS CHRIST, the Son of God, begotten of the Father, [the only-begotten, that is, of the essence of the Father, God of God], Light of Light, very God of very God, begotten, not made, being of one substance (*homoousios*) with the Father; by whom all things were made [both in heaven and on earth]; who for us men, and for our salvation came down and was incarnate and became man; he suffered, and the third day he rose again, ascended into heaven; from whence he will come to judge the quick and the dead.
>
> And in the HOLY GHOST.
>
> [But for those who say: "There was a time when he was not"; and, "He was not before he was made"; and "He was made out of nothing," or "He is of another substance" or "essence," or "The Son of God is created," or "changeable," or "alterable"—they are condemned by the holy catholic and apostolic Church.][34]

The statement is significant both for what it affirmed and what it denied. The word *homoousios*, which was to carry such great significance in the years ahead, is especially interesting. There was some suspicion of this word on the part of the orthodox because of its earlier association with Gnosticism and even Manicheism.[35] Even its defenders experienced some embarrassment about this term because of its identification with the condemned ideas of Paul of Samosata.[36] This term, however, upon which Constantine insisted, was given a special turn of meaning here. What was being affirmed and insisted upon was

33. Pelikan, *Christian Tradition*, 1:203.
34. Philip Schaff, ed., *The Creeds of Christendom*, 6th ed., 3 vols. (New York: Harper, 1931; Grand Rapids: Baker, 1990 reprint), 1:28–29.
35. Arius, *Epistle to Alexander* 3.
36. Hilary of Poitiers, *On the Councils* 81; 86.

that the Son is different, utterly different, from any of the created beings.[37] He is not out of any other substance, but out of the Father. The condemnations attached to the confession also spoke very emphatically to the Arian position, specifically rejecting its major affirmations. Arius refused to sign this statement and was apparently joined by only two other members of the council. The rest, including those supposedly supportive of Arius's position, signed the creed. It is generally agreed that this was a triumph for the views of Alexander, and that the primary architect of it was Athanasius, strongly supported by Amphilocius and Didymus in the East and Ambrose and Hilary in the West.[38]

One question that then must be raised, however, pertains to just what the council meant by this statement. On the one hand, the usual meaning of the word *homoousios*, as used by Origen, for example, was generic, namely, "of the same nature." In that sense, it could signify the kind of substance or stuff common to several individuals of a class, as would be true of a collection of humans, for example. On the other hand, it could connote an individual thing as such.[39]

While a large number of scholars have contended that the council used the term in this latter sense, there are good grounds for questioning such a conclusion. Both J. N. D. Kelly and G. L. Prestige argue that whether that is properly the term's meaning, it was this more modest version that they had in mind. Among their reasons are the fact that Arius, prior to the council, objected to the term *homoousious*, but it is apparent that he was repudiating the Son's alleged divinity, rather than the unity of God. Further, the issue before the council, it is virtually universally agreed, was not the unity of the Godhead but rather the coeternity of the Son with the Father, and his full divinity, as contrasted with the creaturehood that the Arians attributed to him. In addition, if Eusebius and his allies had thought that *homoousios* was being used to teach the doctrine of numerical unity of substance, they would have seen this as a concession to Sabel-

37. George Leonard Prestige, *God in Patristic Thought* (London: SPCK, 1956), p. 211.
38. Pelikan, *Christian Tradition*, p. 203.
39. J. N. D. Kelly, *Early Christian Doctrines* (New York: Harper & Row, 1960), p. 234.

lianism and would have vigorously resisted it. Finally, we know that later the most orthodox theologians continued to use the term in the sense of generic unity.[40]

The Continuing Dispute

This did not, of course, settle the dispute in any final fashion. Given the relationship of the church to the empire, the changing convictions of successive emperors became increasingly significant for the theology of the church. Thus, Constantine's successor, his son, Constantius, exerted strong opposition to the Nicene position. During this period Athanasius was deposed and exiled, and a genuinely Arian position was approved at the third council of Sirmium in 357 and the synods of Nicé in 359 and of Constantinople in 360. As a result of this triumph of the extreme anti-Nicenes, the moderates rallied around the *homoiousios* formula. Gradually these homoiousions were converted to the *homoousios* formula.[41]

A bit more attention needs to be given to the *homoiousios* view. This view was that the Son was "of a similar ousia to that of the Father," or "like the Father in every respect," rather than "like the Father," but not in ousia.[42] As a result, said Gibbon, "the profane of every age have derided the furious contests which the difference of a single diphthong" caused.[43] Yet very small variations in spelling can have huge differences in meaning. My church bulletin once almost included an announcement extending congratulations to a newly married couple, who, it said, "were untied in marriage," when it should have read, "united." As small as the verbal variation may seem, there is an immense difference between someone being "similar in nature" to another, and being "of the same nature" as another, when the nature of the latter is deity. It appears that the differences in meaning of the two words were eventually overcome by a moving together of the views of the two parties, the homoousions and the homoiou-

---

40. Ibid., pp. 235–36; Prestige, *God*, chap. 10.
41. Harnack, *History of Dogma*, 4:59–107.
42. Epiphanius of Salamis, *Against Eighty Heresies* 73.13.1.
43. Edward Gibbon, *The Decline and Fall of the Roman Empire* (New York: Peter Fenelon Collier, 1899), 2:252.

sions. Both realized that they were basically in agreement regarding what they wanted to exclude, namely, the Arian view that the Son was a created being. Thus, the agreement came through a further clarification of the unresolved problems of the One and the Three.[44]

We should at this point examine briefly Athanasius's view, since he continued to maintain the Nicene view during a time of widespread rejection. He maintained that God can never be without his Word, just as the light cannot stop shining or the river source cease flowing. So the Son must exist eternally along with the Father.[45] His generation is eternal and mysterious, but he is derived from and shares the Father's nature.[46] This does not mean he is part of the divine substance, separated out of the Father, since the divine nature, being immaterial and without parts, cannot be divided.[47] And although the Son is generated according to the Father's will, since this is eternal it cannot be said to be the result of a specific act of volition in which the Father decided to bring the Son into being.[48] There is a likeness and unity of the Son and the Father, and this is not merely one of will, but of essence.[49] Athanasius especially liked the analogy of the light and its brightness. While distinguishable, they are yet one and the same substance. So the Son is other than the Father as his offspring, but as God they are one. Whatever is predicated of the Son is predicated of the Father.[50] So the Godhead is one unique, indivisible Monad.[51] Yet the Father and Son are one identical substance, this indivisible reality existing in two forms of presentation. It is because they are really two that he is able to speak of them as alike. The Son is the same Godhead as the Father, but that Godhead is manifested rather than immanent.[52]

---

44. Athanasius, *On the Synods of Ariminum and Seleucia* 41.1.
45. Athanasius, *Orations Against the Arians* 2.32.
46. Ibid., 1.26–28; 2.59–60.
47. Athanasius, *On the Decrees of the Synod of Nicea* 11.
48. Athanasius, *Orations Against the Arians* 3.59–66.
49. Ibid., 3.10–11.
50. Ibid., 3.4.
51. Ibid., 3.15.
52. Ibid., 3.6.

The Person of the Holy Spirit

The final element in formulating the understanding of the Trinity was the question of the nature, status, and function of the Holy Spirit. For the Spirit had been relatively ignored during this period of the development of theology. He had, of course, from the very beginning of the church been seen as very important. The baptismal formula, whether one holds that it goes back to Christ himself or is of apostolic origin, was certainly utilized very early, and it gives equal prominence to the Holy Spirit, Father, and Son. Christ had promised that the Holy Spirit would be the one who would come on the disciples and give them power to be able to do even greater works than he himself had done (John 14:12). It was with respect to special works of the Holy Spirit that Paul had found it necessary to write a rather vigorous letter to the church at Corinth. Yet there had not been the intense theological interest in and discussion about the Spirit that there had been with respect to Christ. There had, of course, been a flurry of interest and debate in connection with the views propounded by the Montanists, and Tertullian's joining that party provided him with a special prod to go further into this area of doctrine. The Council of Nicea, however, had merely made the brief statement, "and [we believe] in the Holy Spirit." This seemed to be a doctrine ripe for controversy and for constructive theologizing.

A confusing array of beliefs was held about the Holy Spirit at this time. Harnack points out that this was due at least in part to the accumulated difficulties regarding the Holy Spirit, which were of three types. There was difficulty in the very notion of the Spirit himself, since πνεῦμα was also used to describe both the substance of God and the substance of the Logos. Second, there was great difficulty in recognizing any specific activity of the Spirit in the present time. Third, there was a desire to ascribe to the Logos, rather than to the Spirit, some of the specific works, such as the active working in the universe and the history of salvation.[53] Consequently, there was a wide variety of ideas about the Spirit, as persons struggled to understand in some coherent way who he was. Some considered him an impersonal, unbegotten power whom Christ had promised to send and who therefore be-

---

53. Harnack, *History of Dogma*, 4:108.

came an actual fact only after Christ's ascension. Others thought of him as a primitive power in the history of salvation. Yet others conceived of him as an active power in the world process as well.

A number of persons, taking their cue from the reference to the Holy Spirit as "Paraclete," considered him to be personal. Of these, some thought of him as a created divine being, others as the highest spiritual being or angel made by God. Some referred to him as the second derivation from the Father, after the Son, a permanently existing Being sharing in the Godhead itself. Others identified him with the Son himself. Still others identified the Holy Spirit as the Old Testament Wisdom, and noting that Wisdom is feminine in gender in Hebrew, thought of this person as feminine.

Once the question of the Holy Spirit was raised for discussion, his very absence from earlier discussions presented a problem. Why should there be this silence? Gregory of Nazianzus accounted for it by a theory of the development of doctrine, according to which "the Old Testament proclaimed the Father manifestly, and the Son more hiddenly. The New [Testament] manifested the Son, and suggested the deity of the Spirit. Now the Spirit himself is resident among us, and provides us with a clearer explanation of himself."[54] Probably the best explanation, however, was suggested by Amphilocius of Iconium, who sought to account for the vagueness of the doctrine of the Holy Spirit in the creed adopted at Nicea: "It was quite necessary for the fathers then to expound more amply about the glory of the Only-Begotten, since they had to cut off the Arian heresy, which had recently arisen. . . . But since the question about the Holy Spirit was not being discussed at the time, they did not go into it at any greater length."[55]

This may have sufficed to account for the brevity of the statement at the Council of Nicea. Not only Nicea, however, was silent about the deity of the Holy Spirit. The Scripture itself, Gregory of Nazianzus had to concede, did not "very clearly or very often call him God in so many words, as it does first the Father and later on the Son."[56] This was a source of considerable discomfort

---

54. Gregory of Nazianzus, *Epistle* 58.
55. Amphilochius, *Synodical Epistle*.
56. Gregory of Nazianzus, *Orations* 31.12.

to many of the theologians. In addition, the church's liturgical practice did not seem to provide instances of prayer or worship addressed to him. It was, of course, expected that those who did not call the Son God would also decline to refer to the Spirit as divine and would describe him as created out of nothing. In this situation, however, even some who otherwise were fully orthodox, having rejected the Arian position on the question of Christ as creature, nonetheless "oppose the Holy Spirit, saying that he is not only a creature, but actually one of the ministering spirits, and differs from the angels only in degree."[57] Some considered him to have had a "middle nature," less than that of God but more than that of a creature, being "one of a kind."[58]

This state persisted, even within the orthodox camp, for quite some time. As late as 380 Gregory of Nazianzus summarized the situation by saying that "of the wise men among ourselves, some have conceived of him [the Holy Spirit] as an activity, some as a creature, some as God; and some have been uncertain which to call him. . . . And therefore they neither worship him nor treat him with dishonor, but take up a neutral position . . . of those who consider him to be God, some are orthodox in mind only, while others venture to be so with the lips also."[59] Clearly, although no crisis of the magnitude and severity of the Arian crisis with respect to the Son was present in the doctrine of the Holy Spirit, there certainly was a situation that cried out for thorough and careful treatment.

Athanasius on the Holy Spirit

It was in response to such uncertainties and especially to the teachings of the "Tropici" that Athanasius set forth his understanding of the Spirit. The Tropici combined a belief in the Son's deity with the contention that the Spirit was a creature brought into existence out of nothingness. To be more exact, they said that the Spirit was an angel—the highest of the angels, to be sure, but one of the "ministering spirits" mentioned in Hebrews 1:14. He therefore was "other in substance" than the Father and Son.

---

57. Athanasius, *Epistles to Serapion* 1.1.
58. Cyril of Alexandria, *Dialogues on the Trinity* 7.
59. Gregory of Nazianzus, *Orations* 31.5.

In addition to the Hebrews text, they relied on three others: Amos 4:13 ("he who . . . creates the spirit [or wind, Heb. *rûaḥ*]); Zechariah 1:9 ("the angel who was talking with me answered"); and 1 Timothy 5:21 ("I charge you, in the sight of God and the elect angels"). In response to these, Athanasius asserted that the Spirit is fully divine and consubstantial with the Father and the Son. He refuted the exegeses of the Tropici and then showed that the Scripture unanimously teaches that the Spirit is not a creature, but instead "belongs to and is one with the Godhead Which is in the Triad."[60] Further, the Triad is eternal, homogeneous, and indivisible, and since the Spirit is a member of it he must therefore be consubstantial with the Father and the Son.[61] The close relation between the Spirit and the Son implies that the Spirit belongs in essence to the Son, just as the Son does to the Father. This is seen in their coactivity in the inspiration of the prophets and the incarnation.[62] Finally, the Spirit's divinity can be inferred from the fact that he makes all believers "partakers of God" (cf. 1 Cor. 3:16–17). While Athanasius abstained from calling the Spirit "God," he held that he belongs to the Word and the Father and shares one and the same substance or is *homoousios* with them.[63]

What Athanasius did, therefore, was to extend his teaching about the Word to the Spirit, so that God exists eternally as a Triad sharing one identical and indivisible substance. Moreover, there is an indivisible working of the three, so that what the Father accomplishes he does through the Son and what the Son does he carries out through the Spirit.

The Cappadocians

The Cappadocians—Basil, Gregory of Nazianzus, and Gregory of Nyssa—developed the doctrine of the Spirit, and thus of the Trinity, further. One analogy that they felt worked well for understanding the Spirit was that of the relationship of the human spirit to the human self. This analogy was substantiated bibli-

60. Athanasius, *Epistles to Serapion* 1.21.
61. Ibid., 1.2, 20; 3.7.
62. Ibid., 3.5–6.
63. Ibid., 1.27.

cally by the use of 1 Corinthians 2:11: "For who among men knows the thoughts of a man except the man's spirit within him? In the same way no one knows the thoughts of God except the Spirit of God." Basil claimed that this provided "the greatest proof of the conjunction of the Spirit with the Father and the Son."[64] Yet in actual practice, this did not play a very large part in his argument, perhaps because pressing this too much might easily lead to a Sabellian understanding of the Spirit.[65]

Another argument employed by the Cappadocians was that the application to the Spirit of divine titles, qualities, and operations was tantamount to a declaration of deity. As Gregory of Nazianzus put it, "What titles which belong to God are not applied to [the Holy Spirit], except only 'unbegotten' and 'begotten?'"[66] He then listed the divine titles that were applied to God. One of these was the term "holy" itself. This was "the fulfillment of [his] nature," because he was spoken of as sanctifying, not as sanctified. He was consequently holy not "by participation or by a condition having its source outside him," but "by nature and in truth."[67] To Basil, the very title "spirit" seemed to connote a nature unlimited by change and variation.[68] He was the source of all created good and was "unapproachable by thought"; therefore, he had to be God.[69]

Even more significant, in the judgment of the Cappadocians, were the works of the Spirit. He was the one who regenerated, sanctified, and justified. These works could only be done by one who was truly divine.[70] Especially appropriate to the Holy Spirit was the proof from baptism. The Cappadocians noted, as had the defenders of the Nicene formula against the Arians, the inclusion of the name of the Spirit in the baptismal formula. Basil argued that regeneration came through the grace given in baptism, being thus the divine way of salvation. Rejecting the deity of the Holy Spirit then meant casting away the very meaning of salva-

---

64. Basil of Caesarea, *On the Holy Spirit* 16.40.
65. Epiphanius of Salamis, *Against Eighty Heresies* 62.1.4.
66. Gregory of Nazianzus, *Orations* 31.29.
67. Cyril of Alexandria, *Dialogues on the Trinity* 7.
68. Basil, *Holy Spirit* 9.22.
69. Ibid., 22.53.
70. Gregory of Nazianzus, *Orations* 40.44.

tion itself.[71] This regeneration was through baptism "into the name of the Father and of the Son and of the Holy Spirit."[72]

Basil also argued for the full deity of the Holy Spirit on the basis of liturgical usage. The doxology, just like the confession of faith, preserved the doctrine taught to believers at their baptism. It was not only the doxology, but also the hymn sung each evening at the lighting of lamps that bore on this question, for its wording was, "We praise Father, Son, and God's Holy Spirit." If liturgical practice was to be authoritative for dogmatic confession, it was not legitimate to make an exception in this case.[73] It was this doctrine of the Cappadocians that the church affirmed at the Council of Constantinople in 381.

That doctrine, in its fullness, was indeed a doctrine of the Trinity, stating that the one Godhead exists simultaneously in three modes of being. What was needed was the development of terminology that would protect the doctrine against the charge of Sabellianism. The terms in which the relation of the one and the three came to be expressed were: one ousia, three hypostases. The difficulty with this usage was that the two terms had been understood as virtually synonymous, but the Cappadocians were able to bring about the adoption of this distinction. They did this by defining the hypostasis as "that which is spoken of distinctively, rather than the indefinite notion of the ousia."[74] Together with this was a distinctness in the "mode of origin" of the several persons. The Son is begotten from the Father; the Spirit proceeds from the Father; the Father neither is begotten nor proceeds.[75]

The Cappadocians also introduced the idea of the coinherence, or as it would later be called, the perichoresis, of the three. Basil put it this way: "Everything that the Father is, is seen in the Son, and everything that the Son is, belongs to the Father. The Son in His entirety abides in the Father, and in return possesses the Father in entirety in Himself. Thus the hypostasis of the Son is, so to speak, the form and presentation by which the Father is known, and the Father's hypostasis is recognized in the form of

71. Basil, *Holy Spirit* 10.26.
72. Ibid., 29.75.
73. Ibid., 29.73; 25.58.
74. Basil, *Epistles* 38.3.
75. Basil, *Holy Spirit* 18.46; *Against Eunomius* 4.1.

the Son."[76] The Cappadocians also sought to reply to the charge of tritheism by using the analogy of the Platonic form and its particulars, but did not really make this concept a determinative factor in their doctrine. Indeed, in attempting to avoid the charge of tritheism, Gregory of Nyssa was forced to argue that, strictly speaking, even three men who have the same nature in common should not be spoken of as "three humans," but as one human, since there is but one humanity.[77] If anything, that which was given as the major argument for the unity of the three was their unity of activity. For, said Gregory of Nyssa, "Father, Son and Holy Spirit cooperate in sanctifying, quickening, consoling and so on."[78] In the final analysis, number is indicative only of the quantity of things, not of the real nature of the persons. While each of the persons is designated one, they cannot be added together; thus number should not be used of deity at all.[79]

---

76. Basil, *Epistles* 38.8.
77. Gregory of Nyssa, *That There Are Not Three Gods*.
78. Cf. Basil, *Epistles* 189.6–7 (by Gregory of Nyssa).
79. Basil, *Holy Spirit* 44.

Part **2**

Problems Concerning the Doctrine of the Trinity

4

Is the Trinity Biblical and Does It Make Any Practical Difference?

We come now to a very different set of considerations. Since the fourth-century councils that established the official view of the Trinity, a great deal of time has elapsed and a large number and variety of developments have taken place. Out of these have grown a considerable number of objections to our holding and teaching the doctrine of the Trinity today in the form in which the church fathers enunciated it. In this chapter, we will examine two: (1) that the Trinity is not really a biblical doctrine, and (2) that this doctrine does not make any practical difference for Christian living.

Biblical Problems

In the process of formulating the doctrine of the Trinity, the early theologians drew on a large number of texts. Once the basic concept of threeness in oneness was arrived at, indications of this nature of God were found in many places. For example, the three men who came to visit Abraham in Genesis 18 were said to be a preincarnate theophany of the triune God. The threefold "holy, holy, holy" that the seraphs sang to one another (Isa. 6:3) was also thought to be an indication of this threefold nature of

God. The baptismal formula of Matthew 28:19 and the Pauline benediction of 2 Corinthians 13:14 were also considered indications of the triunity of God. It was thought that Paul's statement in Romans 11:36, "For from him and through him and to him are all things," was indicative of the different ways of relating to the creation by the three members of the Godhead. Although probably not available in this early period of theological construction, the clearest trinitarian proof text was found in the late Vulgate version of 1 John 5:7–8: "For there are three that testify in heaven: the Father, the Word, and the Holy Spirit, and these three are one. And there are three that testify on earth: the Spirit, the water, and the blood; and the three are in agreement."

One of the objections to the traditional view of the Trinity is that it rests on an outdated way of understanding the Scriptures. This is not merely a question of the interpretation of one passage of Scripture or another. Rather, it involves a completely different understanding of the nature and status of Scripture. Some of this happened in relatively simple and undisputed fashion. For example, textual criticism, accepted by both conservative and liberal scholars, concluded that the crucial portion of the 1 John 5 proof text was not part of the original reading of the biblical text, since no Greek manuscript earlier than the sixteenth century contained it. Other issues were more complex and controversial, however.

I have selected as a primary presenter of the objection to the biblical teaching of the Trinity the work of Cyril Richardson, in his small but influential book, *The Doctrine of the Trinity*.[1] This book is cited frequently by process theologians in their reconstruction of the biblical teaching about the Trinity.[2]

The objection that he raises, Richardson says, is not necessarily the common one about the paradoxical nature of the doctrine. He recognizes that such will be present, whether in the usual statement of the doctrine or in the variety of it that he constructs. To speak of God is to deal with contradictions. Rather, the ques-

1. Cyril C. Richardson, *The Doctrine of the Trinity* (Nashville: Abingdon, 1958).
2. E.g., Lewis S. Ford, *The Lure of God: A Biblical Background for Process Theism* (Philadelphia: Westminster, 1978), p. 99; John J. O'Donnell, *Trinity and Temporality: The Christian Doctrine of God in the Light of Process Theology and the Theology of Hope* (Oxford: Oxford University Press, 1983), pp. 83–84.

tion to be dealt with is whether the traditional doctrine of the Trinity expresses these necessary contradictions adequately. Richardson further feels that the concerns that lie behind the doctrine of the Trinity are very real ones. His intention is to show that the traditional position does not adequately express these concerns, and therefore engenders bewilderment instead of true faith.[3]

Part of the difference Richardson finds in the biblical teaching about the Trinity, as contrasted with the traditional way of expressing it, is the understanding of the nature of the New Testament writings. He assumes that the New Testament writers were trying to do the very thing we are, namely, to find appropriate language and symbols to express their faith in the God who had revealed himself in Jesus Christ. They did this by employing many different forms of thought and religious symbols. A key element in understanding these writings is to recognize "that the New Testament betrays a marked development in the understanding of the revelation in Jesus Christ, and is not all of one piece so far as the symbols used are concerned. They differ considerably from one writer to another."[4] He believes that failure to recognize this fundamental characteristic of the New Testament writings was one of the sources of confusion in trinitarian theology. Those who formulated the doctrine in the early centuries treated the biblical material as all of one piece, failing to see this development within the canon proper. Texts were torn from their contexts and misused to a large degree; certain symbols were absolutized independently of their original meaning.[5]

Richardson grants that the New Testament writers had two advantages over later theologians. For one thing, they were nearer to the dramatic events by which God unveiled himself in Jesus Christ. Further, the measure of their inspiration was greater than that of later theologians. Yet we have the benefit of something that they lacked, namely, two thousand years of Christian reflection and experience. Consequently, although we must listen humbly to what they have to say, we must evaluate critically what they wrote and attempt to express in ever clearer

3. Richardson, *Trinity,* p. 15.
4. Ibid., p. 16.
5. Ibid.

and more satisfactory ways the message they recorded. We are to engage in critical construction, using the materials supplied by the New Testament writers, as well as other insights, rather than simply accepting and repeating uncritically the thoughts that they articulated.[6]

Richardson observes that the doctrine of the Trinity is not a biblical doctrine, in the sense of being specifically found in the New Testament writings. It is a creation of the fourth-century church. While there are elements in the New Testament that point toward it, there are other elements that point away from it. There is a reason why the New Testament may not be used in an absolutistic and final fashion as the basis for our doctrine. Whereas the church theologians treated the Bible as unconditioned, Richardson holds that its conditionedness must be seen and taken into account. When he speaks of understanding the New Testament teachings in context, he is not merely referring to the surrounding biblical materials. Rather, he is thinking of the whole intellectual context from which it sprung. He says: "But the important thing is this: The background of thought in Judaism and Hellenistic culture, whence the New Testament symbols for understanding Jesus Christ were drawn, was not necessarily the best."[7] This background has given theology innumerable problems. Attempts to demythologize the New Testament have perhaps been unduly radical, but they point to the need for continued evaluation of the New Testament symbolism. It is not just the church fathers who, failing to understand this background, misunderstood it. The New Testament writers themselves were apparently affected by their backgrounds more than they realized. So, Richardson says, "We, then, like the New Testament writers, seek to express as adequately as possible the nature of this God who disclosed himself in Jesus Christ; and we should not feel bound by their particular symbolism if we find it at times detracts from, or confuses, the basic message it sought to convey."[8] There is apparently, in effect, a canon within a canon, a criterion by which evaluation and selection of the biblical symbols are made.

6. Ibid., p. 17.
7. Ibid.
8. Ibid.

The central problem around which Richardson's investigation and discussion revolves is the relationship between the Father and the Son stipulated in the New Testament. As important as are the questions of how God can be three and also one, and of the place of the Spirit in the Trinity, these are less fundamental. Not being recognized as such, however, the difference between the Father and the Son is often insufficiently examined. Of the several terms applied to Jesus, the ones that finally came to prevail in expressing the difference between him and God were Father and Son. After briefly tracing the development in Scripture of the concept of Jesus' sonship, Richardson says that this concept of a relation between God and a supramundane being involves the idea that God works through agents, which are angelic beings. In the case of Jesus the relation involves more than that. "It means," he says, "that the Word or Son is that aspect or 'mode of being' of God whereby he comes into relationship with the world, whereby he creates and reveals himself."[9]

This idea grows out of the paradoxical nature of God. He is absolutely transcendent and yet related to the world. This paradox is required philosophically, by the one and the many. God is both the absolute and the Creator of all that is. It is also important religiously, which from the Christian standpoint is ultimately more important. Being a jealous God, who can tolerate no rivals, Jehovah has no consort like the gods of the nature religions. He stands alone, not needing anyone or anything else. Yet he is related to his creatures, and this relatedness is expressed in various ways. Sometimes he acts directly, like a great king leading his armies personally in battle. At other times he acts by means of his "Spirit" or "wisdom" or "name," or his "angel" or "messenger."[10] In fact, Richardson says, "the more God's transcendent glory is stressed, the more need there is for intermediaries."[11] It was out of this background of the need for intermediaries that the ideas of the Son of God in Paul and the Logos or Word in John arose. The distinction between Father and Son is maintained in order to preserve this paradoxical character of God. Thus, says Rich-

9. Ibid., p. 21.
10. Ibid., p. 22.
11. Ibid., p. 23.

ardson, "God is *beyond* and yet he is *related;* that is the essence of the distinction between Father and Son."[12]

Richardson is quick to affirm, however, that these categories are inadequate to express the relationship. For one thing, there was an ambiguity in the concept of Father itself. It did, of course, represent the transcendent dimension of God in contrast to his relatedness. It also, however, included the idea of the Father showing love and pity for his children.[13] More serious, however, was the fact that this relationship was transferred from the situation of Jesus' earthly life to the eternal realm. Thus, the idea of eternal begetting was attached to the Father-Son relationship. That, however, is misleading, because it assumes the priority of God's beyondness to his relatedness, of his transcendence to his immanence. We have no reason to suppose this, however, says Richardson. His capacity for action is not secondary to or derived from, his absolute character.[14]

When examining the biblical teaching regarding the Son, Richardson maintains that "First and foremost in the New Testament the sonship of Jesus means the dependence of the man, Jesus of Nazareth, upon his heavenly Father."[15] It came to mean that in a special way Jesus was God's Son. That is to say, he had been given the vocation of the Messiah and fulfilled it according to God's purpose. As to the time of Jesus becoming the Messiah, however, there is no uniform testimony in the New Testament. Rather, what we find is indication of development. That development, as Richardson reconstructs it, would be that the earliest Christian preaching may be that in Acts 2:36; 5:31; 13:33, reflecting the primitive notion that Jesus became Son in this special sense, and hence Lord and Savior, at his resurrection. If he was Messiah then, however, he must also have been so before, and must have been given and responded to his vocation at his baptism. Further, however, if Jesus was already Messiah at his baptism, he must have been such by his birth, and thus we have the story of the nativity and the conception. Yet even this could not adequately account for the mighty acts done by God in Jesus.

12. Ibid.
13. Ibid., p. 30.
14. Ibid., pp. 35–36.
15. Ibid., p. 39.

This must have been someone who descended from the heavenly sphere. Hence we get the conception of the preexistent being, becoming incarnate in Jesus. The climax of this process of development comes in John's attribution to him of the Logos idea.[16]

Richardson is not prepared to declare that this development is strictly chronological. It may be that these differing ideas existed side by side in different geographical locations. What is important to notice, however, is the way in which the title "Son," originally used of the earthly sphere, is transposed to the heavenly realm. Instead of being God's adopted Son—the idea Richardson believes lies behind the use of Psalm 2:7—in John's and Paul's writings Christ now is God's "*own* son." By contrast, human beings can become sons only by adoption. Richardson summarizes this process: "What occurred then in the development was the granting of a truly divine status to Jesus the Christ."[17]

Richardson believes that the terms "Father" and "Son" are inadequate symbols for describing the nature of God's being. Their use introduces confusion into our thinking, producing a variety of "unnecessary and insoluble problems." While appropriate when applied to the humanity of Jesus of Nazareth, the term "son" should not be applied to a distinction within the Godhead.[18] His argument at this point is summed up well:

> A distinction in the Godhead certainly we have to make. He who is absolutely transcendent is at the same time the one who is related to us and unveiled in Jesus. To fail to make the distinction is to compromise the divine transcendence. Yet the distinction cannot be adequately made by the terms Father and Son. They derive originally from a relation of God to the creature and never can be sufficiently divested of their origin to illuminate or express a distinction within the Godhead itself.[19]

The final phase of Richardson's examination of the New Testament material is his treatment of the Spirit. He finds the primary notion of the Spirit in the Bible to be that of God's dynamic

16. Ibid., pp. 39–40.
17. Ibid., p. 41.
18. Ibid., pp. 43–44.
19. Ibid., p. 44.

activity. He develops three central themes: the Spirit as creative; the Spirit as the power of ecstasy; and the Spirit as connected with the end of history. The Spirit is generally distinguished from Christ in the New Testament, particularly as the divine power by which Jesus is conceived in the womb and adopted for the messianic mission at his baptism. As the effort was made to press the divine reality back further in the history of Jesus, however, it became difficult to say in what way he differed from the Spirit.[20]

In particular, Richardson finds a variety of conceptions about the nature of the Spirit in Paul's writings. He says, "it is evident that Paul had not thought the matter fully through; consequently he introduced some inconsistency into his thinking."[21] Paul presents the Spirit as the source or seat of God's vitality, his self-consciousness, his very being, the center of his "person." Whereas Christ is God's image, the Spirit is his inner being. Paul also, however, in Romans 8:26–27 treats the Spirit as if he were an entity distinct from the Father. Here, the Spirit comes very close to being the same as the indwelling Christ. Richardson thinks these two conceptions of the Spirit are irreconcilable; not only does Paul not try to reconcile them, but he also never resolves the issue of the contrast between Christ and the Spirit.[22]

There are other conceptions of the nature of the Spirit in the New Testament as well. The fact is that the symbolism in the New Testament was in a very fluid state, and no well-defined doctrine had emerged. As to the question of whether the Spirit is personal in the New Testament, Richardson says that the difficulty that has led to such extensive debates on this subject really lies in what we mean by "personal." He says that the best way to put it is that the Spirit is God's active approach to us. "Where the Spirit is given a personal quality such as teaching, revealing, witnessing, interceding, creating, and so on, it is not as an entity distinct from God, but as God himself doing these things and yet not compromising his transcendence."[23] It appears to be significant that Richardson put the question as he did. He asked whether the

20. Ibid., pp. 45–47.
21. Ibid., p. 50.
22. Ibid., pp. 50–51.
23. Ibid., p. 53.

Spirit is personal, rather than whether the Spirit is a person. By putting the question in adjectival rather than nominative form, he can answer in the affirmative.

Richardson develops his view at considerable length, by examining various conceptions of the Trinity that were propounded over the centuries of the church's history. Space does not permit us to note all of those comments. Nor would it be profitable to scrutinize his view that thoroughly. It is as representative of a whole that his view benefits us. For the value of this statement is to a large extent in its raising for us the whole question of the degree to which the traditional or classical doctrine of the Trinity really is based on the biblical revelation.

Our response to the challenge laid down by Richardson will be twofold. First, we will examine what the biblical revelation as a whole teaches us, for that is our ultimate authority in matters such as this. That response will come, both explicitly and implicitly, in the three chapters on the biblical material (Part 3). Second, we will make some evaluative comments on Richardson's thesis and argument.

There are several points at which Richardson's argument appears vulnerable.

1. Richardson displays an apparent lack of awareness, or at least, lack of acknowledgment, of the major assumptions underlying his case. So, for example, he does not consider the possibility of real inspiration of the biblical authors, and particularly, for the sake of this argument, of Paul. That Paul's thought contains contradictory elements Richardson seems to explain by saying that Paul had not really thought through his view on this matter. This, in turn, prevents him from seeking ways of harmonizing those ideas as strongly as he might if he considered those writings to have been produced through divine inspiration.

2. Richardson has a tendency to favor diversity over unity in attempting to understand the biblical materials, perhaps stemming from unconscious existentialist assumptions.

3. Richardson seems to make a latent evolutionary assumption. While he considers the diversity of biblical witnesses regarding the Son to be possibly geographical rather than chronologically ordered, the underlying belief seems to be that this development took place over time. Yet Richardson provides no

real documentation from Scripture. What one would expect is that he would try to show by the dating of the Pauline letters, for example, that what he considers earlier conceptions come from earlier writings. It seems suspiciously as if the framework has already been adopted, and that dating was then made to fit. But this may then be simply an instance of the nineteenth-century views of development of the more complex from the less complex.

4. Perhaps the most serious objection is to Richardson's basic thesis that the Father is God considered in his transcendence or independence of the world and that the Son is God from the perspective of his immanence or relating to the world. The problem, however, is that the data do not fit neatly into this schematism. In particular, the immanence of God is not restricted to his presence in the Son or in the Spirit, or at least is not in every case identified as being by that means (cf. e.g., Matt. 5:45; 6:25–30; 10:29–30). To be sure, Richardson speaks of the ambiguous nature of the image of Father, but perhaps that would not be the way he would view God's involvement in the world if he had not so sharply reassigned those dimensions of God to the separate persons. Conversely, it is not really possible to restrict the understanding of the Son to the immanent or relatedness dimension. In part because he regards the preexistence concept as something of a late inference, and because he mentions but does not really develop the idea of the present intercessory ministry of Jesus, Richardson is able to ignore some of these data.

5. Richardson does not grapple with some of the problems created by his interpretation. In effect, what he has done is to develop a type of modalism. Yet modalism has some serious and rather well-known problems attached to it. For example, modalism does not consider or deal with the fact that the different "persons" speak to and of one another in terms that seemingly imply that they are persons, individuals, rather than personal manifests of a single subject's activities. One of the reasons for rejecting the traditional trinitarian interpretation is because of the problems, especially the contradictions, which it contains or produces. Richardson has stated that he does not reject the Trinity because of its paradoxical nature, because any consideration of the doctrine of God must inevitably involve paradox. He does not really indicate his criteria for preferring one of these para-

doxical constructions over another, however. A common way of responding would be to say that one gives preference to that view that leads to fewer or less serious paradoxes, but it is not at all clear that this is the case with Richardson's view. Indeed, as we have sought to show above, some of the contradictions that he finds may well be products of the inappropriate presuppositions he brings to the consideration.

6. We should note the nature of the "biblical" argument that Richardson presents. While it purports to be biblically based, it frequently relies less on citation of specific Scripture than on logical arguments regarding the difficulty of a certain concept. It is, however, a different matter to say, "The Bible says this, but that is an untenable contention," than to say, "The Bible does not say this."

7. Richardson relies on a certain understanding of the conclusiveness and utility of biblical criticism that may not be currently justified. Richardson makes clear that the church fathers, in formulating the doctrine of the Trinity, utilized the Bible in a way that is no longer accessible to us.[24] To be sure, the rejection of an approach that takes texts out of context is desirable, and in a sense, indisputable. There are, however, certain elements of Richardson's argument that are now somewhat dated, and which are not made sufficiently specific or argued at great enough length to justify their use—statements such as "The background of thought in Judaism and Hellenistic culture, whence the New Testament symbols for understanding Jesus Christ were drawn, was not necessarily the best. This background has bequeathed to theology innumerable problems."[25] One could not, of course, hold Richardson, who published this book in 1958, responsible for the work that has been done since that time, considerably reducing the customary statements about the "assured results of biblical criticism." We, however, who live at this later point in time, which may well be termed the "postcritical," may find some of his contentions to be less impressive. This is not to say that there is not considerable controversy and debate about the current status of critical study, but the point is that one can no longer uncritically utilize biblical criticism. This is especially the

---

24. Ibid., p. 17.
25. Ibid.

case because Richardson seems to be drawing conclusions regarding his interpretations based on some such critical views, but without specific documentation and argumentation.

8. Finally, Richardson displays something of the "chronological snobbery" that C. S. Lewis[26] and others have criticized. He does, to be sure, concede that the New Testament writers were closer to the revelatory events than we are and even that they had a greater measure of inspiration than do we—a point which, as we noted above, does not really seem to play a significant role in his thinking. Then, however, he says rather blatantly, "Yet it is equally true that we profit from a benefit denied to them, viz., two thousand years of Christian reflection and experience."[27] The assumption seems to be that such additional reflection and experience will lead us closer to correct conclusions. That, however, depends on whether the assumptions underlying the thought are more adequate. For in a sense, the assumptions are like one of the premises of an argument. If that premise is false, the conclusion does not follow as true. It is the contention of some that this indeed is the case, that the more recent views are contaminated by assumptions incompatible with the material being interpreted. Indeed, a small but increasing number of theologians are undergoing a change of conviction on this very subject.[28]

There is another, more general objection against the doctrine of the Trinity. It is essentially an argument from the apparent silence of the Bible on this important subject. This contention notes that there really is no explicit statement of the doctrine of the Trinity in the Bible, particularly since the revelation by textual criticism of the spurious nature of 1 John 5:7b. Other passages have, in many cases, been seen on closer study to be applicable only under the greatest of strain. There are, to be sure, still a number of passages intimating something that contributes to the formulation of the doctrine. The question, however, is this. It

26. C. S. Lewis, *Christian Reflections* (Grand Rapids: Eerdmans, 1967), pp. 157–58.

27. Richardson, *Doctrine of the Trinity*, p. 17.

28. For examples of persons now quite critical of such modern presuppositions that they once held, see Thomas C. Oden, "On Not Whoring after the Spirit of the Age," in *No God but God: Breaking with the Idols of Our Age*, ed. Os Guinness and John Seel (Chicago: Moody, 1992), pp. 189–203; and Royce Gordon Gruenler, *The Inexhaustible God: Biblical Faith and the Challenge of Process Theism* (Grand Rapids: Baker, 1983).

is claimed that the doctrine of the Trinity is a very important, crucial, and even basic doctrine. If that is indeed the case, should it not be somewhere more clearly, directly, and explicitly stated in the Bible? If this is the doctrine that especially constitutes Christianity's uniqueness, as over against unitarian monotheism on the one hand, and polytheism on the other hand, how can it be only implied in the biblical revelation? In response to the complaint that a number of portions of the Bible are ambiguous or unclear, we often hear a statement something like, "It is the peripheral matters that are hazy or on which there seem to be conflicting biblical materials. The core beliefs are clearly and un-equivocally revealed." This argument would appear to fail us with respect to the doctrine of the Trinity, however. For here is a seemingly crucial matter where the Scriptures do not speak loudly and clearly.

Little direct response can be made to this charge. It is unlikely that any text of Scripture can be shown to teach the doctrine of the Trinity in a clear, direct, and unmistakable fashion. What we can do, however, is to look closely at the Bible and see if the wit-ness to the Trinity there may not be clearer and more broadly based than may have been thought. It is this endeavor that will occupy our attention in chapters 8 to 10.

There is one final and quite serious consideration regarding the biblical status of the doctrine of the Trinity. That concerns the texts that seem to argue against it. We do not have in mind so much here the assertions regarding the oneness of God, for those must be part of the positive overall case that we are building. The problem of their relationship to the texts suggesting the deity of each of the three will be dealt with in chapter 12. What we have in mind here are rather the texts that seem to confute the claims for the deity of one or the other, especially the texts used by the Arians and others to argue for the inferiority of the Son to the Fa-ther. While they will be dealt with concretely in chapter 9, we need to note them here.

The first group of texts are those that seem to say that the Son was a creature. Foremost of these, at least historically the text that seemed to lead to the Arian position, was Proverbs 8:22–26, which contains such statements as "When there were no oceans, I was given birth" (v. 24); and "before the mountains were settled in place, before the hills, I was given birth" (v. 25). Other significant texts of this type include Acts 2:36 ("God has made this Jesus, whom you crucified, both Lord and Christ"); Romans 8:29 ("the firstborn among many brothers"); Colossians 1:15 ("the firstborn over all creation"); and Hebrews 3:2 ("He was faithful to the one who appointed him" [ποιήσαντι, from ποιέω, often translated, "make"]).

The second classification of passages is those in which God the Father is represented as the only true God, especially when these are uttered by Jesus himself. The classic example is John 17:3, "that they may know you, the only true God, and Jesus Christ, whom you have sent." Another example of this type is Jesus' response to the ruler who addressed him as "Good teacher." "Why do you call me good? No one is good—except God alone" (Mark 10:18; Luke 18:19).

A third group of texts includes those that seem to imply that Jesus is inferior or subordinate to the Father. The most notable of these is John 14:28, where Jesus says very directly, "the Father is greater than I." A somewhat different text of this type is where the Son subordinates himself to the Father, such as Matthew 26:39: "My Father, if it is possible, may this cup be taken from me. Yet not as I will, but as you will."

The final group of texts appealed to by the Arians as objections to the full equality of the Son with the Father is the whole collection of statements about the limitations on the Son, whether involving ignorance, weakness, suffering, or development. Probably the major one is Jesus' direct statement, "No one knows about that day or hour, not even the angels in heaven, nor the Son, but only the Father" (Matt. 24:36). Such ignorance is also implied in Jesus' requests for information, such as the question directed to the father of the demon-possessed boy, "How long has he been like this?" (Mark 9:21). Luke 2:52 ("Jesus grew in wisdom and stature, and in favor with God and men") is an indication of development, presumably from less perfect to more complete, as is Hebrews 5:8 ("Although he was a son, he learned obedience from what he suffered").

In general, the response to these texts has been to point out that they refer to Jesus' time of earthly abode during his incarnation, or the state of humiliation. Not all of these texts can be easily disposed of, however, and we will need to examine them more closely in Chapter 9.

Practical Problems

An entirely different type of objection pertains to the practicality or relevance or pertinence of the doctrine of the Trinity. In general these objections can be classified into two groups: those that contend on principle that the doctrine does not, and virtually cannot, have any practical significance, and those that argue empirically, that in reality it does not, and therefore, presumably cannot.

The person who first raised the former variety of pragmatic objection was the philosopher, Immanuel Kant. He had begun his consideration of the relationship of propositions to reason in his *Critique of Pure Reason.* In this work he considered the necessary conditions for obtaining theoretical knowledge and concluded that we cannot have such knowledge of supersensible objects. Those must then be the concern of the practical reason. Many traditional religious teachings fall here.

If religion is primarily a practical (or ethical) rather than a theoretical (or doctrinal) matter, then its doctrines and passages of its Scriptures must be interpreted in this light. So Kant says, "Passages of Scripture which contain certain *theoretical* doctrines, proclaimed as sacred but going beyond all the concepts of reason (even the moral ones) *may* be interpreted to the advantage of the latter; and those which contain statements contradictory to reason *must* be so interpreted."[29] His first example of such doctrines is that of the Trinity: "From the doctrine of the Trinity, taken literally, nothing whatsoever can be gained for practical purposes, even if one believes that one comprehended it—and less still if one is conscious that it surpasses all our concepts."[30] It makes no difference, says Kant, whether we worship three gods or ten, because "it is impossible to extract from this difference any different rules for practical living."

29. Immanuel Kant, *Der Streit der Fakultäten* (Hamburg: Felix Meiner, 1975 [Philosophische Bibliothek, Band 252]), p. 33.
30. Ibid., p. 34.

An example of the other kind of practical problem can be found in the writings of Karl Rahner. He contends that in actual practice, the doctrine of the Trinity has no bearing on the lives and practices of Christians. In their practical lives, Christians are almost mere "monotheists." He says, "We must be willing to admit that, should the doctrine of the Trinity have to be dropped as false, the major part of religious literature could well remain virtually unchanged."[31] Some will surely object, claiming that the incarnation is at the very heart of the Christian faith, both religiously and theologically, thus making the Trinity also crucially important. This, however, according to Rahner, also is irrelevant, for in actual practice the belief of these persons is that "God" became man, and that "one" of the divine persons took on flesh, rather than specifically that the Logos became incarnate. He comments, "One has the feeling that, for the catechism of head and heart (as contrasted with the printed catechism), the Christian's idea of the incarnation would not have to change at all if there were no Trinity."[32] Rahner is referring to what I have termed "unofficial theology"—that belief we actually hold in practice, regardless of what we hold in our official creedal belief. Note that here the contention is not that the Trinity has, or cannot have, any practical significance, but that in practice it does not. This contention, however, if sustainable, must inevitably push us back to the earlier form posed by Kant.

Underlying both of these positions, although probably not recognized by the advocates of the latter view, is a definite ideology. In the version of the former that we saw above, it was the Kantian classification of human experience into theoretical or cognitive, practical or moral, and emotional or aesthetic categories. In more recent times, one of the philosophies developed from this scheme is pragmatism. Beginning first as a theory of meaning and later becoming a theory of truth, pragmatism is the evaluation of ideas or systems of ideas on the basis of the criterion of whether they "work," that is, whether they meet generally recognized needs. There are a large number of varieties of this overall philosophy. In fact, Arthur O. Lovejoy wrote an article entitled

31. Karl Rahner, *The Trinity* (New York: Herder & Herder, 1970), pp. 10–11.
32. Ibid., p. 11.

"The Thirteen Pragmatisms."[33] One of the problems for any of these is the question of how to decide the end toward which these philosophies contribute. This involves a choice of values, and that choice cannot be made entirely on the basis of the pragmatic theory alone. If, for example, the view is to be evaluated in terms of whether it contributes to the good of the human, the question becomes, What is the good for the human, and, even beyond that, what is humanity? The other major problem becomes the time span within which to make the judgment. Is that which works for ten minutes the best? For one month? One year? Ten years? These questions frequently are not answered, or even asked, but the answers to them are crucial for pragmatism.

Pragmatism has made its impact in many different fields of endeavor, and not merely on the academic but also on the popular level. It is not uncommon to find its influence in Christian circles, especially among lay persons and practicing ministers. This has always been the case to some extent; pragmatism was fairly widespread in some varieties of liberalism in the nineteenth century. More recently, however, it has exerted considerable force within the "church growth" movement.

This movement, as known in our time, theoretically is concerned about both the quantitative and the qualitative dimensions of growth of local congregations. In practice, however, it is the numerical expansion that gets primary attention and appears to be the goal pursued. Ideology, or more correctly, theology, is not as highly prized. Indeed, it is sometimes either said overtly or implicitly that one problem that has hampered the church has been its excessive concern for theological issues—sometimes unnecessarily minute and specific.[34] The preaching and teaching within this movement do not emphasize doctrine to the extent that was true in an earlier generation. The presence of theological distinctions may be a hindrance to the achievement of numerical success. Denominations, for example, were at one time the result of theological differences. Baptists insisted on believers' baptism by immersion, whereas Presbyterians did not, but

33. Arthur O. Lovejoy, "The Thirteen Pragmatisms," *Journal of Philosophy* 5 (January 16, 1908): 29–39.

34. Os Guinness, *Dining with the Devil: The Megachurch Movement Flirts with Modernity* (Grand Rapids: Baker, 1993), p. 26.

instead insisted on a Calvinistic understanding of the way of salvation, a distinctive that in turn distinguished them from Methodists, whose baptismal practices may have been quite similar.

More recently, churches have become much more denominationally generic. The name of the traditional denomination with which the congregation is affiliated may be dropped from its name. This decision is not an indication, in most cases, of a deep soul-searching about the correctness of the respective denominational doctrines, but rather is a pragmatic matter, a desire to appear as nonexclusive as possible, so that a greater number of persons will be willing to attend.

This can be seen in other areas as well. Seventh-Day Adventists worship on Saturday because they are convinced, on biblical and theological grounds, that the observance of the Sabbath is still mandatory. Some churches now offer Saturday evening services, not because of biblical or theological considerations, but because there are people who, because of work or other commitments, or simply because of convenience, would not attend on Sunday. There is a considerable difference between worshiping at a given time because of biblical and theological conviction and worshiping because of expediency. For that matter, there is a difference of motivation between providing a service on a Saturday because work schedules prohibit one from attending on a Sunday, and doing so because it does not interfere with people's recreational plans.

In this type of environment, complex and controversial doctrines such as the Trinity get little positive exposition and inculcation. I have not heard anyone within the church growth movement speak against the doctrine of the Trinity. Yet I am not aware of much teaching and preaching on the subject. The topics that are addressed are frequently not doctrinal subjects at all. Rather, the concern is with practical matters of life problems. While belief in the Trinity may be quite widely held, it is not something that attracts people to a church, and the fine distinctions that have characterized trinitarian debate can easily be regarded as a waste of time or irrelevant.[35]

35. Os Guinness, "Sounding Out the Idols of Church Growth," in *No God but God: Breaking with the Idols of Our Age*, ed. Os Guinness and John Seel (Chicago: Moody, 1992), p. 165.

5

Is the Doctrine of the Trinity Metaphysically Intelligible and Logically Coherent?

The objections to the doctrine of the Trinity discussed in this chapter do not assume the type of commitment to biblical Christianity that those in the preceding chapter appear to. Those treated here are more purely intellectual objections to the tenability of the doctrine of the Trinity.

The Metaphysical Problem

The view of the Trinity as developed in the first four centuries and fixed in the formulas developed at the Councils of Nicea and Constantinople is very metaphysical. It is couched in terms of essence, substance, hypostases, persons, and other concepts. It is quite clear that this way of conceiving the issues was bound to Greek metaphysics. To the extent that emphasis was placed on the immanent Trinity, or God in his eternal triune nature, it was metaphysical; to the extent that it stressed the economic Trinity, it was historical.

Since the beginning of the nineteenth century, however, the metaphysics of the Trinity has been challenged by a series of crises. Much of this is related to the general decline of metaphysics. There are actually several aspects to this metaphysical problem, or perhaps it would be more accurate to speak of a complex of several different metaphysical problems.

In general, the crisis began with the critical philosophy of Immanuel Kant. More than most philosophers, Kant exerted a strong influence on the direction of theology. In fact, one significant series on the history of Christian thought entitled two of its volumes *Protestant Thought before Kant* and *Protestant Thought after Kant*. Kant stated that David Hume had awakened him from his dogmatic slumbers, but he in turn sought to awaken others, especially theologians, from *their* dogmatic slumbers.[1]

Kant developed his thought in three major treatises, termed critiques. The first of these, the *Critique of Pure Reason*, concerned theoretical reason and its objects of knowledge. Kant maintained that cognition involves two components. The senses provide the content of knowledge, and the forms of understanding, which are part of the mind of the knower, supply the form or structure of knowledge. Both elements are necessary for knowledge. Whereas rationalists had contended that knowledge could be obtained by pure abstract thought, and empiricists claimed that knowledge was a result of sense experience, Kant insisted on both. He said, "Percepts without concepts are blind; concepts without percepts are empty."[2]

The most significant implication of this formula was that it became impossible to have theoretical knowledge of supersensible objects. This covered the usual objects of metaphysics, as well as most of the doctrines of a religion such as Christianity. Theology would have to go in one of several directions in the post–Kant era. It would either have to refute Kant, show that his philosophy was not really antithetical to traditional theology, reformulate doctrine on some other basis than metaphysics, or abandon its enterprise completely. Kant himself did not abandon religion, but relocated its basis. In the *Critique of Practical Reason*, he reintroduced God and some other theological concepts as necessary postulates of the practical reason, essential for the functioning of ethics. Thus, religion became a matter of ethics rather

---

1. Immanuel Kant, *Prolegomena to Any Future Metaphysics* (New York: Liberal Arts, 1951), introduction.

2. Immanuel Kant, *Critique of Pure Reason*, I, second part, first division ("Transcendental Analytic"), book 2, chapters 1 & 3.

than of doctrine, and any theology that was to be developed would have to issue from the practical considerations of ethics and the ethical consciousness, rather than from pure or theoretical reason.

The first major response to this challenge came from Friedrich Schleiermacher. Schleiermacher basically accepted the critical thrust of Kant's first thesis, namely, that religion cannot be based on theoretical reason or intellectual propositions. He also, however, rejected Kant's approach of making ethics, or the practical realm, the locus of religion. For Schleiermacher, a romanticist in philosophy and a pietist in religion, the proper realm of religion was feeling. In this respect, he seemed to have identified religion with Kant's third critique, the *Critique of Judgment,* which dealt with the realm of esthetics. He made quite clear that anything piety might have borrowed either from science or ethics, it gladly gave back.[3]

Religion, for Schleiermacher, was a matter of feeling. There is an alternation in his thought. At times, Schleiermacher appears to say that any feeling at all is piety. At other times, however, he is quite specific, insisting that it is the feeling of ultimate dependence that is piety or religion.[4] Theology, in this view of religion, must also be feeling-based. The doctrines of Christianity are read off from the religious consciousness of Christian persons.[5]

This meant that for Schleiermacher, the Trinity was given a very minor place in the total scheme of things. Because it cannot really be the object of any specific feeling, or one cannot have a consciousness of God as Trinity, it must be at best an inference from a combination of feelings.[6] Consequently, Schleiermacher puts the discussion of the Trinity at the very end of his treatise, virtually as an appendix to the whole of doctrine. The Trinity has lost any position of prominence that it might have had, and even such position is now within a totally reworked conception of doctrine, as virtually a cryptodoctrine, not really a matter of metaphysics but of feeling.

3. Friedrich Schleiermacher, *On Religion: Speeches to Its Cultured Despisers* (New York: Harper & Brothers, 1958), p. 35.

4. Ibid., p. 45.

5. Ibid., pp. 47–50.

6. Friedrich Schleiermacher, *The Christian Faith* (New York: Harper & Row, 1963), 2: §170.

A very different response to the Kantian epistemology was made by Georg Hegel. Kant had argued that one cannot extend the categories of the understanding beyond sensory experience in part on the grounds that when one attempts to do so, the result is antinomies: two mutually exclusive positions, either of which is equally plausible, but between which one cannot choose. What appeared to be the death of metaphysics appeared to Hegel, however, to be the key to the whole of reality. Rather than proceeding logistically, or in straight-line fashion from premise to premise, eliminating contradictions, Hegel instead proceeded dialectically. That is to say, he understood reality to be organized on the pattern of thesis-antithesis-synthesis. This is how history unfolds and how logic proceeds. Thus, the order of the mind or the order of thinking matched well the order of the universe and of history. Rather than being irreconcilable opposites, what Kant termed the antinomies were seen by Hegel as thesis and antithesis, which are eventually reconciled as a synthesis.

In this way of thinking, philosophy is the supreme science. Religion, and specifically theology, must be interpreted philosophically. Philosophy enables faith to understand itself for the first time.[7] The doctrines of Christianity are not to be taken literally. Those who do so, need nothing further. They believe they have the actual, factual truth. Rather, what we must do is to see the doctrine of the Trinity, as well as other doctrines, as philosophical truth, resting on general philosophical premises. This doctrinal analysis will therefore follow the general laws of logic, namely, the triadic or dialectical pattern. The Trinity in particular is especially well suited to this triadic pattern.[8]

In Hegel's understanding, God is absolute Spirit, posited in three forms. Thought of as pure abstract idea, God is Father. He is God in himself. This God, however, may be thought of as going forth from himself into the realm of finite existence, otherness, or physical nature. Here God is the Son, God as other than himself. This is the antithesis to the thesis that is God in himself. God can also be conceptualized as returning to himself, or the Spirit. The Spirit cancels this distinction of God from himself, returning

7. Georg Hegel, *Lectures on the Philosophy of Religion,* trans. E. B. Speirs and J. B. Sanderson (London: Kegan Paul, 1895), 3:148.
8. Ibid., 1:7–33.

home enriched by this outgoing as the synthesis of the thesis and antithesis.[9]

This approach makes the Trinity a thoroughly metaphysical matter. It is not, however, the type of metaphysic usually thought of as the Trinity. Here the doctrinal formulations are symbolic and pictorial, rather than in any sense literal representations of truths. The incarnation is not a one-time occurrence, but a symbol of the continued or repeated truth of God going forth from himself. The generation of the Son is a symbol for the creation of the world. Thus, although the Trinity was metaphysical, it was a rather different metaphysic from that which had characterized the previous articulations of the doctrine. It was a metamorphosis of the metaphysic. In the judgment of most orthodox Christians, it so transformed the understanding of the Trinity that this formulation scarcely deserved to be called the Trinity. And, with the decline of Hegelianism, it also receded as a genuine option in most persons' thinking.

The next major nineteenth-century theology was that of Albrecht Ritschl, whose thought was to become the source of probably the most popular form of liberal theology in that century. Ritschl basically accepted Kant's analysis of the nature of knowledge and of religion. Unlike Schleiermacher, he also accepted Kant's solution to the problem. That is to say, religion is seen as focused in the practical realm, or in the area of value judgments. Ritschl insisted on the independence of religion. Religion is not to be judged by general philosophical principles, but "from the standpoint of the redeemed community of Christ."[10] Consequently, Ritschl was opposed to Hegel's view, with its reduction of Christian doctrine to comprehensive philosophical categories. He was also opposed to formulating doctrines from religious consciousness, as Schleiermacher and his followers had done.

As noted, Ritschl accepted Kant's distinction between theoretical or cognitive and religious knowledge. The latter type of knowledge consists solely of independent value judgments of faith. He stated, "We know the nature of God and Christ only in

9. Ibid., 3.2; *Encyclopaedie*, § 564.
10. Albrecht Ritschl, *The Christian Doctrine of Justification and Reconciliation* (New York: Scribners, 1900), 3:5. Cf. p. 202.

their worth for us."[11] When applied to doctrine, this approach eliminated any possibility of a disinterested knowledge of God. The type of scientific or dispassionate objective study of religion that was to characterize the "scientific study of religion" movement and the comparative study of religions was clearly precluded by this approach. Religion, in this conception, is essentially a practical matter; metaphysical theory is of no importance for value judgments. In making religion a practical matter, Ritschl was not denying the objectivity of the matters to which he was referring. He was merely excluding from theology all assertions that could be considered speculative or metaphysical in nature.

What, then, are the implications for the doctrine of the Trinity of such a way of conceiving of religion? In Ritschl's judgment, the Trinity was a matter of speculative thought, not of practical issues. It cannot be the object of value judgments. Consequently, he nowhere includes the Trinity in his doctrinal scheme. As far as God is concerned, "Personality is the form in which the idea of God is given through revelation. As theology has to do with the God revealed in Christ, this is justified scientifically as the only practical form of the conception of God."[12] His full description of the biblical revelation of God is: "God and Father of our Lord Jesus Christ." Nothing more than this is intended when we use the terms "Father, Son, and Holy Spirit." Ritschl says, "for the name denotes God in so far as He reveals Himself, while the Holy Spirit is the power of God which enables the community to appropriate His self-revelation through His Son."[13] Beyond this it is not possible to say anything about God "in himself," or even about distinctions in his nature as he reveals himself to us.

What, then, can we say about Christ? Only that he, in his personal character, is the bearer of the revelation of God. That, however, is not a theoretical judgment, but a value judgment of the most direct sort.[14] What of the various statements of christological formulas, such as those of the Chalcedonian type? These belong to the sphere of disinterested scientific knowledge, and are

11. Ibid., p. 212.
12. Ibid., p. 237.
13. Ibid., p. 273.
14. Ibid., p. 389.

therefore not of the nature of religion. This is even more true of the doctrine of the Trinity. It is largely irrelevant to theology's main business. Ritschl himself did not discuss the Trinity in any systematic fashion. Some of his many and varied disciples did, however.

As is generally the case with any influential founder of a new school of thought in any field, Ritschl's followers divided into right and left wings. Those on the right wing included Wilhelm Hermann, Theodore Häring, and Julius Kaftan. They were more tolerant of doctrinal formulations than was Ritschl. Hermann and Häring were embarrassed by the doctrine of the Trinity, and while not wishing to abandon it, were hard pressed to know how to incorporate it into their teaching. Kaftan, however, restored it to a central place in the doctrine of God.[15] The left wing was represented by Adolf von Harnack, who in many ways represented the culmination of Ritschl's views and the pinnacle of this variety of liberalism.

In Harnack's thought we find the same anti-metaphysical atmosphere that characterized Ritschl's work. The revelation of God is limited to his Fatherhood. There really is no such doctrine as the Trinity here. Jesus' message was in no sense about himself, but rather about the Father. Jesus called us to believe with him, not in him. Harnack says, *"The Gospel, as Jesus proclaimed it, has to do with the Father only and not with the Son."*[16] Jesus' message involved only three major points: the kingdom of God and its coming; God the Father and the infinite value of the human soul; the higher righteousness and the commandment of love.[17] This was the sum and substance of his message, and this is what he invites us to believe.

As noted, Jesus had nothing to say about himself. He associated himself with all men in his relationship to the Father. God is the Father of Jesus just as he is the Father of all men. Thus, any customary understanding of the relationships within the Trinity is dissolved in favor of a more generalized father-son relationship of all persons to God. To be sure, Jesus knew the Father in

15. Claude Welch, *In This Name: The Doctrine of the Trinity in Contemporary Theology* (New York: Scribners, 1952), pp. 20–22.

16. Adolf Harnack, *What Is Christianity?* (New York: Harper & Brothers, 1957), p. 144.

17. Ibid., p. 51.

a new way and sought to communicate this to all men. This was all he came to seek to accomplish, however. He "desired no other belief in his person and no other attachment to it than is contained in the keeping of his commandments."[18]

Harnack went beyond Ritschl and the more conservative Ritschlians by seeking to account for the early presence in the Christian tradition of such metaphysical conceptions as the Trinity. His massive *History of Dogma* is an attempt to trace the growth of the tradition from the initial nondoctrinal and nonchristological message of Jesus to the complex metaphysical theology of Nicea and Chalcedon. He finds the Christian community borrowing heavily from Greek philosophy.[19] It was from these foreign sources, not from Jesus himself, that the doctrine of the Trinity, the incarnation, and related conceptions grew.

All of these approaches rendered questionable the traditional view of the Trinity, either by moving religion and theology out of the realm of metaphysics, as in the case of Schleiermacher, Ritschl, and Harnack, or by insisting on a different type of metaphysics, as in the case of Hegel and his followers. In the twentieth century, a more thoroughgoing and violent assault on the possibility of any sort of metaphysical inquiry took place. This was found in the revolutionary developments within the field of philosophy. Some of that will be dealt with in the latter part of this chapter, since it formulated what was a logical objection to metaphysics.

We do want to examine briefly, however, a twentieth-century objection to the traditional type of metaphysics involved in the Trinity that was not, however, an objection to metaphysics per se, an alternative approach to metaphysics. We have in mind here the school of thought known as process theology, which was based on process metaphysics.

Usually cited as the founder of process thought is Alfred North Whitehead. He insisted, as have all those who have followed him in process thought, that the basic unit of reality is not the substance, as has been customarily thought, but the event. Further— and this is key for our purposes here—God is not outside the usual categories of metaphysics that apply to all other reality, but

18. Ibid., p. 125.
19. Adolf Harnack, *History of Dogma* (New York: Dover, 1961), 2:13–14.

is part of it. Thus, Whitehead wrote, "God is not to be treated as an exception to all metaphysical principles, invoked to save their collapse. He is their chief exemplification."[20] Traditional or classical metaphysics had emphasized the difference between God, who is infinite and unchanging, and the creation, which is finite and changing. On this view, however, whatever laws govern the created universe also govern God. In Whitehead's metaphysics, the fundamental building blocks of reality are called actual entities, each of which has two poles—the physical pole and the mental pole. The mental pole is this actual entity's desire for and realization of ideal forms, or, as Whitehead terms them, eternal objects. These are the essences or universals. Whitehead once said that the history of Western philosophy was a series of footnotes to the thought of Plato, and it is here that we see this admiration and dependence. Whitehead's eternal objects correspond to Plato's forms or ideas, at least on one interpretation of them. The physical pole, on the other hand, is this actual entity's direct rapport with the environment from which it springs.

As we noted, Whitehead insists that God is bound by and involved in the same metaphysical processes and rules applicable to anything else. Thus God, whom he speaks of as the nontemporal actual entity, must have both a mental pole and a physical pole.[21] Whitehead calls the former God's primordial nature, and the latter, God's consequent nature. His primordial nature is the realm of possibilities, existing in abstraction from all particular matters of fact. His consequent nature is his concreteness in his relatedness to the world and as the world's events are objectified in him. God is acted on by the world, receiving from it the effects of its actions.

Charles Hartshorne, a disciple of Whitehead, reworked the concept of God. He draws a distinction between the divine existence and the divine actuality. The divine existence is necessary. It is necessarily the case that God exists; it could not be otherwise. Hartshorne considers the ontological proof valid, because it is not conceivable that the most perfectly conceivable being not exist. Yet God's actuality is contingent. He must necessarily

20. Alfred North Whitehead, *Process and Reality: An Essay in Cosmology* (New York: Macmillan, 1929), p. 521.
21. Ibid., pp. 521–24.

exist, but how he exists, or in what particular state he exists, is contingent. With respect to what he is like, or his concrete side, God is of the same logical class as other individuals. He is a "product," as it were, of the concrete and finite existents to which he is related. The difference between him and other individuals is that for him the class of his possible states could not have been empty, but for them there might not have been any such states. God has no options regarding whether he exists or does not exist, but he has options as to *how* he exists or in what particular states he exists.[22] God, then, is bipolar. The abstract pole is necessary, eternal, and unchanging; the relative pole is contingent, temporal, and changing. Hartshorne's understanding of God is as "the self-changing whole which includes all other beings and its (more or less) self-changing parts."[23]

Another theologian who has attempted to relate this metaphysical conception of God specifically to the doctrine of the Trinity is Schubert Ogden. According to Ogden, God is not merely an individual but the supreme individual, the one whose own reality constitutes reality itself or as such. It is appropriate to refer to him as both transcendent and immanent. "Thus, while God as individually distinct from the world is affirmed to transcend it, he is also affirmed to be immanent in the world as its primary source, even as the world is immanent in him as its final end."[24]

In Ogden's view, which he refers to as "neoclassical theism," "God" and "the world" are regarded as correlative terms. God is essentially God precisely as the source and the consequence of the world; the world is essentially the world as having its beginning and end in God. "God" refers to one unique individual. "The world," on the other hand, is actually a collective term, referring to all these other individuals and events of which God is the source and end. Thus far, this sounds much like classical theism. The major difference, however, emerges when Ogden specifies more fully the nature of this relationship: "his [God's] relation to

22. Charles Hartshorne, *Creative Synthesis and Philosophic Method* (LaSalle, Ill.: Open Court, 1970), p. 144.
23. Charles Hartshorne, *Man's Vision of God and the Logic of Theism* (New York: Harper & Brothers, 1941), p. 349.
24. Schubert M. Ogden, "On the Trinity," *Theology* 83 (March 1980): 97.

the world is internal as well as external. It is essential to him that he should be the ever-growing whole of reality itself, who grows in reaction to the growth of his world, or of the nondivine individuals and events, of which he alone is the final end."[25] God's very essence is to grow, but this is not to say that his essence grows. The one respect in which God never grows is that he never ceases to grow as the ever-growing source and consequence of all growth.

This interrelationship with the world is what process theologians like Ogden mean by love. The symbolization of the reality of God as the first principle of reality is "pure unbounded love." God is "at once the eminent subject and the eminent object of love, the one individual whose essence is both to love and to be loved by *all*—himself as well as others."[26] How, then, does this understanding of God relate to the doctrine of the "immanent Trinity"? Ogden began his article by affirming that an appropriate account of Christian revelation requires speaking of God as essentially triune, thus requiring both the concept of an economic and an immanent Trinity. What would this mean in this sort of metaphysical framework?

Ogden seeks to relate the one substance and three persons by use of the distinction between individual and individuality. There is a parallel between the relationship of individual to individuality and between person and personality. The person is "the concrete unity of a certain sequence of human experiences"; the personality is "the complex of abstract traits or characteristics which identify all the experiences in this sequence as belonging to one human being rather than another."[27] Thus, the one divine substance is God himself, the eminent individual, who both loves and is loved by himself and all others. Thus he is the primal source and the final end of reality as such. There are then the three divine persons, who are, respectively, *"Father*, or the essence of the eminent individual as both loving and loved by himself and all others, i.e., the divine *individuality* as such; *Son*, or the essence of the eminent individual as loved by himself and all others, i.e., divine *objectivity* as such; and *Holy Spirit*, or the es-

25. Ibid., p. 98.
26. Ibid.
27. Ibid.

sence of the eminent individual as loving himself and all others, i.e., divine *subjectivity* as such."[28]

In this Trinity, then, the customary categories of substance metaphysics have been translated into process categories. Instead of one substance in three persons, we have one substance, God himself in Father, the divine individuality as such; Son, the divine objectivity as such; and Holy Spirit, the divine subjectivity as such. Ogden believes these terms are appropriate, for the divine individuality as such is the fountain of the whole Trinity, both loving and loved by all individuals, himself and others, so that here we are dealing with both divine subjectivity and divine objectivity in their primordial unity.[29]

Another process theologian who has sought to develop the doctrine of the Trinity using process categories is Lewis Ford. His is one of the clearer statements of process thought. He begins his exposition by noting the present evil days on which trinitarian reflection has fallen. It once was a cutting-edge response to a pressing need, namely, how to sort out the biblical symbols for God and his activity, and especially, how to relate the two central symbols, "Christ" and "God." Then, however, under the threat of heresy, it crystallized into dogma, becoming not the goal of theological reflection but at best its starting-point and at worst a bit of cultural baggage the continued presence of which had to be explained and rationalized.[30]

In more recent years, the doctrine has been used as a means of relating the question of God's transcendence of and immanence within the world. It is not, however, obvious that such an endeavor requires a triunity of principles. Ford proposes to take the endeavor one step further. Whereas classical theism saw only a single problem, namely, the question of God's transcendence and immanence, to which a twofold solution is quite adequate, Ford notes that from the standpoint of process theism there is a double problem—one aspect concerning God's transcendence of and immanence within the world, and the other aspect consisting of the world's transcendence of and immanence within God. The

28. Ibid.
29. Ibid., p. 99.
30. Lewis Ford, "Process Trinitarianism," *Journal of the American Academy of Religion* 53.2 (June 1975): 199.

solution of this double problem, he maintains, will require a triunity of principles within God. He argues that if it can be shown that this is the case and that this triunity is intimately correlated with the basic biblical symbols of Father, Word, and Spirit, then we will have gone a long way toward showing how these symbols may be appropriated today. Thus, he says, trinitarian speculation may have spoken more wisely than it knew, providing the basic coordinates of a problem that did not even arise on the horizon of classical theism.[31] Hence, he would in effect contend, process theism deals with the real problem of God, the problem which in the classical orthodox way of understanding did not even require the Trinity. It might be said that Ford believes that contrary to the idea that process theism eviscerates the Trinity, it alone truly preserves it. He sets himself a threefold task: to show how the three symbols of Father, Word, and Spirit can be expressed using the terms of Whitehead's process theism; to correlate these expressions with the threefold structure of his concept of God; and to show why this threefold structure is necessary in order to express the mutual transcendence of God and the world.[32]

Whitehead rejects what he terms "the fallacy of simple location," the idea that each actuality occupies its own spatiotemporal place distinct from the places of all other actualities. This is actually an instance of the broader "fallacy of displaced concreteness," which considers past occurrences to be as concrete and exclusive as present experiences. Actually, they continue to exist as constituents of present experiences. This is belief in radical immanence, for past events are literally part of present experiences. They are actually there, not as mere representations or copies of them. This is possible because of Whitehead's concept of "eternal objects," which are atemporal and thus indifferent to whether they are past or present. It is literally the same event in both cases, although in the latter it is part of a larger whole. Thus one can speak of the cause as immanent within the effect, and can speak of God as causally influencing the world, or in more traditional terms, can speak of God's activity as the Holy Spirit.[33]

31. Ibid., pp. 199–200.
32. Ibid., p. 200.
33. Ibid.

We usually think of past causes as actively producing present effects, which are simply passive outcomes of those causes. In Whitehead's thought, however, such is not the case. Instead of such a deterministic causation, there is a reversal of this active/ passive relationship. Present effects actively produce themselves out of their past, objectified, passive causes. There need not be just one way in which the past is appropriated in the present creative unification. This unification may take place in more than one combination. That there can be such creativity and such novelty going beyond mere repetition of the past, requires a source of such novelty transcending the past world. This stems from an ideal toward which each actuality is inspired to strive, and this ideal is derived from God. And, since this causality is also immanent, God is present within the actuality in this ideal.[34]

The Spirit is God at work in us in many ways. One is the awareness of the divine aims in terms of the ethical aspiration so vividly evident in the Hebrew prophets. Another is the discovery of the novel possibilities hitherto unactualized in the world. Finally, it is by the Spirit that we learn to respond to God, since it is through awareness of those values first purposely entertained by God that we seek out their divine source. This should be understood as a prompting by God, however, not a determination. We are radically free, independent even of God in our self-causation.[35]

The divine aims, which constitute God's presence within us as Spirit, are derived from God's primordial nature, the divine Logos. All structure is derived ultimately from God's primordial nature, and is communicated to each creature both directly and indirectly—directly through the divine aim that it receives and indirectly through the divine aims actualized in the past that it inherits. While the Spirit ranges over all the aims presented to the world from the primordial nature, the Logos comprises a special subclass of extraordinary aims. The Logos articulates the structure of peculiarly emergent possibilities, by which Ford means rendering relevant for actualization in the world a flood of previously inaccessible possibility. For example, without the

34. Ibid., pp. 200–201.
35. Ibid., p. 201.

emergence of man, the entire range and diversity of human culture would not have been "relevant for actualization."[36]

If this helps us understand the Logos and the Spirit, however, what about the Father? Here we encounter a difficulty under which trinitarian thinking has always labored. On the one hand, God the Father, according to the classical formula, can constitute only one member of the Trinity. On the other, however, he is addressed by Jesus simply as God. This difficulty stems in part from supposing that God in Christ must be a second divine subjectivity distinct from the Father's, and in part from the lack of an adequate understanding of immanence (one actuality can be objectively present within the experience of another without destroying its integrity as a distinct individual actuality). Ford says, "By God as Father we mean God in his own individual actuality, known to us either by metaphysical reflection upon the generic features of experience, or by revelation manifesting God's contingent actions on our behalf."[37]

God as Father is the chief exemplification of the metaphysical principles, which implies a distinction and interaction between him and the world. "This is a philosophy of self-creation, in which God is conceived as creating himself through his primordial, nontemporal envisagement of all possibility."[38] God creates the structure of his own being. God acts by his Word and his Spirit; but they reveal the Father from whence they came. Ford summarizes his treatment of the three persons of the Trinity: "The Father is constituted by the primordial nature as it expresses the nature and activity of God, the Logos as it provides emergent possibilities for the on-going creation of the world, and the Spirit as it expresses the immanence of God within every creature as its particular creative possibility."[39]

Ford thus explains in process categories a trinitarian formulation that he hopes does justice to the biblical symbols. That does not require precisely three factors, however. To go beyond the primordial nature to the role of the consequent nature, and to address the problem of God's simultaneous transcendence and im-

36. Ibid., pp. 202–3.
37. Ibid., p. 204.
38. Ibid.
39. Ibid., p. 205.

manence requires another triad of principles, which correspond to the three "persons": the divine creative act, the primordial nature, and the consequent nature.[40]

Ford makes clear the relationship of this process triunity to the traditional or classical view. His triunity "cannot be interpreted as implying a plurality of subjects in personal interaction within the Godhead, even though these principles are formally distinct from one another."[41] The idea of "one substance in three persons" could mean either "one actuality having three distinct aspects" or "three distinct subjectivities inhering in one divine substratum." The former is precluded because the idea of substance as a divine substratum in which the three persons inhere is "just that sort of vacuous actuality devoid of its own subjectivity which Whitehead rejects." The latter, the social interpretation, is excluded by Whitehead's categories, according to which "no meaning can be attached to a subjective process of becoming which does not terminate in some sort of substantial unity." Three persons would entail three substances, while one substance would entail three persons. Hence, the orthodox doctrine of the Trinity must be rejected.[42]

The Logical Problem

There is a fundamental difficulty that lies at the heart of the discussion of the doctrine of the Trinity: the doctrine seems to be impossible to believe, because at its very core it is contradictory. Stephen Davis has summarized the problem quite well, stating the doctrine of the Trinity in a series of five statements.[43] With variations, one finds these in a number of statements of the doctrine and the problem:

1. The Father is God.
2. The Son is God.
3. The Holy Spirit is God.

40. Ibid.
41. Ibid., p. 207.
42. Ibid.
43. Stephen T. Davis, *Logic and the Nature of God* (Grand Rapids: Eerdmans, 1984), pp. 134–35.

4. The Father is not the Son and the Son is not the Holy Spirit and the Holy Spirit is not the Father.
5. There is one and only one God.

The problem is that these statements seem to constitute an inconsistent set, that is, a set of statements not all of whose members can be true. This can be shown easily, since 1, 2, 3, and 5 entail:

6. The Father, the Son, and the Holy Spirit are one thing.

and 4 entails:

7. The Father, the Son, and the Holy Spirit are separate things.

Since 6 and 7 are obviously inconsistent, 1–5 must be an inconsistent set of statements, in which case they cannot rationally be believed. If Christians are required to affirm both 6 and 7, as it seems they must, it then appears to be the case that they are obliged to contradict themselves.[44]

We have here a dilemma that resembles in some ways the dilemma that faces Christians in connection with the problem of evil. The truth of one premise, namely, "God is one," seems to imply the falsity of the other, namely, "God is three." How to resolve this tension has been the logical problem of the Trinity. Three major efforts have been made.

1. Some approaches have modified the threeness in such a way as to make it variations or manifestations of the oneness. These are basically modalistic in character. This is not to say that they are modalistic in the more extreme sense that was true of modalistic Monarchianism. That approach basically said that the three were simply the one playing different roles, or appearing in different costumes, as it were. It was merely one person, pretending to be three. In less extreme forms, this approach treats God as being basically one, existing in three modes of consciousness.

2. There are approaches that have so emphasized the threeness at the expense of the oneness that they have virtually lapsed

44. Ibid., p. 135.

into tritheism. These emphasize the three persons, especially noting the passages of Scripture in which the three interact or refer to one another, and see the three interrelated in a closeness of communion and harmony that binds them to one another. While relatively few theologians have held this view in any official way, it is likely that a fairly large percentage of ordinary Christians have taken this position in an informal fashion, often combined with some sort of subordination of the persons.

3. The third approach is to redefine the concepts of person and substance, or whatever terms are used for the threeness and oneness, so that they are seen to be more compatible with one another. This approach usually seizes on the fact that a formal logical contradiction is present only when something is A and not-A at the same time and in the same respect. This then suggests that God is not three in the same respect that he is one, so that there is no actual contradiction.

The problem then focuses more sharply on the question of the difference between the threeness and the oneness of God, or in what respect he is one, and in what respect he is three. Put in terms of the classical formulation of Nicea and Constantinople, what does "one substance and three persons" really mean? Here theologians face a specific form of the general problem of religious language that has been so prominent in the twentieth century. Indeed, the focus on the meaning of language can in many ways be said to be *the* question of twentieth-century philosophy.

For much of its history, philosophy had focused on the issue of truth: Is that particular idea or system of ideas true? While closely related, the question of meaning is a distinct and in many ways prior question. For unless we know what it is that we are considering, we will have great difficulty determining whether it is true.

This question was magnified sharply by the movement known as logical positivism. Its beginnings can be traced to a seminar in philosophy taught by Moritz Schlick at the University of Vienna in 1923. The seminar enrollees consisted of ex-scientists who had become philosophers, and practicing scientists with an interest in philosophy.[45] Their concern was the meaning of the propositions with which they were dealing. They classified all proposi-

---

45. Morton White, "Logical Positivism," in *The Age of Analysis: 20th Century Philosophers,* ed. Morton White (New York: Mentor, 1955), pp. 203–4.

tions in terms of two sets of categories familiar in philosophy. There are a priori and a posteriori sentences, referring to whether these statements are logically independent of or dependent on sense experience, respectively. Propositions can also be classified as analytic or synthetic, depending on whether the predicate simply makes explicit that which is implicit in the subject or whether it adds something to it. This resulted in a combination of four types of propositions: a priori analytic, a priori synthetic, a posteriori analytic, and a posteriori synthetic. The philosophers involved then asked what the meaning of each of these types of sentences was.[46]

The meaning of a priori analytic propositions can be arrived at fairly easily, for these are mathematical-type sentences, in which the content of the predicate is already contained in the subject, such as "2 + 2 = 4." If one knows the meaning of the symbols, "2," "+," and "=," one has the conclusion, namely, 4. The meaning of the sentence is found in a deductive analysis of its elements. No external sense data are needed.[47]

A second group of propositions comprises the a posteriori synthetic, or scientific-type sentences. These cannot be dealt with as the first type was, for the predicate contains content not deducible from the subject. These were propositions of great importance to these men with their interest in natural sciences. Here their conclusion was that the meaning of such propositions is the set of sense data that would in principle confirm or falsify the proposition. Thus, if I say, "A is heavier than B," and you ask me, "What do you mean by 'heavier than'?" I would reply as follows. "If you place A in one pan of a balance scale and B in the other, you will then have a sense experience of seeing pan A go down and pan B go up. That is what I mean by 'A is heavier than B.'" The issue is not that of truth, for a false statement could be meaningful if I knew what sense data would result if it were false. Thus, if instead of seeing pan A go down and pan B go up, I saw the reverse, I would know that the sentence was false, but it would at least be meaningful, for I would know what would count against it.[48]

46. Ibid., pp. 206–9.
47. Ibid., pp. 207–8.
48. Rudolf Carnap, "The Rejection of Metaphysics," in *The Age of Analysis*, pp. 209–11.

Note that it is only necessary that such propositions be in principle testable. There may be some propositions we cannot put to this test because of technical reasons; however, we know what we would experience if they were true. For example, prior to the advent of space travel, the proposition, "The other side of the moon is made of green cheese," was meaningful, even though we could not observe the other side of the moon. We knew what we would observe if the statement were true, if only we could place ourselves in that location.

When examined on this basis, many propositions that on first glance appear to be meaningful, when examined more closely, can be seen not to meet this "verification principle." Many metaphysical statements are of this type. "Reality is basically one," or "reality is at root of the nature of mind," are examples. If we ask, "What is the set of sense data that would verify that statement?" we are hard put to reply. The problem is that these propositions are literally "non-sense" statements, and therefore meaningless.[49] So we find that a large collection of propositions that in the past have been thought to be very important have no cognitive meaning. The fourth classification, a posteriori analytic statements, is in a sense superfluous. For if the content of the predicate is contained within the subject, then it is unnecessary to test them by sense experience. This leaves us with only two types of meaningful propositions: a priori analytic, or mathematical-type propositions, and a posteriori synthetic, or scientific-type propositions.

Is there, however, no meaning to sentences that do not meet these criteria? Since so many people have used them, vehemently in some cases, they must surely have thought them to have some sort of meaning. They do indeed have meaning, but not of the cognitive type, which is restricted to the representative propositions, such as we have examined. Rather, these are expressive or emotive. They tell us something, not about the apparent object of the proposition, but about the subject, the speaker, the author. They are a means of venting the speaker's emotions, rather than describing an objective state of affairs.[50] When someone says something like, "There is a purpose and a design that

49. Ibid., pp. 212–16.
50. Ibid., pp. 218–21.

governs the universe," he is not telling us anything about the universe, but expressing his feelings about that universe, saying, in effect, "I feel good about the universe." This is an expression of optimism, versus the pessimistic statement, "There is no pattern to the events of our world."

This means that the history of philosophy, which purported to be the account of the nature of things, was actually just a very sophisticated series of grunts and groans. Hence some of these logical positivists had a considerable contempt for the earlier history of philosophy. One university philosophy department, interviewing a young candidate for a teaching position, sought to ascertain his areas of competency. He was asked whether he could teach history of philosophy, and replied in the affirmative. Then he was asked, "Can you teach ancient philosophy?" "Oh, yes," replied the candidate, "I can teach early Bertrand Russell."

When these criteria are applied to theology, interesting developments result. There is a famous parable, told by John Wisdom. Two explorers happen upon a clearing in which are growing many flowers and also many weeds. One of them says, "Some gardener must tend this plot." The other disagrees: "There is no gardener." So they decide to settle their difference of opinion by setting a watch over the clearing, but no gardener is ever seen. Thinking, however, that this may be an invisible gardener, they set up a barbed-wire fence, electrify it, and patrol the area with bloodhounds. There are, however, no shrieks, no movements of the wire, no outcry from the bloodhounds. The believer of the two explorers is not deterred from his faith in a gardener, however: "But there is a gardener, invisible, intangible, insensible to electric shocks, a gardener who has no scent and makes no sound, a gardener who comes secretly to look after the garden which he loves." Finally, however, the skeptic despairs: "But what remains of your original assertion? Just how does what you call an invisible, intangible, eternally elusive gardener differ from an imaginary gardener or even from no gardener at all?" Antony Flew comments on this situation: "A fine brash hypothesis may thus be killed by inches, the death by a thousand qualifications."[51]

51. Antony Flew, "Theology and Falsification," in *New Essays in Philosophical Theology*, ed. Antony Flew and Alasdair MacIntyre (New York: Macmillan, 1966), pp. 96–97.

This is the problem with theological propositions, or for that matter, any propositions that fall outside the realm of sensory perception. They are not susceptible to the kind of verification or falsification that would enable us to determine what we really mean by them, or at least, what we exclude by them. For on this criterion, immunity to falsification is no guarantee of meaningfulness. That which does not contradict anything really does not affirm anything either.

Suppose, for example, we took the proposition, "God answers prayer," a fairly common and important belief among Christians. We might seek to determine what that means by dividing a group of Christians into two subgroups, one of which prays fervently about the matters of greatest concern to them, and the other of which simply wishes for those things that it wants to come to pass. At the end of six months, it would be possible to determine what percentage of desired effects had come to pass, assuming they were sufficiently specific. What if there were no statistically significant differences between the two groups? Probably the response of the praying group would be that which such persons usually give when prayer does not appear to be answered: "It wasn't God's will to answer that prayer." But now the death by a thousand qualifications has occurred.

It was not too long before even philosophers began to see that the verification principle was too restrictive a criterion of cognitive meaning. For what, after all, was the logical status of this principle? Is it merely a definitional matter, which most would not think it to be? If not, what is the set of sense data that would verify or falsify it? It became apparent that on its own terms, the primary criterion of meaning was meaningless. There would therefore have to be some revision, some broadening of the understanding of meaning.[52]

This first form of analytical philosophy was sometimes referred to as "ideal-language" philosophy. This philosophy was stipulative in its definitions. It set up an ideal of the most meaningful type of language, and then measured language against this. Later varieties of analytical philosophy were "ordinary-language" philosophies; they did not stipulate an ideal of language to be ful-

---

52. Frederick Ferré, *Language, Logic and God* (New York: Harper & Row, 1961), pp. 53–54.

filled, but instead asked how language functioned in the usual forms of human communication. If the former type of language philosophy was termed "verificational analysis," this was "functional analysis." Instead of insisting on how language must work, it asked how it actually functioned. It observed that there are different languages or "logics" of ethical-type statements or religious propositions than those that pertain to scientific statements.[53]

The question then, however, becomes how propositions "mean" in each of these realms or languages. With respect to theological language, what are these alleged assertions really doing? In what way can they be seen to be meaningful? Specifically, for our purposes, what do we mean when we say that God is one and God is three? How can we elucidate the meaning of a proposition such as this?

The formula that has been used in one fashion or another for more than sixteen centuries now is that God is one substance and three persons. What is meant by these terms, however? Unless their content can be elaborated, this formula seems to be saying, "God is one x and three y," or perhaps simply, "God is x and y." It may, of course, be the case that God really is both x and y, but unless we know what we are asserting by the use of these two expressions, there is no way to assess their truth or falsity. We are not even communicating.

How can we know what this formula means, then? One answer that has sometimes been given is the "logic of encounter." On this way of thinking, God does not communicate truth about himself to us; rather, he presents himself. This means that the truth of statements about him can only be known, and indeed, that the meaning of those statements can only be understood, in a direct encounter with him.[54] There is a problem here, however. What is it like to encounter God as three in one, versus simply encountering him as one, or encountering three gods? This is a question that at best is very difficult to answer. For without some intersubjectivity, one person cannot really indicate to another what he or she means by such a statement, and the two persons have no basis for knowing whether they are referring to the same thing, or for that matter, whether what they are encountering is

53. Ibid., pp. 58–61.
54. H. H. Farmer, *Revelation and Religion* (London: Nisbet, 1954), pp. 42–70.

something objective, rather than simply their own subjective emotions.

This, then, is the task of a theology of the Trinity: to make clear in some fashion what it means by its statement that God is both three and one, and what difference this really makes. To fail to do this is to seem to engage in meaningless chatter.

6

Is Trinitarian Christianity the Only Way for Salvation for All Persons?

We turn now to a different type of objection to the Trinity, based more on cultural or anthropological considerations than biblical, theological, or philosophical concerns. Christianity has traditionally maintained that it is the only way of salvation, the one divinely appointed channel to fellowship with God. Besides that exclusiveness, however, it has also maintained its universality: it is available to all persons. This way of salvation is very much tied up with the distinctive doctrinal content of Christianity, including the doctrine of the Trinity. In our time there are challenges to both dimensions of the trinitarian theology.

Objection to the Universality of Trinitarian Christianity: Feminist Theology

One source from which challenge to the traditional understanding of the Trinity has come is the feminist movement within theology. In general, the problem is perceived as being the conflict between the designation of the members of the Trinity as Father and Son, two gender-linked conceptions, and the desire for women to have full religious status and to be able to consider feminine characteristics as legitimate and appropriate for women as the more conventional masculine characteristics are

139

for men. Many feminists find it difficult to relate to a God thought of as masculine. Kate Marlin refers to as "not atypical" a woman who said that God the Father was "nobody I could talk to. You couldn't say nothing to the dude."[1]

One who has enunciated this concern in a broad context is Sally McFague. She places the objection to the traditional doctrine of God in the setting of a nuclear and ecological age. Thus, she says that we must hold a holistic view of reality. We live in the twilight years of the twentieth century. One senses that by this she means not simply the fact that the year 2000 is near, but that the modern era is fading in favor of postmodernism. Yet despite this fact, we are living anachronistically, calling ourselves, one another, and our earth by names from another era.[2] In our imaginations and our feelings we live in a bygone world, which is under the guidance of a benevolent but absolute deity, a world populated by individuals who relate to one another and to other forms of life individualistically and hierarchically. That, however, is not our world, and to continue to do theology on these assumptions is detrimental. This undermines our ability to accept the new sensibility of our time, a sensibility that is holistic and responsible, inclusive of all forms of life and acknowledging the interdependence of all life.[3]

Just what does McFague mean by saying that this approach is inclusivistic? She observes that for the past twenty years, feminist theologians have made a strong case against the androcentric, hierarchical Western religious tradition. They have insisted that the humanity of women be given equal status and that divisions that separate people be minimized in order to create an inclusive vision. These divisions are male and female, rich and poor, old and young, white and colored, straight and gay, and Christian and non-Christian. She quotes Elisabeth Schüssler-Fiorenza, who says, "Not the holiness of the elect but the wholeness *of all* is the central vision of Jesus."[4]

1. Kate Anders Marlin, "The Underground Ecumenist," *Christian Century*, 22.29 (August 1990): 757.

2. Sally McFague, *Models of God: Theology for an Ecological, Nuclear Age* (Philadelphia: Fortress, 1987), p. 3.

3. Ibid.

4. Elisabeth Schüssler-Fiorenza, *In Memory of Her: A Feminist Theological Reconstruction of Christian Origins* (New York: Crossroad, 1983), p. 121.

McFague not only endorses this statement, but wants to extend it to the nonhuman world also. She notes that those who have given the greatest attention to that world have for the most part been those involved in Goddess traditions and witchcraft, since for them the body, earth, and nature's cycles are critically important. Yet even these efforts have not been focused on the intrinsic value of the nonhuman world sufficiently to bring about the needed change of consciousness. She affirms that the feminist theology that she represents has much in common with other forms of liberation theology, but it places a greater emphasis on the nonhuman components of reality.[5] We must feel our oneness with the whole of creation. The Western religious tradition, exemplified by Augustine, has been very individualistic in outlook. In so doing, it is neglecting a vital part of the biblical tradition, according to which the whole creation "groans" for fulfillment (Rom. 8:22). This individualistic approach has led to domination and even ruthlessness.[6]

There is something very inappropriate about the traditional way of conceiving of God. This can be traced, at least in part, to the fact that we now live in a nuclear age—an age of potentially universal destruction. In this kind of world we are literally dealing with life and death matters. McFague says: "Language that supports hierarchical, dualistic, external, unchanging, atomistic, anthropocentric, and deterministic ways of understanding [the relationships of God to world and human to world] is not appropriate *for our time*, whatever its appropriateness might have been for other times."[7] Her objection, in other words, is not just on behalf of women, but for all other members of the creation.

The traditional way of thinking of God focuses on the idea of the power of God. God is "almighty," the creator, redeemer, and sustainer of all that is. This concept of power does not necessarily move in the direction of domination. Rather, the power may be seen as providential and loving. The point, however, is that the power is all God's.[8]

5. McFague, *Models*, p. 7.
6. Ibid., p. 9.
7. Ibid., p. 13.
8. Ibid., p. 16.

A somewhat different approach to the problem of the Trinity is taken by Rebecca Oxford-Carpenter in her article, "Gender and the Trinity."[9] She raises questions about the historical propriety of the doctrine of the Trinity. The doctrine is not biblical, in the primary sense of that word. The word "Trinity" is not found in the Bible. The only trinitarian-like passage is Matthew 28:19, which is more liturgical than theological. Nor was the doctrine quickly and universally accepted in the church. It arose out of a period called the "twilight zone" of Christianity, so called because of its evolutionary and dialectical aspects. It evolved over a period of many years, involving struggle in church councils. The apostolic age was actually binitarian rather than trinitarian. The Holy Spirit, though mentioned in the Bible, really was not clearly part of the Trinity until the Council of Nicea (A.D. 325) and was only accepted as equal with the other two persons in the declaration of the Council of Constantinople in 381. Oxford-Carpenter's understanding of the Trinity is that it is not a formal, logical statement, but a dialectic.[10] She cites with approval Tillich's statement that the doctrine "does not affirm the logical nonsense that three is one and one is three; it describes in dialectical terms the inner movement of the divine life as an eternal separation from itself and return to itself."[11] This definition is quite similar to that of Hegel; the doctrine did not refer to specific persons or to events (specifically, the incarnation) which occurred at particular times and places, but is a symbol of the ongoing process or relationship of God to the world.

Oxford-Carpenter sees the main twilight zone aspect as being the Trinity's all-masculine image. This came to be accepted late in the second century A.D., when women lost the roles of authority they had held in the early church. Prior to this time, women had a great deal of ecclesiastical power, and androgynous images of God flourished. Then, however, "cultural and political trends led toward the development of an increasingly patriarchal church, and God's image became masculinized." With the accep-

9. Rebecca Oxford-Carpenter, "Gender and the Trinity," *Theology Today* 41.1 (April 1984): 7–25.
10. Ibid., p. 8.
11. Paul Tillich, *Systematic Theology* (Chicago: University of Chicago Press, 1951), 1:56.

tance of Augustine's interpretation, the patriarchal model has dominated. Only a few theologians and mystics dared to challenge the masculine image of God from the time of Augustine until the twentieth century, when a handful of feminist theologians, both female and male, advocated breaking the monopoly of the all-masculine divine image.[12]

Although not stated overtly, the contours of Oxford-Carpenter's argument are plain to see. The doctrine of the Trinity arose in a period during which the political or cultural model was being formulated. As the original egalitarian church structure became increasingly male-dominated, the originally androgynous models of God came to be replaced by more exclusively masculine views. Thus, the doctrine of the Trinity, with its persons of Father and Son, as well as Holy Spirit, was a function of the politics of the time. Politics produced theology, and the doctrine of the Trinity is culturally accounted for.

The importance of the doctrine is sketched by Oxford-Carpenter. She sees these twentieth-century "liminal" thinkers as shattering the boundaries of conventional religious thought, just as did Jesus, Paul, and Luther before them. Yet the masculine image of God remains dominant at this point in Christian history. Christianity, Oxford-Carpenter says, is one of only three major world religions (along with Judaism and Islam) that do not have a feminine deity of some kind. The Trinity gender problem is very important because of the very nature of religion. Religious symbolism is important for humankind in general and for particular cultures, because it is an expression of humanity's ultimate concern for meaning, value, and a ground of being. Symbols, dreams, images, and myths express the yearnings, primarily unconscious, of individuals and society and also have socially motivating effects. Thus, "how the divine is to be symbolized is the heart and soul of the gender-Trinity issue."[13]

There have been various attempts to respond to this challenge of the apparent incompatibility of the conventional view of God and the feminist consciousness. We first examine some of the more radical of these, and then seek to evaluate them in turn.

---

12. Oxford-Carpenter, "Gender and the Trinity," p. 8.
13. Ibid., p. 9.

Perhaps the most extreme is the rise of Goddess religion. This is not simply a parallel to, or a supplementation in similar form, of the traditional view of God, as the all-masculine Trinity or God the Father. Starhawk, a modern leader of Goddess religion, puts it this way: "The symbolism of the Goddess is not a parallel structure to the symbolism of God the Father. The Goddess does not rule the world; she *is* the world. Manifest in each of us, she can be known internally by every individual, in all her magnificent diversity."[14] Contrasted with traditional theism, then, this is a form of pantheism.

Goddess religion is not new, by any means. Its devotees claim that this kind of worship goes back 35,000 years, being broken only by the last 5,000 years of primarily patriarchal religion. It is sometimes known as "witchcraft" or "Old Religion." Because it is a nature-oriented or pantheistic religion, it also has a great deal in common with many other movements, both ancient and recent. It has affinity with what some would consider the original religion. Starhawk asserts that worship of the Goddess is close in spirit to Native American spiritualism, Arctic shamanism, and the religion of Faeries, Picts (Pixies), and Druids.[15] Because this worship has to do with that which is present within each one of us, it is a realizable possibility for all. A common denominator of all forms of Goddess religion is magic, which is the art of changing consciousness at will, other elements being poetry, myth, legend, ritual, and nature worship.[16] Because of the characteristic of nature worship, Goddess-worshipers are frequently in the forefront of the ecological movement.

Carol Christ identifies four necessary aspects of Goddess symbolism: female power as opposed to patriarchy; the female body and the life cycle; the female will as ritualized in magic and spell-casting; women's heritage and bonding among women.[17] Goddess religion goes back to the ancient fertility worship of Egypt and the Near East. McFague contends that fertility goddesses

14. Starhawk, *The Spiral Dance: A Rebirth of the Ancient Religion of the Great Goddess* (San Francisco: Harper & Row, 1979), p. 9.

15. Ibid., pp. 2–5.

16. Ibid., p. 18.

17. Carol P. Christ, "Why Women Need the Goddess: Phenomenological, Psychological, and Political Reflections," in *Womanspirit Rising: A Feminist Reader in Religion,* ed. C. P. Christ and J. Plaskow (San Francisco: Harper & Row, 1979), pp. 273–87.

were worshiped as superior to gods, before people knew of the contributions of the male to the generation of life.[18]

There might quite naturally be a tendency to treat Goddess religion as a sort of mirror image of traditional masculine-oriented theism, with parallel or countering doctrines. This is really not the case, however, for there is no real symmetry between the two. Goddess religion is not primarily a doctrinal system, with a well-worked-out set of beliefs. It is more subjective, more a matter of poetry than of theology, since the basic truths of the religion cannot really be verbally communicated.[19]

There is variation among Goddess groups in their conception of the proper status of the male principle. Some hold that the Goddess is to be permanently and fully ascendant, while the male principle or God remains secondary—a son or lover, but not the equal of his mother. In some forms of this religion, the God, if there is one, often dies in the service of the Goddess or life-force.[20] This Goddess is not necessarily personal in nature. Rather, she is more nearly a synonym for nature or life-force, and thus everything else, including any God(s), would have to be thought of as a product of this force. Starhawk says: "The Goddess is the Encircler, the Ground of Being; the God is That-Which-Is-Brought-Forth, her mirror image, her other pole. She is the earth; He is the grain. She is the all-encompassing sky; He is the sun, her fireball. She is the Wheel; He is the Traveler. His is the sacrifice of life to death that life may go on. She is the Mother and Destroyer; He is all that is born and is destroyed."[21]

There are more conservative and less conservative varieties of Goddess religion, from the standpoint of Christianity. To put it another way, there are varieties of it that emphasize continuity with Christianity, and attempt to amalgamate Goddess religion and traditional Christianity. There are other forms of it in which Goddess worship clearly supplants or replaces any element of traditional Christianity. Even in the former types, however, the role usually played by God is taken over by the Goddess, as the

18. Sally McFague, *Metaphorical Theology: Models of God in Religious Language* (Philadelphia: Fortress, 1982), p. 156.

19. Starhawk, *Spiral Dance*, p. 7.

20. Ibid., p. 98.

21. Ibid., p. 95.

object of worship. If "A Mighty Fortress Is Our God" is a good expression of typical masculino-centric religion, then, it is sometimes said, the counterpart for Goddess worshipers would be, "A Mighty Goddess Is Our Forte."[22]

A somewhat different approach is that of Quaternity, or the expansion of the Trinity to include a fourth, feminine, member or principle. The primary advocate of this concept has been the psychoanalyst, Carl G. Jung. Jung was much more charitable toward religion than was his predecessor, Sigmund Freud, and sought to integrate religion and psychology. Like Freud and the rest of the psychoanalysts, Jung strongly emphasized the reality and the influence of the unconscious, and also stressed the need for myths and symbols to express the deepest contents of the unconscious.[23]

Jung believed that the fourth element has always existed in the religious representations, but has become separated from God. The unconscious, however, is capable of reuniting what has been separated, by transforming the Trinity into a Quaternity. The identity of this fourth or feminine principle varies in Jung's writings. Sometimes it is the devil; other times it is the Virgin Mary.[24]

This particular formulation of the idea has not drawn a great deal of support. Indeed, L. I. Sweet has referred to it as an idea "whose time will never come."[25] We will note shortly some of the problems with it. In the meantime, however, we need to observe the values that this view is seeking to preserve and the needs that it attempts to meet.

Many women have a difficult time finding a role model. In a church in which there are no female leaders, and in the official theology of which there are at least two masculine divine persons, but none who are clearly feminine, it is difficult to relate one's faith to one's conception of gender. This is particularly a problem for Protestant Christians.

Roman Catholics have the Virgin Mary as a person to whom they, and especially women, can relate. Although only a human

22. Marlin, "The Underground Ecumenist," p. 757.

23. C. G. Jung and M. L. von-Franz, eds., *Man and His Symbols* (New York: Doubleday, 1964); also Christ and Plaskow, *Womanspirit Rising*, p. 2.

24. Jung and von-Franz, *Man and His Symbols*, p. 225.

25. L. I. Sweet, *New Life in the Spirit* (Philadelphia: Westminster, 1982), p. 41.

vessel God used to accomplish the incarnation, she had a status that in some respects experientially approached that of deity. The Roman Catholic Church, in the process of making explicit dogma of what had previously been implicit tradition, progressively upgraded Mary's status. The dogma of the virgin birth, or the perpetual virginity of Mary, meant something more than what Protestants have usually designated by the expression "virgin birth." Actually, the view as held by most Protestants, could probably best be referred to as the "virginal conception," the idea that Mary was a virgin when Jesus was conceived, and remained so until his birth, but not during or after that birth, and that she later had other offspring, conceived in the normal fashion. Traditional Roman Catholicism, however, held to the perpetual virginity of Mary: she was a virgin, before, during, and after the birth of Jesus, and continued as one throughout her lifetime. Jesus was born by a sort of spiritual Caesarian section. Thus, Mary is clearly set apart from other women and from other human beings in general. The church also propounded as dogmas the immaculate conception (Mary was miraculously cleansed of any sin, so that Jesus would not be born with original sin), and the bodily assumption (Mary did not die and was buried, but rather was taken directly and bodily to heaven). Prior to the Second Vatican Council, some theologians were arguing the doctrine that Mary was co-redemptrix of the human race, a development that the council tended to cut short.[26] Note, however, how close that would have brought Mary to equal status with the members of the Trinity.

Clearly, Protestants have nothing to match the emotional power and appeal of a person such as Mary. No one stands out. There is almost an avoidance of the subject of Mary by most Protestants, perhaps because of a sort of Catholicophobia. There are no feminine persons of such status as to be venerated, let alone anything more. There is a gap unfilled by any sort of feminine object of worship.

Now let us evaluate these two views. Goddess religion is in many ways a radical reaction against what are perceived as the flaws and extremities of patriarchal trinitarianism. In this re-

---

26. C. O. Vollert and J. B. Carol, "Mary, Blessed Virgin, II (in theology)," *New Catholic Encyclopedia* (New York: McGraw-Hill, 1967), pp. 356–64.

spect, it resembles the black power movement in the black cultural revolution. Just as the latter was a backlash against white supremacy, so Goddess religion is a radical rejection of masculine ascendancy, whether within society, the church, or the doctrine of God. As such, however, it really is not a corrective, but an alternative. It is difficult to know how one can really forge a combination of this philosophy with the more traditional elements of Christianity and the more traditional interpretation of that. One may be able to find a view here with which feminists, especially female feminists, can relate, but it would appear that this is virtually at the expense of surrendering most of what distinguishes Christianity as Christianity.

In particular, Goddess religion does not seem to be an ideology suitable for all segments of the human race. It appears to aim, not at the equality and unity of the male and female halves of the race, but at the supremacy of women. The status of women has been achieved by a subordination of men. While there is a place for men, and some covens have men within their numbers, they really are not thought of as counterparts or equals. In the desire to reject the sort of dominance that has sometimes characterized Christianity, Goddess religion has fallen into a new sort of dominance or domination. Some proponents, such as Carol P. Christ, leave open the question of the ascendancy of the feminine aspect,[27] while others seem to advocate something parallel to communism's "dictatorship of the proletariat," a temporary feminine supremacy and emphasis on the feminine dimensions of life and worship, to be followed someday by a more egalitarian form.[28] Budapest, on the other hand, advocates the permanent ascendancy of the feminine principle and worship for women only.[29]

Even where there is openness to some sort of future equality, there does not seem to be much positive effort by adherents of the view to bring it about. Thus, it is quite possible that we have only traded one problem, relatively more familiar in the history of religion, for another, less common, one. This would then be reverse sexism, which from the standpoint of women might be preferable to the older sexism, but from the position of the wel-

---

27. Christ and Plaskow, *Womanspirit Rising*, pp. 13ff.
28. Ibid., p. 15.
29. Ibid., pp. 14–15.

fare of the human race, might not be an improvement—and might even be worse. Beyond that, however, there is the possibility that Goddess worship could in effect lead to the oppression of women, because of the stereotyping of feminine qualities. McFague sees these stereotypical qualities found in Goddess religion as a variant of Freud's axiom, "biology is destiny."[30]

Equally problematic, in its own way, is the Jungian Quaternity. Part of the difficulty stems from the ambivalence regarding the relationship of femininity and evil. Indeed, ambivalence seems too weak a term. Jung seems to hold that there is some sort of inevitable linkage between evil and the feminine. And that, as Oxford-Carpenter puts it, is a rather startling assertion from a feminist theologian. She considers this to be "extraordinarily sexist."[31] The solution to the problem seems to be virtually worse than the problem it is ostensibly intended to solve.

Beyond that, however, even if this effort to expand the Godhead from three to four were successful, it would still present a deity in which three of the four persons were masculine, which still appears to some to be inherently sexist. Yet, in a sense, that is not really a problem, for the difficulty lies in such a suggested expansion. The Trinity is not a club to which anyone, male or female, can apply for membership. There is no way to obtain entrance. Its membership is simply not something that humans have the ability or right to enlarge, and in fact, it is safe to contend that even God cannot expand its membership. The makeup of the Godhead is not something that is that way because of choice or action. It is simply the way God is.

Of course, Jung would contend that it is not a literal doctrinal enlargement that he is talking about. Rather, it is a matter of symbolism, or myth, or experience, which experience can enlarge. That, however, is what must be established. The difficulty with the doctrine of the Trinity for feminists came because it was thought to be some sort of at least partially literal description of the way God is. If this were merely a matter of myth and experience, of symbolism, the problem would not be especially severe, or at least the resentment would not be directed at God, but at those who had so construed him. Thus, to the extent that this

---

30. McFague, *Metaphorical Theology*, p. 159.
31. Oxford-Carpenter, "Gender and Trinity," p. 20.

Goddess religion is helpful, it is unnecessary. It seems unlikely to be a solution that will have widespread acceptance or efficacy. Sweet has probably put it well.

Objection to the Uniqueness of Christianity: Generic Religion

Another objection to the essentiality of the Trinity has come from the area of comparative religions or interreligious discussion. There are both similarities to and differences from the feminist objection. Underlying the discussion here is the idea that Christianity has been unduly provincial and exclusivistic, insisting that its teachings are alone true and that any who would come to a proper relationship with God must do so by accepting its teachings and acting on them. One assumption of the persons whose thought we will be examining here is that interreligious dialogue is a good thing. Indeed, in the shrunken world in which we live, the fewer dividing factors there are among members of the human race worldwide, the better.

There is agreement that extensive doctrinal statements of the participating religions tend to be a hindrance to mutual dialogue. The Christian doctrines of the incarnation and the Trinity especially present major obstacles to any sort of genuine interchange among religious dialogue partners. John Hick, for example, considers the situation of a Christian and others engaged in dialogue. One of the basic points on which the Christian would undoubtedly insist would be the claim that Jesus Christ is God the Son incarnate. The Muslim in the discussion would undoubtedly respond that Jesus is indeed the greatest of the prophets preceding Mohammed, and would even acknowledge the biblical claim that Jesus was born of a virgin. To claim that Jesus is actually and literally God, however, as a member of the Trinity, would be utterly blasphemous to him. This would conflict with the very central tenet of Muslim belief, namely, monotheism: "There is no God but Allah, and Mohammed is his prophet." The Hindu might well respond that Jesus is indeed an incarnation of God, but not *the* incarnation of that God. He is one of a long series of such incarnations, which continues perhaps to Sri Ramakrishna and Mahatma Gandhi in the nineteenth and twentieth centuries.

Such dialogue is hardly dialogue, but a series of monologues. Each soliloquy assumes that one's own position is the only correct one. It assumes the wrongness of the other person's position. Such interaction must have one of two results: either the conversion of one partner to the view of the other, or the hardening of each of the positions. Occasionally it will be the former, but unfortunately more often it will be the latter.[32] This idea is repeated frequently in Hick's writings. If Jesus was indeed the incarnate second person of the Trinity, "it is then very hard to escape from the traditional view that all mankind must be converted to the Christian faith."[33] He acknowledges that this idea of Jesus as the second person of the divine Trinity living a human life was the very centerpoint of the older theological tradition within Christianity: "It follows from this that Christianity, and Christianity alone, was founded by God in person on the only occasion on which he has ever become incarnate in this world, so that Christianity has a unique status as the way of salvation provided and appointed by God himself."[34]

It should be noted that this is in many ways the same type of objection raised to the doctrine of the Trinity as that propounded by the feminists. If the doctrine is insisted on, then Christianity is not a real option for many people, who for one reason or another are unable to accept it. In the case of the feminists, the seemingly inherently patriarchal view conflicts with egalitarian consciousness. In the case of the other religions, it is the seeming absoluteness of a doctrine of the Trinity according to which the only God became incarnate in just one person at one point in history. With this in mind, several attempts have been made to understand the Trinity and the incarnation in such a way as not to inhibit interreligious dialogue.

One rather conspicuous solution has been propounded by Raimundo Panikkar. His strategy is not to minimize the integral character of the doctrine within Christianity, but to reduce the uniqueness of Christian doctrine. He states this rather clearly: "It is simply an unwarranted overstatement to affirm that the trinitarian conception of the Ultimate, and with it of the whole of re-

32. John Hick, *God Has Many Names* (Philadelphia: Westminster, 1980), p. 121.
33. Ibid., p. 19.
34. Ibid., p. 26.

ality, is an exclusive Christian insight or revelation."[35] On the face of it, this may seem to be a difficult assertion to maintain, in light of John Hick's statements noted above. Part of the resolution of this paradox, however, comes from scrutinizing Panikkar's understanding of the nature of a symbol. As he puts it, the question begins as a semantic problem, or in Thomas Aquinas's way of putting it, the "misery of terms."[36] The earlier way of understanding the symbols that constitute our language is that they represent a reality external to us. In Panikkar's way of thinking, however, the symbol represents not only the symbolized "thing" but also the consciousness of it. It encompasses and unites both. He says, "The moment that words say only exactly what you mean and do not leave room for what I may also mean, the moment that they become only signs and cease to be symbols, the moment that they only signal something else and are no longer the expression, the manifestation and with it the veil itself of that 'else,' in that moment they degenerate even as words."[37]

The problem with such an approach, says Panikkar, is that real communication breaks down as a result. Words become means of oppression, tools of power in the hands of those who dictate their meaning. This action frightens the one who should be the partner in the dialogue.[38] Panikkar proposes a better solution, namely, an approach that would not be isolated to meanings that one group gives to a set of symbols, but would incorporate the meanings that others find in them. He puts it thus: "The author, however, believes that he expresses not a private opinion, but a paradigm of an experience which is bound to become more and more frequent in our time: the experience of gathering or rather concentrating in oneself more than one of the human phyla in which mankind's fundamental insights have accumulated. We want to be no longer sons of Manu or Israel or Ishmael alone, but children of Man."[39]

To take this observation back to the initial point made earlier, the trinitarian conception is not unique to Christianity. It would be unique if the meaning of symbols is only in their objective di-

35. Raimundo Panikkar, *The Trinity and the Religious Experience of Man* (New York: Orbis, 1973), p. viii.
36. Ibid.
37. Ibid., p. ix.
38. Ibid., p. x.
39. Ibid., pp. x–xi.

mension, in terms of the object that they represent. Then they have the meaning that those who propound them give them. If, however, the meaning is an amalgam of the objective meaning and of the consciousness of the symbol, then others may also contribute to that meaning. Panikkar cites with favor the approach of those in India, who called sentences *sutras*, which, like sutures, link us with the great intuitions of humankind. Specifically, then, he says of the Trinity:

> The different traits here taken into account are brought together to form a tress which represents one of the deepest intuitions man has had and is still having, from different points of view and with different names: the intuition of the threefold structure of reality, of the triadic oneness existing on all levels of consciousness and of reality, of the Trinity. We are not saying that the idea of the Trinity can be reduced to the discovery of a triple dimension of Being, nor that this aspect is a mere rational discovery. We are only affirming that the Trinity is the acme of a truth that permeates all realms of being and consciousness and that this vision links us together.[40]

This endeavor is of fundamental human concern. A nontrinitarian God could not "mingle" and even less unite himself with Man without destroying himself in the process. Conversely, a nontrinitarian Man could not step outside himself, could not become what he wants and longs for, without destroying himself. Just as God would cease to be God if he became Man, so Man would cease to be Man if he became God. In light of this, the question of the Trinity is one of the deepest ones Man can ask about himself and about God. It is a basic issue at the root of our human situation, and has direct relevance to questions such as a more just society and a more integrated human personality. It is both one of the theoretically most important and one of the practically most urgent questions that can be asked.[41]

What Panikkar is calling for is a sort of transformation of the current understanding of the Christian faith. He emphasizes that it has undergone considerable change over time. What we now call Christianity is only one possible form of living and realizing

40. Ibid., p. xi.
41. Ibid., p. xii.

the Christian faith. This present form is a form that it has adopted little by little over the years, but it is by no means the only or even necessarily the best form, and we have no right to identify this particular sociological form with the essence of Christian faith itself. It is not, however, possible to jettison the results of this process, and get back to some pure or pristine form. Rather, we must assimilate new values, and that not so much by substituting them for the old content so much as by adding, by assumption rather than rejection.[42] It may, of course, occur to someone to ask why he takes Christianity as his point of departure. This, he says, is not out of partiality or sectarianism, but because it is necessary to start somewhere and he believes that Christianity is especially called to "suffer" this purifying transformation.[43]

Panikkar's essential thesis is that there are three kinds of spirituality found in the majority of religions, and that they are symbolized by Christianity under the imagery of the Trinity. He therefore proposes to study these three most characteristic forms of spirituality, and then attempt to weigh the *theological* problem of the Trinity, which he says is "that mystery which out of a kind of reverential awe has been virtually allowed to atrophy in a great part of Christianity."[44]

Panikkar begins by defining any given spirituality, pragmatically and even phenomenologically, as being "one typical way of handling the human condition." In more religious terms it can be stated by saying that it "represents man's basic attitude *vis-a-vis* his ultimate end." There are three kinds of spirituality, *vis*. of action, love, and knowledge. To put it another way, there are spiritualities centered about iconolatry, personalism, and mysticism. They can be briefly summarized as follows:

1. Iconolatry is adopting an image, an idol, an icon, which is simultaneously outside (attracting), inside (inspiring), and above (directing).[45]
2. Personalism refers to a relationship with the Absolute. There is a mystery hidden deep within the human soul

42. Ibid., pp. 4–5.
43. Ibid., p. 6.
44. Ibid.
45. Ibid., p. 10.

that can be unveiled by an intimate human relationship, a dialogue. In this view, God is the essential pole that orientates the human personality, but is also its constitutive element.[46]

3. Mysticism is the suprarational experience of a "reality." In Hinduism, God does not speak; he is not Word. Rather he inspires; he is *Spirit*. This is God in the dimension of immanence. One cannot speak to or think about this one.[47] Panikkar shows the Hindu equivalent for each of these concepts. Thus he correlates iconolatry with *karmamarga*, personalism with *bhaktimarga*, and mysticism with *jnanamarga*.[48]

Panikkar proceeds to explore the meaning of the Trinity, believing that in the light of it, the three forms of spirituality described above can be reconciled. He describes his aim, however, as being "simply so to enlarge and deepen the mystery of the Trinity that it may embrace this same mystery existent in other religious traditions but differently expressed."[49] To put it another way, "In the Trinity a true encounter of religions takes place, which results, not in a vague fusion or mutual dilution, but in an authentic enhancement of all the religious and even cultural elements that are contained in each."[50]

What Panikkar then does is to examine in turn the concepts of Father, Son, and Holy Spirit, giving each this more generalized meaning. As an example, he maintains that the term "Lord" should be used for a principle found in many religious traditions and referred to by a variety of names. So he says, "I would propose using the word Lord for that Principle, Being, Logos or Christ that other religious traditions call by a variety of names and to which they attach a wide range of ideas. . . . Each time that I speak of Christ I am referring (unless it is explicitly stated otherwise) to the Lord of whom Christians can lay claim to no monopoly. It is Christ, then, known or unknown—who makes religion possible."[51] Panikkar is not affirming an identification of

---

46. Ibid.
47. Ibid., p. 31.
48. Ibid., pp. 11–40.
49. Ibid., p. 42.
50. Ibid.
51. Ibid., p. 53.

Christ with Jesus of Nazareth. Phenomenologically, this title represents the role of mediator between divine and cosmic, eternal and temporal, which other religions call by different names.[52] He had earlier developed this same concept at greater length in a separate work.[53]

---

52. Ibid., p. 54.
53. *The Unknown Christ of Hinduism* (London: Darton, Longman & Todd, 1964).

Part 3

A Contemporary Statement of the Doctrine of the Trinity

7

The Trinity in the Old Testament

We have seen the classic understanding of the Trinity as it came to be constructed in the first four centuries of the church's thought. We have also seen the objections that have been raised to this doctrine. We must now make some response to those problems, starting with the question of whether the doctrine of the Trinity really is taught in the Bible.

When we discuss the biblical material that forms the basis for the doctrine of the Trinity, we must first turn to the Old Testament. It is important to note clearly what the issue is with which we are concerned in this chapter. We are not coming to the text with the expectation of finding the doctrine of the Trinity taught therein. We will not even find a full-fledged and explicit doctrine within the New Testament. Given the nature of progressive revelation, we should not, therefore, expect to find as much in the Old Testament as in the New. Until the incarnation of the Son and the sending of the Spirit at Pentecost, it would be very difficult to reveal much about the second and third persons of the Trinity in a fashion that would be comprehensible to the recipients of that revelation. The help that the Old Testament revelation can be to us is much more modest than that.

What we will be seeking here are indications, hints, of the understanding of God by the Old Testament writers that go beyond the mere or normal understanding of God on a monotheistic model. To put it another way, are there any indications of complexity or the composite character of God in the Old Testament?

Are there references that are in some sense consistent with or may even implicitly contain, trinitarian conceptions? Are there hints within the Old Testament revelation of this trinitarian understanding that await the fuller revelation of the New Testament to make it complete?

The Cultural Form of the Old Testament Revelation

Before we intentionally address this question, however, another preliminary issue must be faced: the cultural form in which that revelation came. It is commonplace to understand that God chose the people of Israel out of the sinful, rebellious human race to be his covenant people. This meant that they were in some special way to be the initial and perhaps even primary objects of his fellowship and favor and thus his redemption and reconciliation. Beyond that, however, we understand that their election by God was not exclusive but inclusive. They were not to be merely the recipients of God's grace, but agents of its transmission.

This meant that the revelation that came to them was of importance to all persons. The revelation of God's will and holiness, found in the Ten Commandments, for example, was a normative manifestation of truth about God. The promises of future blessing were truth that would benefit all peoples and were intended to be the object and basis of faith and hope.

If God chose the people of Israel, did he also choose their language and their mind-set? Since the revelation came through that language and in a sense is colored by its peculiar characteristics, may we rely on the resulting characteristics? Or, to put it differently, are we required to accept those characteristics? Are they authoritative or normative? Or are they to be treated as somehow primitive or obsolete, to be replaced by more modern or Western forms of thought?

I am here proposing the thesis that the selection of the people of Israel also involved the choice of their language as a vehicle for the conveyance of divine truth. There was an appropriateness of their ways of thinking to the truth God was seeking to make known to humans.[1] Whether the language should be regarded as

---

1. G. A. F. Knight, *A Biblical Approach to the Doctrine of the Trinity* (Edinburgh: Oliver and Boyd, 1953), p. 6.

a preexisting factor or as something that itself was the product of God's providential working is another issue. If one holds that God foresees and plans from all eternity what he then infallibly brings to pass within time, then the Hebrew language was not merely discovered or adopted, but was prepared as a means by which the truth could be conveyed. If this is truth, then it is especially important that we get back to that original, normative language as what is normative, rather than rely on a particular translation of it.

This rather general and formal point takes on more significance when we bear in mind that the form of the Old Testament to which most Christians had access was itself a translation, the Greek Septuagint, usually designated by the abbreviation LXX. Part of the difficulty, according to G. A. F. Knight, stemmed from the enmity between Jews and Christians during the early period of the history of the church, the time when much of the formation of Christian theology was taking place. Thus, there was an aversion to studying the Old Testament Scriptures in Hebrew, and to even consulting the Jews for understanding of those same Scriptures. Very few theologians were capable of reading the Hebrew Old Testament. Since the LXX was written in the same koine Greek as the New Testament, this meant that by the time the New Testament was canonized, the entire Bible was available to the church as a Bible written in one language throughout.[2] Jerome, who translated the Bible into Latin (the Vulgate), attempted to learn Hebrew, but never really mastered it. Given his inadequate knowledge of Hebrew, Jerome was reluctant, at those points where the LXX differed from the meaning of the Hebrew, to seek to change the whole climate of thought. Consequently, any distortions of the Hebrew thought occasioned by the translation into Greek became perpetuated and even amplified by his translation work. Now, with the Vulgate becoming the official text from which Catholic theologians operated, theological work was, with respect to the Old Testament, already two steps removed from the original. The concepts, in other words, had already gone through two filters, with some resulting modification. Knight believes that this was a radical distortion. He says,

2. Ibid., p. 2.

"But what is of real consequence is that the LXX even provided the Church with dogmatic presentations of the Faith that are not in accord with the original text."[3] Wainwright, however, maintains that Knight has overstated the case, and that while the LXX does eliminate anything that might be construed as favoring polytheism, it nonetheless retains much that does not easily harmonize with the most rigid form of monotheism.[4] Having said that, it is nonetheless still the case that the thought world out of which the LXX koine Greek came was both strongly hostile to polytheism and also favorable to a rather static view of reality in general and of God in particular.

There has, to be sure, been too strong a contrast sometimes drawn between the Hebrew and Greek ways of thinking. In such a construction, the supposedly Hebrew mind became a framework into which twentieth-century existentialist and functionalist categories and content were often read. The extremes to which this conception of the "distinctive biblical mentality" were carried have been quite accurately depicted and evaluated by Brevard Childs and James Barr.[5] Yet there is a difference, nonetheless. Further, we are not necessarily bound to the Hebrew way of thinking as an adequate set of conceptions for us in our modern and Western world. The concepts must be translated into a contemporary context. What we are here concerned about, however, is that this not be done too soon, and that it be a second step, carefully and self-consciously taken after the first step of accurately determining what the Hebrew author was really saying. To make the transition too quickly would be to cause ourselves to be led astray. This means that we must consciously and definitely make an effort to set aside our presuppositions and attempt to enter as fully as possible into the world and the mind of the Old Testament.

One characteristic of the Old Testament and Hebrew way of thinking is its concreteness. The Hebrew language has a scarcity of abstract nouns, and also tends to avoid adjectives. Instead of

3. Ibid., p. 4.

4. Arthur W. Wainwright, *The Trinity in the New Testament* (London: SPCK, 1962), p. 23.

5. James Barr, *The Semantics of Biblical Language* (Oxford: Oxford University Press, 1961); Brevard Childs, *Biblical Theology in Crisis* (Philadelphia: Westminster, 1970), pp. 44–47, 70–72.

an adjective, which would be an abstraction, Hebrew often uses instead a noun of quality with a possessive. For example, instead of "a righteous man," it might say, "a man of righteousness." Knight believes that this grammatical peculiarity is related to the desire of the Hebrew to see something with the mind's eye. As an example he notes Isaiah 63:1–2, where instead of speaking of the wrath of God against sin, Isaiah speaks of a blood-spattered warrior. Similar references are found in the psalmist's "The Lord is my Shepherd" and "Like as a father pitieth his children."[6]

There is a considerable amount of anthropomorphism in the early Old Testament material. In part this is due to the fact that, believing themselves to have been created in the image of God, it seemed natural for the Hebrews to think of God as being like themselves. The depictions of the divine nature exhibit a certain complexity. We cannot expect to find a view of the Trinity in the idea of God, either explicitly or implicitly. What we do want to determine, however, is whether within this understanding of God, there is sufficient breadth to be at least not incompatible with the trinitarian conception.

The Hebrew Concept of Extended Personality

The Hebrew conception of the makeup of the human person is instructive. There was not, in Hebrew thought, the sharp distinction between body and soul sometimes found in some varieties of Greek thought. The person is not limited to the soul, but is the whole of him or her. Yet this unity is a unity in diversity. Thus, the psalmist prays, "Examine me, O LORD, try my kidneys as well as my heart" (Ps. 26:2). In the creation account, Jehovah makes the man out of earth and breathes into it. It is this whole that is then called *nephesh*, or soul. This is what Johannes Pedersen has called the "grasping of a totality."[7]

Beyond this, however, there is what can be called the concept of the extension of the powers and personality of the individual. Part of this is seen in the individual's word. A clear example of this is in Genesis 27:33–37. Isaac pronounces a blessing on Ja-

6. Knight, *Biblical Approach*, pp. 8–9.

7. Johannes Pedersen, *Israel, Its Life and Culture*, I–II, (Oxford: Oxford University Press, 1926), pp. 106–33.

cob, mistakenly thinking he is Esau, and then is unable either to retract or to nullify those words. Similarly, the importance attached to the name of the person demonstrates this extension of powers. The practice of levirate marriage was instituted to preserve the individual's name. Bildad's description of the fate of the wicked is that his memory perishes from the earth; he has no name in the land, for there is no offspring to perpetuate his name (Job 18:17–19).

A man's personality extends throughout his entire household. Thus, the household of Achan was treated as a psychical whole; all of them were stoned for his sin. Further, a household head is thought of as present in the person of his servant or steward. So, Joseph's brothers address his servant as Joseph himself, for in their understanding he was present in that servant.[8] Even a man's property could be understood as an extension of the personality. So, for example, when Elisha sent his servant Gehazi ahead of him with his staff as the instrument for restoring the Shunammite's son to life, he warned him against even giving a greeting to anyone whom he might meet (2 Kings 4:29). It was as if this would dissipate a power that was to be preserved for the intended recipient of the blessing.[9]

Extended even further, this conception leads us to the Hebrew idea that the individual is never to be thought of merely as an isolated unit. Rather, he lives in constant reaction toward others— both those with whom he is close-knit within the sphere of his social unit as an extended or larger self and those who fall outside this sphere. The household is seen as a psychical whole representing the extended personality of the man as its head, and it is the nucleus of the social unit or kinship group. The social unit or kinship group, however widely conceived, is a single *nephesh* or person. For example, the people of Israel complained during the period in the wilderness, "Our soul is sick of this cursed food" (Num. 21:4–5). So also when the Israelites were put to flight at Ai, their heart melted and became like water (Josh. 7:5). David, after appealing for the loyalty of the people of Judah on the ground of their kinship, "won over the heart of all the men of

8. Aubrey R. Johnson, *The One and the Many in the Israelite Conception of God* (Cardiff: University of Wales Press, 1961), pp. 4–5.

9. Ibid., pp. 6–7.

Judah as if they were one man" (2 Sam. 19:14). In each of these references, the word "heart" is in the singular in the Hebrew.[10] This characteristic even helps account for the tendency of some to treat the Genesis narratives as dealing not with individuals but with personifications,[11] or to interpret the "I" of many of the psalms in terms of these collective units.[12] This particular characteristic of Hebrew thought and writing is not limited to the Hebrews, however, but is also found in the Tell el-Amarna tablets.[13] In both the tablets and the Hebrew account, there is what Johnson calls an oscillation between thinking of the social unit in question as an association of individuals, in which case the plural is used, and as a corporate personality, in which case the singular is used.[14] The frequency of this phenomenon can be seen in major analyses in Psalms by H. Wheeler Robinson[15] and in Isaiah 40–55 by Robinson[16] and O. Eissfeldt.[17]

We now note the relevance of this consideration for the Israelite understanding of God. Belief that man was made in the image of God meant that God was also conceived of in terms of the human himself. Thus, anthropomorphism was frequently employed in the attempt to discuss God. We have seen that the Israelite conception of man was of a unified psychical whole, and that the power of this whole was thought of as extending beyond the body through "extensions" of the personality. Similarly, this idea of the extension of the power of God is found in Hebrew thought. This is seen, for example, in the idea of the Spirit of God, by which the prophets and judges were able to perform superhuman acts. The Spirit "dons" Gideon like a garment (Judg.

10. Ibid., p. 9.

11. A. Kuenen, *The Religion of Israel to the Fall of the Jewish State,* trans. A. H. May (London: Williams and Norgate, 1882), 1:111.

12. Rudolf Smend, "Ueber das Ich der Psalmen," *Zeitschrift für die Alttestamentliche Wissenschaft* 8 (1888): 49–147.

13. Tablet number 100, lines 1–10 and 31–36. *The Tell El-Amarna Tablets,* ed. Samuel A. B. Mercer (Toronto: Macmillan of Canada, 1939), 1:338–41.

14. Johnson, *The One and the Many,* pp. 11–12.

15. H. Wheeler Robinson, "The Hebrew Conception of Corporate Personality," in *Werden und Wesen des Alten Testaments,* ed. Johannes Hempel, *Beihafte zur Zeitschrift für die Alttestamentliche Wissenschaft* (Berlin: Alfred Töpelmann, 1936), 66:57–58.

16. Ibid., pp. 58–60.

17. O. Eissfeldt, "The Ebed-Jahwe in Isaiah 40–55 in the Light of the Israelite Conceptions of the Community and the Individual, the Ideal and the Real," *The Expository Times* 44.6 (March 1933): 261–68.

6:34), and rushes on Samson (Judg. 14:6, 19; 15:14) and Saul (1 Sam. 10:10). The description is such that it can hardly be regarded as the work of an impersonal force. Johnson comments:

> In light of the Israelite conception of man, however, it would seem that this רוּחַ, as a member of Yahweh's heavenly Court (or 'Household'!), should be thought of as an individualization with the corporate רוּחַ or 'Spirit' of Yahweh's extended Personality; in other words, that we must be prepared to recognize for the Godhead just such fluidity of reference from the One to the Many or from the Many to the One as we have already noticed in the case of man.[18]

The point of what we are saying is this. It is not that there is any claim of a teaching of the Trinity in these Old Testament conceptions. Nor is there even an implicit concept of Trinity here. What we are saying, however, is that the Hebrew conception of God included the idea of a unity that had an extension beyond itself. Thus, there was sufficient breadth of the idea that we are not compelled to hold that the conception precluded the doctrine of a Triune God.

Plural References in the Old Testament

We wish now to examine another significant concept, that of the plural references in the Old Testament. These occur in both noun and verb form. The noun is the common *ĕlōhîm*. There of course are singular words for God. The word *ĕloah* occurs some fifty-seven times, almost always in poetry or very late prose. More common is *ĕl*, which occurs a total of 217 times. Almost always it is combined with an attribute, such as *gibor*, *chah*, or *shaddai*, and consequently is to be understood as describing an aspect of God's nature. Not every case of the singular is accounted for in this fashion, but, says Knight, "even if we could do so, the fact is not altered that אלהים is used most peculiarly (from our point of view) to cover an aspect of the Godhead which is specifically Hebraic, viz., the conception that God is both singular אל and plural אלהים at one and the same time."[19]

18. *The One and the Many*, p. 16.
19. Knight, *Biblical Approach*, p. 19.

One method of ascertaining the meaning of Hebrew terms is to look at the cognate Semitic languages for similar terms, on the assumption that this will give us insights into the Hebrew. When we consult the cognate languages of Arabic and Aramaic on this specific point, however, we find that the respective word is singular. In fact, this presented a problem for the Hebrews in translating *ʾĕlōhîm* into Aramaic, when they adopted that language as their own. It also presented a problem for the Septuagint translators, since the Greek language had no way of translating this plural form without an apparent commitment to polytheism.

The common way of dealing with this phenomenon is to regard it as the plural of majesty.[20] Knight, who says he has even seen the suggestion that this represents the "we" of the newspaper editor, feels that this and similar explanations rest consciously or unconsciously on Greek assumptions. He says of the plural of majesty explanation, "surely that is to read into Hebrew speech a modern way of thinking."[21]

Knight suggests what he believes to be a preferable explanation. There is in Hebrew what he terms the quantitative plural. He notes that the words for "water" and "heaven," for example, are both in the plural. Water can be thought of in terms either of individual rain drops or of the mass of water in the ocean, yet in both cases it is equally water. He believes that the plural vowel pointing of the noun *Adhonai,* used as a parallel to the plural concept behind the word *Elohim,* is another example of this. Although plural in form, singular verbs are used with it. He comments: "what we have before us is an example of this diversity in unity in regard to the nature of God which we have already noted as a characteristic of Hebrew thought."[22]

The issue also occurs in connection with plural verb forms. The first and most widely cited of these is in Genesis 1:26: "Then God said [singular], 'Let us make [plural] man in the image of us.'" Just as with the name of God, this has frequently been explained as a plural of majesty.[23] Even the Koran (which, of

---

20. S. R. Driver, *The Book of Genesis,* 14th ed. (London: Methuen, 1943), p. 14.
21. Knight, *Biblical Approach,* p. 20.
22. Ibid.
23. Driver, *Genesis,* p. 14.

course, was strictly monotheistic) uses the plural.[24] On the other hand, however, this and the other plural passages seemed to the Jews to require some explanation. The Book of Jubilees (written in the second half of the second century B.C.) gives an account of the Genesis story, in which the statements that create theological difficulties are either omitted or altered. The creation story is told in such a way that the plural verb in 1:26 is dispensed with: "And after this, he created man, a man and a woman created he them" (Jubilees 2:14). The words of God are omitted from this account. Similarly, Philo's comments on Genesis 1:26 indicate that this passage caused him difficulty. He argued that God was the sole creating agent of other things, but that he was assisted by subordinate powers in his creation of man. Since he was only able to create good, the evil in man must necessarily be created by others. So, when God is quoted as saying, "Let us make man," he was addressing these subordinates, who were his inferiors. Consequently, his uniqueness is not affected by this consideration.[25] In the Jerusalem Talmud it is argued that because 1:27 refers to one God, 1:26 must also.[26] Although the Talmud does not provide certain evidence of first-century Judaism, Wainwright feels that there is no reason to suppose that this is untrue to the spirit of Judaism at that time.[27]

One consideration which, from the point of logical analysis, is of considerable significance is the shift in number within this verse. The verb in the statement, "Then God, said . . . ," is in the singular. The statement "Let us make man," is plural. If this is to be interpreted as a plural of majesty, we must conclude that God uses the plural of majesty while the author of this passage does not, which would seem most peculiar, if the Jews were familiar with and used the plural of majesty. The pronominal suffix "of us" on the "image of God" is yet another consideration beyond the name, Elohim, that we may rather be dealing here with that concept of oneness in plurality of God that we have referred to earlier.

24. Johnson, *One and Many*, p. 28, n. 1.
25. *On the Creation of the World* 24.
26. *Berakhot*, 9:1, VI, A–G. *The Talmud of the Land of Israel* (Chicago: University of Chicago Press, 1989), 1:307–8.
27. Wainwright, *Trinity*, p. 25.

A second significant passage is Genesis 3:22, which reads, "And the LORD God said, 'The man has now become like one of us.'" This also presented difficulties for the Jews. In the account of the expulsion of Adam and Eve from the Garden of Eden, the Book of Jubilees includes no verse corresponding to Genesis 3:22. Pappias, a Palestinian rabbi who lived at the end of the first century A.D., held that the verse implied that Adam had become like an angel.[28] The Targums also are instructive to us on this passage. Onkelos, the earliest, follows closely the original Hebrew in 1:26 and 11:7, but in 3:22, it says, "And the Lord God said, 'Behold, man is become singular in the world by himself.'" Here is an actual and considerable alteration of the original wording of the passage. The Palestinian Targum explains the plural verbs on the basis that God was addressing angels; the Jerusalem Targum makes a similar interpretation of 3:22.[29]

Another Genesis passage pertinent to our purposes is 11:7, which reads, "[The Lord said,] 'Come, let us go down and confuse their language.'" Here again we have the shift in number of the verb from singular to plural. Philo's explanation was that God is surrounded by potencies, although he himself is one. When he said what he did above, then, he was addressing these potencies. Philo notes: "In the first place, then, we must say this, that there is no existing being equal in honour to God, but there is one only ruler and king, who alone may direct and dispose of all things. . . . God is one, he has about him an unspeakable number of powers, all of which are defenders and preservers of everything that is created."[30] These powers were the ones who went down and confused the tongues of the persons who were building the tower of Babel. They had to do this; God himself could not carry out this punishment, which is an evil.

The account of the encounter between Abraham and the three men at Mamre in Genesis 18 offers special considerations. There is a series of oscillations between the singular and the plural in this passage. The introduction says, "The LORD appeared to Abraham" (v. 1). When Abraham looks up, however, he sees three

28. C. G. Montefiore and H. Loewe, *A Rabbinic Anthology* (New York: Schocken, 1974), p. 664.

29. Wainwright, *Trinity*, p. 25.

30. *On the Confusion of Languages* 33–34.

men (v. 2). When he speaks, he addresses his visitors in the singular, "My lord" (v. 3), but in the following verse speaks to them in the plural. The alternation continues throughout the passage: "The Lord"—verses 10, 13, 14, 17, 19, 22; "the men"—verses 16, 22; and "you all"—verse 4. Further, in chapter 19, two angels appear to Lot, who addresses them as "lord" (v. 18).

This passage provoked quite a lot of explanatory activity from Jews. The Targum of Onkelos follows the usual meaning of the Hebrew quite closely, but the Palestinian Targum attempts to offer an explanation of the juxtaposition of singulars and plurals. According to that Targum, the three angels were sent at once rather than only one because each carried out a single mission. One gave the message announcing the birth of Isaac, another warned Lot, and the third was to destroy Sodom and Gomorrah. There is no comment on the fact that Abraham addressed them as "my lord." In verse 10 the explanation is that only one angel was speaking to Abraham. In verse 20 the Targum makes quite clear that "the Lord" is not to be identified with the three men, saying, "And the Lord said to the ministering angels."

Philo gives a very different interpretation of this incident. He claims that in this vision, there is really only a single object, God. Like an object that may cast two shadows at once, however, God may have a threefold appearance. Thus, the three men whom Abraham met were simply a triple manifestation of a single God. To those who are more advanced in the faith, God reveals himself as three; to those less advanced, he appears as one. The lower classes do not worship God for his own sake, but for the benefits they receive from him or to avoid divine punishment. God, the supreme being, is capable only of doing good and so leaves the task of inflicting punishment to these lower beings, the two angels, who consequently destroy Sodom and Gomorrah.[31]

Another passage involving plurals is Isaiah 6:8, which has received less attention than the Genesis passages. Of special significance is the shift between singular and plural: "Then I heard the voice of the Lord saying, 'Whom shall I send? And who will go for us?'" The Targum solves the problem by removing the plural pro-

---

31. *A Treatise on the Life of the Wise Man Made Perfect by Instruction, or, on the Unwritten Law, That is to Say, on Abraham*, 24–28.

noun, so that it reads: "Whom shall I send to prophesy, and who will go to preach?"[32]

To sum up this section on the plural used with respect to God, we have noted a limited but impressive number of such occurrences. The standard explanation, of the plural of majesty, may actually stem more from the period of the interpreter than from the ancient period of the writer. Even if that explanation were accepted, one still faces the fact of the oscillation between singular and plural usages in some of these passages. Further, there is also the question of whom the speaker of the plural statements is addressing. In short, there appear to be logical eccentricities present in some of these passages, even when one attempts to approach them from the Hebrew perspective. Johnson's statement seems well put:

> In the circumstances does not such fluidity of reference seem best explained in terms of that oscillation as between the one and the many which we have seen to be characteristic of the Israelite conception of man and also present on occasion in, say, the Assyrian conception of deity? In short, may one not suggest with a degree of probability that any Israelite who thought his אֱלֹהִים, to be Many also thought his אֱלֹהִים to be One?[33]

The Angel of the Lord

Another significant consideration for our purposes is the angel of the Lord. There are a large number of such references (Gen. 16:7, 9, 11; 21:17; 22:11, 15; 24:7, 40; 31:11; Exod. 3:2 [cf. v. 4 and cf. Acts 7:30–34]; 14:19 [cf. Num. 20:26]; 23:20–26; 32:33–33:17 [cf. 63:9]; possibly Josh. 5:13–6:2; Judges 2:1–5; 6:11–40).

In some passages there is an apparent identification of the angel of the Lord with Yahweh. In Genesis 31:11–13 the angel actually says, "I am the God of Bethel." In Genesis 32:24–30, Jacob wrestles with a man, but says, "I saw God face to face." Hosea 12:4 says of this incident, "He struggled with the angel and overcame him." In Genesis 48:15–16, the angel is identified with God in the action of, or as the instrument of, redemption. He is the

---

32. *The Targum of Isaiah*, ed. J. F. Stenning (Oxford: Clarendon, 1949), pp. 22–23.
33. Johnson, *One and Many*, p. 28.

go'ēl, although according to Isaiah 44:6 there is no *go'ēl* but God. The narrative of the sacrifice of Isaac (Gen. 22) begins with the simple statement, "God said" (v. 1). Later in the passage, it is the angel of the Lord who appears and speaks (vv. 11, 15), yet at the end it is seemingly God who speaks: "I swear by myself, declares the LORD" (v. 16). In Exodus 3:2–6 the angel of God appears to Moses (v. 2), but it is as Yahweh and as Elohim that the divine visitor speaks (vv. 4, 5, 6, and to 4:17). Moses hides his face, because he is afraid to look at God (v. 6). In Judges 2:1–5 the angel of Exodus 14:19 reappears and speaks as if he were Yahweh: "I will never break my covenant with you" (v. 1). Presumably, however, only God can make covenants of this kind with human beings, so that would argue that the angel is God himself.

Judges 6:11–24 is somewhat different. In verse 12 the angel appears to be distinct from the Lord, for he says, "The LORD is with you, mighty warrior," giving the definite impression of a third person statement. Yet in verse 14 he becomes Yahweh himself, and in verse 15 Gideon addresses him as "Lord." In verses 22–23 we find both aspects at once: "When Gideon realized that it was the angel of the LORD, he exclaimed, 'Ah, Sovereign LORD! I have seen the angel of the LORD face to face!' But the LORD said to him, 'Peace! Do not be afraid. You are not going to die.'" The fear that he will die indicates that Gideon considered the angel of the Lord to be God himself. A distinction also can be seen in Judges 13:2–23. The angel of the Lord appears to Manoah's wife (v. 3). She refers to him as "a man of god" who looked like "an angel from God" (v. 6). Manoah prays to God that he would send the man of God to them again (v. 8). God hears Manoah (v. 9), and the angel of God comes again (vv. 9, 13, 15, 16, 17, 21). Manoah tells his wife that they are doomed to die, because "we have seen God" (v. 22).

It appears that in this rich and varied usage of the expression, "angel of the LORD," we have a contrast. On the one hand, he is distinguished from God or the Lord, who sends him and of whom he speaks. On the other hand, the angel speaks as if he were the Lord himself speaking directly, and is regarded as the Lord by those to whom he appears. We are drawn to the conclusion that in some way, not really explicated in Scripture, the angel of the Lord is both the Lord and not the Lord.

The Nature of the Unity of God

The Hebrews, of course, were strongly monotheistic in their belief and worship. They were warned that they were to have no other gods besides Jehovah (Exod. 20:3). This was necessary because of the propensity of the Israelites to adopt the deities of the peoples around them. The difficulty was not that they ceased to believe in Jehovah and substituted other deities for him. Nor was it even that they gave greater devotion and commitment to some other deity or deities than to Jehovah. It was simply that their religious devotion to Jehovah was not exclusive. Literally, what this commandment says is, "You shall have no other gods to my face," or in the presence of Jehovah. He did not want to divide people's commitment with any other claimed gods, which were not gods at all. Jehovah was the only true and living God. This command, however, does not tell us anything about the nature or makeup of that God.

This prohibition was supported by other texts, the best known of which is the Shema of Deuteronomy 6:4–5: "Hear, O Israel: The LORD our God, the LORD is one. Love the LORD your God with all your heart and with all your soul and with all your strength." Ostensibly, this is an argument that because there is only one God, there is to be no dividing of the commitment of one's total being to this Lord. We need, however, to examine more closely what is meant by the oneness that is here attributed to God. There are two Hebrew words for one. The first is יָחִיד, *yāḥîd*, which means unique, the only one of a class. This word is used of Isaac, in Jehovah's command to Abraham, to take his only son and offer him as a sacrifice. He was the only son, and there was no other. It is also used of an only child of his mother in Proverbs 4:3. In Amos 8:10 it also is used of an only son. It is also used in that fashion in Zechariah 12:10, as "an only child." If this were the word used here, it would simply be telling us of the uniqueness of God, the fact that he is the only one in his class. That of course is a truth found in Scripture, and all Christians believe it. Yet that word alone would not tell us anything about the nature of that God. It would be quite possible to hold that view and be a unitarian. And unitarianism is quite a different matter from monotheism as such.

There is another Hebrew word for one. It is the word אֶחָד, (ʾeḥād). It is derived from a verb form meaning to unify, that is, figuratively, to collect (one's thoughts). The numeral derived from this means properly, united, that is, one. It is this word that is used of God in Deuteronomy 6:4. It is also used in Genesis 2:24, which says that "a man will leave his father and mother and be united to his wife, and they will become one flesh." There the unity is not uniqueness, but the unity of diversity. It speaks of union, rather than aloneness. And it is this same word that is used of God in Deuteronomy. In fact, in Zechariah 14:9, both words are used: "On that day there will be one LORD, and his name the only name."

8

The Trinity
in the New Testament

When we come to the New Testament material on the Trinity, we face something of a paradox. On the one hand, the references are clearer and more direct than those in the Old Testament, for we now have a more advanced stage in God's progressive revelation. By the New Testament, we have the incarnation of the second person of the Trinity and the coming into the world of the third person. Consequently, the material is more directly usable in constructing our doctrine, since the issues are brought more to the fore. Yet, on the other hand, we still do not have a clear-cut statement on the Trinity.

The New Testament can be utilized in a variety of ways. For those who accept it as God's authoritative revelation, written under the inspiration of the Holy Spirit, it is fully authoritative. The issue of its use in the construction of a doctrine of the Trinity is, therefore, rather simple. It is just a matter of determining what it says or what it teaches. That is then true and binding on us. It would not even be necessary to engage in some of the critical endeavors that sometimes characterize New Testament exegesis. If, however, we wish to extend our discussion beyond those who hold a similar view of the New Testament, it will be necessary to interact with the critical methodology and the critical objections to use of the biblical texts to establish the doctrine of the Trinity. Two possibilities lie open to us: (1) refute the critical theories to demonstrate our right to use the Bible in a more traditional fashion; or (2) show that even if one accepts the critical methodology, it is still possible to demonstrate the existence of an implicit belief in the Trinity. In other words, it is not necessary to appeal to the Bible as the inspired Word of God. It can be utilized as simply a historically reliable source for determining what the church held in its earliest period. We will follow this latter approach in our employment of the New Testament documents.

The Status of Doctrine and Doctrinal Formulations in the New Testament

We begin our consideration by noting the status of doctrine and doctrinal formulations in the New Testament. There was no official creed in the earliest days of the church. Some have, of course, claimed that the Apostles' Creed actually went back to the original group of Jesus' intimate circle. Tyrannius Rufinus, writing about 404, reported a view that was rather widely held at that time. As the apostles were to go their respective ways in their ministry following the imparting to them at Pentecost of the ability to speak different languages, they decided that they should agree on the basic content of the message. To minimize the divergence among them, they met at one spot and, under the filling of the Holy Spirit, each contributed a part he felt should be included. They then agreed on this content, as the standard teaching to be given.[1] This tradition was elaborated on in a form reported in the series of sermons, *De symbolo,* falsely attributed to Augustine. According to the first of these, the tradition reports what each of the twelve contributed to the creed.[2]

This general understanding continued into the Middle Ages. It proved somewhat difficult to try to divide the creed into exactly twelve articles. Thomas Aquinas, who found this a somewhat embarrassing requirement, instead organized it in terms of seven articles dealing with the Godhead and seven pertaining to Christ's humanity.[3] The church, however, found the story of the creed's origin useful in reinforcing the authority of what had be-

---

1. Tyrannius Rufinus, *Commentary on the Apostles' Creed* 2 (*Corpus Christianorum, Series Latina* 20, 134f).
2. *Sermon* 240, in *Patrologia, Series Latina,* 39, 2189.
3. *Summa Theologica,* II, 2 Q. 1, art. 8.

come a sacred formula. So the Apostles' Creed continued well into the fifteenth century to be considered as the actual creed of the apostles. In the fifteenth century, however, dispute broke out at the Council of Florence (1438–45) between the Latin church, which accepted the apostolic authority of the creed, and the Greek church, which did not. Shortly thereafter, the idea of the apostolic origin of the creed was sharply criticized by Lorenzo Valla, and then by Reginald Pecock, who in a less brutal and theologically more skillful fashion, denied the apostolic authority of the creed and rejected the article regarding the descent into hell.[4] Because these views were repressed (Valla had to recant; Pecock was forced to resign his bishopric) and because this issue was soon thrust into the background by the more prominent disputes related to the Reformation, the issues did not really surface again until the seventeenth century.

In the nineteenth century, the skepticism was carried further. Doubts were expressed whether there was any creed at all, or whether any organized body of doctrine could have existed during the New Testament period. If there had been such a creed, so went the argument, there surely should be some unmistakable reference to it or some plausible quotation from its text. Certainly if the church had possessed such a creed, it would have survived in at least a fragmentary form. It would have possessed great authority, and the known development of the creeds of the second and third centuries would have been rendered unlikely by the existence of such a creed. Further, such a creed would not have been possible that early in a church in which the faith had not yet attained such a developed form.[5]

It must be remembered that the period from 1860 to 1914, in which this view of early doctrinal statements was being formulated, was dominated by a specific theory of Christian origins. Under the influence of men such as Harnack, a sharp antithesis was frequently drawn between the Spirit-guided, spontaneous New Testament phase, and the second century, which was believed to have seen the beginning of more formal organization and thought.[6] Thus, there was no room for any complete creed at

---

4. *Book of Faith*, pt. 2, chap. 5.
5. J. N. D. Kelly, *Early Christian Creeds* (Essex: Longman, 1972), p. 6.
6. Adolf Harnack, *History of Dogma* (New York: Dover, 1961), 1:141–43.

this early point. Rather, formulated creeds did not come into existence until the middle of the second century, or possibly somewhat earlier. Any doctrinal formulations must have been of the simple sort of brief baptismal confessions, such as "Jesus is Lord" or "Jesus is the Son of God."

This hypothesis, however, deserves further examination. What was the nature of the early church and the state of doctrinal formulation? Here it must be agreed that there was not in the apostolic church any official, fixed confession of faith. It appears that J. N. D. Kelly is correct, however, when he suggests that the alternatives usually considered are insufficient. There is agreement that there were no fixed, stereotyped creeds. Nonetheless, there may early have been creeds of a looser sort than the fixed official formulations, but definitely foreshadowing them.[7]

It is apparent that the early church was from the beginning what we would today call an evangelistic or missionary church. It definitely knew what it believed and considered beliefs important. It was a preaching church, and that preaching was to a large extent doctrinally oriented or at least doctrinally based. Thus the contrast propounded by Harnack and others between the early, noncreedal church and the more highly institutionalized church of the second century is simply inaccurate. Indeed, its very origin and continuation under the circumstances in which it existed refute that. Kelly puts it thus:

> Had the Christians of the apostolic age not conceived of themselves as possessing a body of distinctive, consciously held beliefs, they would scarcely have separated themselves from Judaism and undertaken an immense programme of missionary expansion. Everything goes to show that the infant communities looked upon themselves as the bearers of a unique story of redemption. It was their faith in this gospel which had called them into being, and which they felt obliged to communicate to newcomers.[8]

We must also look at the nature of the apostolic literature. One useful contribution of form criticism to our understanding of the Gospels has been in showing us that these were not merely ob-

---

7. Kelly, *Creeds*, p. 7.
8. Ibid.

jective biographies, given simply to convey to us neutral, factual information about Jesus. They are evangelistic treatises. They were written to convince readers just who Jesus was. They were written from positions of faith, with the desire of bringing others to the faith as well. The terminology used by some to describe this material as propaganda may be too strong, given the connotations of that word. It must, however, be acknowledged that the authors have persuasion as a major part of their intention. The epistles presuppose a common faith shared by the writer and the reader. They could only have come into being from a community with strong and quite well-defined convictions.

This can be seen by examining the texts that emphasize the transmission of the tradition, a collection of authoritative doctrine. Various expressions for this received body of teaching are found throughout the New Testament. In Jude, the author refers to "the faith that was once for all entrusted to the saints" (v. 3). Later he speaks of "your most holy faith" (v. 20), again using the expression to mean an accepted body of beliefs, that is, the content of their faith. The pastoral epistles, noted for their concern for the continuation of ministry, are filled with expressions such as "pattern of sound teaching" (2 Tim. 1:13), "sound doctrine" (2 Tim. 4:3; Titus 1:9), "good deposit" (2 Tim. 1:14), "the faith" (1 Tim. 1:19; Titus 1:13), and "the good teaching" (1 Tim. 4:6). The writer to the Hebrews makes frequent reference to the confession to which his readers are to hold fast at any cost (3:1; 4:14; 10:23), and in 6:2 he refers to "instruction," a rather elementary stage in Christian education, which involves instruction in doctrine as well as ethics and the sacraments.

One specific reference is to "the Word of life" in 1 John 1:1. This occurs in an opening sentence, which has challenged interpreters. One rather common interpretation is that this expression is to be seen as a reference to the incarnate Logos of whom John speaks in the prologue to his Gospel, assuming the common authorship of the Gospel and the first Epistle.[9] Another interpretation, however, is that this expression is to be understood in the same fashion as in Philippians 2:16 ("as you hold out the word of life") and Acts 5:20 ("the full message of this new

9. R. J. Drummond and Leon Morris, "The Epistles of John," in *The New Bible Commentary*, ed. F. Davidson (Grand Rapids: Eerdmans, 1953), p. 1151.

life").[10] On this analogy, the reference would be understood as pertaining to the message of salvation announced by the church. Yet these two interpretations may not be mutually exclusive. The incarnate Lord was certainly regarded as the true Word of God, but the gospel that the early church proclaimed was most assuredly the Word as set forth in what he was and what he had done. The content of the letter supports this. John is writing, at least in part, to combat false teachings that were threatening the received message, and these represented denials of the person of the Word, Jesus Christ. Thus, John appeals to his hearers to continue steadfast in the teaching they had heard from the beginning (1 John 2:24).

On the old assumption of the late date of the Johannine epistles, it was thought that this indicated a fixing of the tradition into a hard-and-fast outline only near the end of the first century, since the letters were thought to have been written in the final decade of that century. Two considerations, however, suggest an earlier dating for this development. One of these is the adoption of earlier dating for the Gospels. John A. T. Robinson was instrumental in this. While this development does not directly affect the issue of the dating of 1 John, there is some tendency to associate it with the Gospel, in light of the similarities of style between the two. More pertinent is the fact that Paul gives indication of such developments earlier. In Galatians 3:1 he reminds his readers that before their eyes Jesus Christ had been "clearly portrayed as crucified." He pleads with the Thessalonians to "hold to the teachings we passed on to you" (2 Thess. 2:15). The verb διδάσκω here hints of doctrine. In Romans 6:17 Paul is more explicit, speaking of "the form of teaching" that they hold. He also refers in 1 Corinthians 11:23 and 15:3 to the tradition passed down (παρέλαβον and παρέδωκα) and received. In the former case, the reference is to the Lord's Supper and in the latter to the resurrection.

There are other references of this type in Paul's writings. For example, he speaks of "the gospel" (τὸ εὐαγγέλιον) in Romans 2:16; 16:25; 1 Corinthians 15:1; Galatians 2:2. He speaks of "the preaching" (τὸ κήρυγμα) or "the preaching of Jesus Christ" (Rom.

---

10. Brooke Foss Westcott, *The Epistles of St. John* (Grand Rapids: Eerdmans, 1952), p. 4; C. H. Dodd, *The Johannine Epistles* (New York: Harper & Brothers, 1946), pp. 1–6.

16:25; 1 Cor. 15:1). A more general term is "the faith" (ἡ πίστις) and the related verb (πιστεύω), in Galatians 1:23; Ephesians 4:5; and Colossians 2:7. In Ephesians 4:5 he appeals to "one Lord, one faith, one baptism." It is with respect to the gospel that he speaks of "the word of God" or "the word of the Lord" (1 Cor. 14:36; Gal. 6:6; Phil. 1:14; 1 Thess. 1:6; 2 Thess. 3:1). Rather than being a radical theological innovator, Paul had great respect for the deposit of teaching that had been authoritatively handed down in the church.

In general, it must be said that the apostles were concerned about declaring the message of what had been entrusted to them. Much attention has therefore been given to the kerygma, as found especially in the sermons in the Book of Acts. The work of Feine, Dodd, and others has enlarged our understanding of this basic set of themes. The one problem with concentrating on the sermons is that preaching was only one of the activities of the early church. The emphasis on the person of Christ in those sermons was obvious since this was primarily missionary activity. This may lead us to overlook the strong belief in the Fatherhood of God, which of course the fledgling church shared with Judaism. It may also cause us to underestimate the strength of the trinitarian motif. Kelly says:

> Similarly the profoundly Trinitarian strain in early Christianity is liable to be ignored in the approach which we are examining. The Trinitarianism of the New Testament is rarely explicit; but the frequency with which the triadic scheme recurs (as we shall see in the following section) suggests that this pattern was implicit in Christian theology from the start. If these gaps are filled in, however, we are entitled to assume with some confidence that what we have before us, at any rate in rough outline, is the doctrinal deposit, or the pattern of sound words, which was expounded in the apostolic Church since its inauguration and which constituted its distinctive message.[11]

From a rather early date a movement toward formulation and fixity was taking place. To be sure, there are no formal introductions of or recitations of creeds. Yet indications of their existence

---

11. Kelly, *Creeds*, pp. 12–13.

can be detected. There were certain creed-like slogans and catchwords that at the time of their writing were already beginning to be crystallized through popular practice. In addition, there are longer passages that betray their origin through their style. Their context, rhythm, and general pattern identify their origin in the community tradition, rather than merely the writer's invention. For example, the rhythm of Philippians 2:6–11 suggests that it had previously existed as a hymn, and the same can be said of 1 Timothy 3:16. A sensitivity to the presence of parallelism, common to Hebrew and Aramaic poetry, can indicate in some cases the previous status of the material.

The Baptismal Formula

One key text is the baptismal formula in Matthew 28:19, which is an apparent indication of the linkage of the three persons in such an intimate fashion as to imply equality: "Therefore go and make disciples of all nations, baptizing them in the name of the Father and of the Son and of the Holy Spirit." Since this appeared to be taught by Jesus as the fashion in which baptism was to be administered, this seemed to be especially significant. To some extent, its weight rested on this apparent authenticity of the words.

There have, however, been several assaults on this apparent authenticity. They have been of varying types. The first has come from the direction of textual criticism, arguing that these words are not legitimately part of the biblical text. One who has argued this way is Conybeare, who maintained that the original text was "Go and make disciples of all the nations in my name."[12] In part, his content was based on a similar objection by Eusebius. There is, however, little basis for such a reconstruction of the text. There is no evidence for this contention in any of the manuscripts and versions. Other explanations have been given of Eusebius holding the view that he did. It may have been that he conflated this text with Mark 16:17, Luke 24:47, or the "name of Jesus" passages in Acts.[13]

---

12. F. C. Conybeare, *Zeitschrift für Neutestamentliche Wissenschaft* 2 (1901): 275–88.

13. Jules Lebreton, *History of the Dogma of the Trinity; from Its Origins to the Council of Nicaea* (New York: Benziger, 1939), 1:438.

The second objection to the claimed authenticity of this formula comes from literary criticism. Here the major thrust is the fact that the verse has no parallels in the Synoptic Gospels or elsewhere. The closest resemblance to this passage is Mark 16:15–18, where there is no mention of the threefold name. That passage, however, is not considered to be textually reliable. Consequently, we are left without any parallel to the passage in question. The absence of a similar expression is therefore not so surprising.

The final, and in many ways the most serious, objection comes from historical criticism.[14] In the Acts of the Apostles, baptism was in the name of Jesus Christ, not in the threefold name. The question then arises, however: How could Acts record baptism in one name, if Jesus himself had commanded it in the threefold name? Further, Paul speaks of being baptized into Christ or into Jesus Christ. These phrases are closer to Acts than they are to Matthew. If Jesus had commanded the threefold formula for baptism, should we not find it referred to somewhere?

Crehan has proposed a solution to this problem. He draws a distinction between the status and the function of the two formulas. The disciples were authorized by Jesus to use the trinitarian formula, but the language of Acts refers to the part taken in the rite by the candidate. Crehan notes that the active voice is used in Matthew 28:19, whereas the passive voice is employed wherever baptism in or into the name of Jesus Christ is mentioned in Acts or the writings of Paul. In other words, the disciples were commanded to baptize in the name of the Father, the Son, and the Holy Spirit, whereas baptizees were commanded to be baptized in the name of Jesus.[15] This solution, however, seems somewhat artificial and forced. Further, it is not clear even in the writings of the first four centuries that such a distinction was drawn.

What are we to make of this historical enigma? It appears that the smoothest resolution of the problem is to draw the conclusion that both are authentic (although that word takes on a somewhat different sense with respect to the passages in Acts

---

14. William Frederick Flemington, *The New Testament Doctrine of Baptism* (London: SPCK, 1948), pp. 107–9; Herbert George Marsh, *The Origin and Significance of the New Testament Baptism* (Manchester: Manchester University Press, 1941), p. 115.

15. Joseph Hugh Crehan, *Early Christian Baptism and the Creed; A Study in Ante-Nicene Theology* (London: Burns, Oates, & Washbourne, 1950), pp. 76, 88.

than those in the Gospels). It is important to bear in mind the reduced time that we must now conclude was involved in the period between the events and the recording of them in the Gospel.
Thus, the opportunity for a tradition to change and grow is reduced. Further, in light of this fact, it is highly probable that eye-
witnesses to the original commission given by Jesus would still
have been alive when the materials began to circulate. Surely if
these words were not authentic, objection would have been
raised. How then could such a view (namely, that Jesus had commanded this form of baptismal formula) have arisen if the other
form, the short form involving baptism only in the name of Jesus,
was being practiced exclusively?

It may be most helpful to think of these two formulas as not
being exactly parallel, that is, of not being of the same status. If
one were a prescribed formula and the other simply a statement
of the nature of the baptism, there really is no conflict. For example, if the statement made by Jesus is a formula, a prescription of
the exact way in which the ordinance is to be administered, and
the passages in Acts are mere descriptions (not prescriptions) of
the fashion or identity of the baptism, then being baptized in the
name of Jesus is not in conflict with the requirement of baptizing
in the name of the Father, Son, and Holy Spirit. It would only be
a conflict if this is purported to be an exact prescription, that one
is to be baptized in the name of Jesus *and only of Jesus*. Certainly,
the way in which the statement in Matthew is expressed gives the
impression of such a mandatory and precise formula, but the
Acts passages do not display such a character.

If, indeed, this is an authentic prescription from Jesus, it is of
considerable significance for our purpose of finding a biblical
basis for the doctrine of the Trinity. For not only are the three
names stated in a similar fashion, implying equality of the three,
but the reference is to the singular *name* of the three persons,
thus implying their unity.

Triadic References: Pauline Writings

There are numerous other places in Scripture where the three
names are grouped together. We turn first to the writings of Paul.
There are a number of passages where he mentions the three

names together. One of the most prominent is 2 Thessalonians 2:13–14. Here he tells his readers that God chose them to be saved and called them to this salvation through the gospel. They were saved through the sanctifying work of the Spirit and through belief in the truth. The end or purpose of this is that they might share in the glory of the Lord Jesus Christ.

Another significant passage is 1 Corinthians 12:4–6. This is part of the letter in which one of the major themes is the unity of the church, which is threatened by a party spirit within the church. Paul reminds his readers of the oneness that the Spirit brings about, not conflict or separation. Then he relates this step by step to each member of the Godhead: "There are different kinds of gifts, but the same Spirit. There are different kinds of service, but the same Lord. There are different kinds of working, but the same God works all of them in all men." There seems to be a definite parallelism here. As is customary in Hebrew poetry, with which Paul was familiar, gifts, service, and working are very similar if not synonymous. Then it must appear here as if "Spirit," "Lord," and "God" are virtually synonymous as well. In any event, there is a closeness and an intimacy of connection among these three persons that is worthy of note.

Another important and conspicuous passage is the benediction in 2 Corinthians 13:14, which reads: "May the grace of the Lord Jesus Christ, and the love of God, and the fellowship of the Holy Spirit be with you all." This is a close association of the three persons in a combined or at least coordinated working (the conferring of blessings) that suggests equal status. It is presented as if they all have the right to do this.

There also are a large number of passages where there is a more subtle type of trinitarian suggestion. For the most part these coordinate the respective workings of the three in close proximity. Many of these are in Pauline writings. In Galatians 3:11–14 Paul is discussing justification "before God" (v. 11), which cannot be by the law. Rather it is Christ who has "redeemed us from the curse of the law by becoming a curse for us" (v. 13). This is so that "the blessing given to Abraham might come to the Gentiles through Christ Jesus, so that by faith we might receive the promise of the Spirit" (v. 14). Here is close linking of the three persons in the matter of justification. It is before God that they are justified, but by the redemptive work of Christ, to receive the promise of the Spirit.

Another interesting and significant text is Galatians 4:6: "Because you are sons, God sent the Spirit of his Son into our hearts, the Spirit who calls out, '*Abba*, Father.'" The dynamics of this verse are both complex and informative. Because we are sons, God sends the Spirit of his Son into our hearts. It is the Father who sends the Spirit and to whom the Spirit in our hearts calls out. And it is the Spirit who enables us to address the Father. Thus all of the members of the Trinity are involved in the relationship of the believer to God.

Another text that speaks of the involvement of the Trinity in the life of the believer is 2 Corinthians 1:21–22. God makes believers stand firm in Christ. He anointed them, set his seal of ownership on them, and put his Spirit in their hearts. The Spirit is a deposit, guaranteeing what is to come. And it is in Christ that they stand firm. In the context, it was the Son of God, Jesus Christ, who was preached to them, and in whom the promises of God are all yes (v. 19). It is through him that they are able to say "Amen" to the glory of God (v. 20). In 2 Corinthians 3:3 Paul describes his readers as a letter from Christ, written on the tablets of human hearts by the Spirit of the living God.

Romans 14:17–18 speaks of the kingdom of God. It is not a matter of eating and drinking, but of righteousness, peace, and joy in the Holy Spirit. This is because anyone who serves Christ in this way is both pleasing to God and approved by men. We please God by serving Christ, and we serve Christ in the Holy Spirit. It appears from this that relationships to the members of the Trinity are not separable. If indeed the three constitute a Trinity, then one cannot relate to them independently of one another. In Romans 15:16–18, Paul relates this threefold ministry to his own ministry. He has been given the grace of God (vv. 15–16) to become a minister. It is the gospel of God that he proclaims (v. 16). The purpose of this is that the Gentiles might become an offering acceptable to God (v. 16) and might obey God (v. 18). Paul's service is to God (v. 17). He is a minister of Jesus Christ (v. 16), he glories in Christ Jesus in his service (v. 17), and he proclaims the gospel of Christ (v. 19). Yet he has been sanctified by the Holy Spirit (v. 16), and what he has said and done by the power of signs and miracles, he has done through the power of the Spirit (v. 19). Paul urges his readers to join in his struggle by praying to God for him (v. 30). They are to pray that by God's will he may come to them (v. 32), and he says, "The God of peace be with you all" (v. 33). This entreaty for them to pray, however, is "by our Lord Jesus Christ and the love of the Spirit" (v. 30).

The other Pauline epistles contain similar references. In Philippians 3:3 Paul speaks of those who worship by the Spirit of God, who glory in Christ Jesus. In Colossians 1:3–8 he thanks God, the Father of our Lord Jesus Christ (v. 3), because he has heard of his readers' faith in the Lord Jesus Christ and their love for all the saints (v. 4). They have heard the gospel and understood God's grace in all its truth (v. 6). They have learned it from Epaphras, who is a minister of Christ, and who told him of their love in the Spirit (v. 8).

Even though it is a relatively short book, Ephesians is especially rich in these triadic references. In 2:11–22 Paul engages in a lengthy discussion of the Gentiles and their relationship to Israel and to God. Formerly they were separate from Christ, without hope and without God in the world (v. 12). Now, however, in Christ Jesus these who were far away have been brought near through the blood of Christ (v. 13). He is the one who has made the two one and who has reconciled both to God through the cross (v. 16). Through Christ they both have access to the Father by one Spirit (v. 18). As a result, the Gentiles are now fellow citizens with God's people and members of God's household, built with Christ Jesus as the chief cornerstone of a holy temple in the Lord (v. 21), a dwelling in which God lives by his Spirit (v. 22).

Ephesians 3:14–21 comprises a lengthy prayer for the Ephesians and a benediction on them. Paul kneels before the Father (v. 14), and prays that he may strengthen them (v. 16). He prays that they may be filled to the measure of all the fullness of God (v. 19), and that there might be glory to the Father throughout all generations (v. 21). His prayer is that Christ may dwell in their hearts through faith (v. 17) and that they may grasp the measure of the love of Christ (v. 18). The glory that he wishes to God is in the church and in Christ Jesus (v. 21). God's strengthening of them in their inner being is through his Spirit (v. 16).

The final Pauline reference is in Titus 3:4–6, although of course some would not consider this, or any of the pastoral epistles, to be of Pauline authorship. Paul writes that, when the kindness and love of "God our Savior" appeared (v. 4), he saved us through the "washing of rebirth and renewal by the Holy Spirit" (v. 5), whom he "poured out on us generously through Jesus Christ our Savior" (v. 6). All of the persons of the Trinity are actively involved in salvation, each in his own respective fashion.

Triadic Passages: Non-Pauline Material

There are triadic references in non-Pauline New Testament passages as well. In 1 Peter 1:2 Peter greets his readers as having been "chosen according to the foreknowledge of God the Father, through the sanctifying work of the Spirit, for obedience to Jesus Christ and sprinkling by his blood." The eternal basis of salvation, the execution or implementation of it, and its outcome in the life of the believer are all identified in this single verse, one of the most condensed outlines of the plan of salvation to be found anywhere in the New Testament. In 1 Peter 4:14 Peter speaks of the insults they are to suffer: "If you are insulted because of the name of Christ, you are blessed, for the Spirit of glory and of God rests on you." Here all the persons of the Godhead figure in the suffering, both in terms of the reason for the suffering and insults and also the compensation for or relief from it.

The Book of Jude envisions much the same sort of suffering and persecution as does the Book of 2 Peter. Jude urges his readers to build themselves up in the "most holy faith" and to pray in the Holy Spirit (v. 20). He instructs them to keep themselves in God's love as they wait for "the mercy of our Lord Jesus Christ to bring you to eternal life" (v. 21).

The Book of Hebrews has at least two references that display this triadic framework. In 6:4–6 we have probably the best known of the famous warning passages. The author describes these who have "shared in the Holy Spirit, who have tasted the goodness of the word of God" (vv. 4–5). If these then fall away, it is impossible to bring them back to repentance, since "they are crucifying the Son of God all over again" (v. 6). Just as faith is related to the members of the Trinity, so is apostasy. In 10:29 there is no explicit mention of the Father, but there is a parallel between the Son and the Spirit: "How much more severely do you think a man deserves to be punished who has trampled the Son of God under foot, who has treated as an unholy thing the blood of the covenant that sanctified him, and who has insulted the Spirit of grace?"

There is one additional text that bears on this discussion. In Acts 20:28 Paul is speaking to a group of elders. He says to them, "Guard yourselves and all the flock of which the Holy Spirit has made you overseers. Be shepherds of the church of God, which he bought with his own blood." There is no explicit reference to Jesus Christ, the Son, but it would certainly appear that he is being referred to as the one who has bought the church with his blood. If this is a correct interpretation, then this constitutes a statement of the relationship of the Trinity to the church. It is the church of God, which the Son has bought with his blood, and it is the Holy Spirit who has made them overseers of the church.

This completes the discussion of the specific texts of the New Testament that contain triadic references. We have seen that they are numerous, and although especially concentrated in the Pauline epistles, are found throughout the various books. They relate each of the persons of the Trinity to the experience of salvation, to the church and its leadership, to the living of the Christian life. It is apparent that for these several writers, to be a Christian was to be related to the Triune God, and to be related to each of the three persons of the Trinity in terms of the unique, specific ministry of each.

Internal Organization of Pauline Books

Even the way some of Paul's writings are organized reflects the triadic pattern. The evidence is in some ways the more impressive, for it reveals an underlying conception, a permeating understanding which undergirds everything written. Although a given book may be focused on one of the three persons of the Trinity, all are mentioned and in such a way that the outline of the book focuses successively on the different persons. Each of these persons is discerned in the consideration of various works of God. It is apparent that Paul really could not think about what one member of the Trinity does without thinking of the others. He could not conceive of any of them existing or acting in isolation from the others. It should be noted that this triadic organizational pattern is not so obvious in all of Paul's writings. This tendency is the most obvious, however, in the books that seem to be the most carefully and consciously crafted.

The Book of Romans, Paul's longest and most doctrinal book, displays this characteristic quite clearly in its first eight chapters. From 1:18 to 3:20 Paul expounds the judgment of God on Gentiles and Jews. Then, from 3:21 to 8:1, he writes about justification through faith in Jesus Christ. In 8:2–30 he focuses heavily on the Holy Spirit and life in him.

In 1 Corinthians Paul is dealing to a large extent with the issue of the unity of the church, in light of the problems within the Corinthian church. Here there is some alternation and overlapping of the treatments of the different persons. Paul initially speaks of Christ as the power and wisdom of God, as contrasted with the wisdom of the world or the wisdom of men (1:18–2:9). He then discusses the instruction given by the Spirit (2:10–16) before returning to expound Jesus Christ as the foundation for men's work (3:10–15). This is followed by a treatment of humans as God's temple in which the Holy Spirit dwells (3:16–17). Later in the book (chaps. 12–14), Paul discusses the gifts of the Spirit and the Spirit's sovereign concern for the welfare of the body of Christ as a whole, in which each member is important. Chapter 11 is a discussion of the Lord's Supper, in which the analogy of the church, the metaphorical body, to the body of Christ is pivotal. Paul does not attempt to work out the relationship between Christ and the Spirit, and the topics and the accounts of their work frequently overlap. To a large degree, what he is doing is descriptive, rather than analytical or even expository and definitive.

Galatians is strongly oriented to the issue of justification. The two opening chapters are largely concerned with establishing Paul's authority as an apostle, and insisting on his message of justification, in distinction from the message that was being enunciated by the Judaizers. Then, he goes on to argue for the uniqueness of the justification by faith in the redeeming work of Christ (3:1–22). This leads him to a discussion of the status of believers as children of God, experiencing the freedom of sons

(3:23–4:31). He then again comes back to the freedom accomplished by Christ's work (5:1–15), drawing a contrast between freedom in Christ and bondage to the law. In the following portion (5:16–6:10), the emphasis is on life by or in the Spirit, and the contrast is between the fruit of the Spirit and the works of the flesh.

In all of this there are clear traces of the triad of Father, Son, and Spirit. The order of presentation varies. Even when the order is "Son and Spirit," rather than "Father, Son, and Holy Spirit," it is clear that the Father has priority. Wainwright correctly points out that here we have revelations of Paul's personal belief and ways of worship.[16] He maintains that they were not here part of Paul's public teaching, but were not the less significant for this. Here, however, there may be some illicit inference on Wainwright's part. The assumption is that the public teaching is restricted to the content of the writing, rather than the form that the content takes, as if these two were not interactive. The further assumption seems to be the equation of intention with conscious intention. What really is involved is the resulting affirmation, whether consciously intended or not.

Paul really does not in any formal fashion address the trinitarian problem, that is, the issue of the nature of the relationships among the three members of the Trinity. At times he seems to reveal awareness of the problem. This is seen, for example, in his statement in 1 Corinthians 8:6: "yet for us there is but one God, the Father, from whom all things came and for whom we live; and there is but one Lord, Jesus Christ, through whom all things came and through whom we live." While Paul does not elaborate on the statement, and the respective meanings of God and Lord are not completely clear, it appears that the uniqueness and distinction of the two persons and also the close connection of the two were within his thinking.

In 1 Corinthians 15 Paul speaks of the work accomplished by the Son in his death and resurrection. He says that Christ will hand over to the Father the kingdom after he has destroyed all dominion, authority, and power (v. 24). There appears to be a subordinationist note to Paul's statements here.

16. Arthur W. Wainwright, *The Trinity in the New Testament* (London: SPCK, 1962), p. 259.

In the well-known passage in Philippians 2:1–11, Paul discusses the self-humiliation of the Son, Christ, in emptying himself of the prerogatives of deity and of equality with the Father. As a result of that, however, God has exalted him to the highest place and given him the highest name. He points forward to a time when at the name of Jesus every knee will bow and every tongue confess that he is Lord. Yet that is said to be to the glory of God the Father (v. 11).

The Holy Spirit receives a more complete treatment by Paul in Romans 8 than anywhere else in Scripture, with the exception of the lengthy discourse by Jesus in John 14–16. It is clear that Paul regards the Holy Spirit as a person, and adds the unique description of him as an intercessor. He does not always make clear, however, a distinction between the indwelling Christ and the indwelling Spirit. This is most apparent in verses 9–11. Here Paul says "the Spirit of God lives in you" (v. 9), and speaks of "his Spirit, who lives in you" (v. 11). Yet he also says, "if Christ is in you" (v. 10). Perhaps the key is his statement, "And if anyone does not have the Spirit of Christ, he does not belong to Christ" (v. 9). It appears from this statement that if a person has one, he or she also has the other. Yet neither here nor anywhere else does Paul identify Christ with the Spirit or confuse the two. He has, however, not clarified the exact relationship of the Spirit to the Father and the Son.

9

The Trinity in John's Gospel

When we come to the Gospel of John, we are on somewhat different ground. John is the most theological of the Gospels, and the one that gives the most direct and conscious attention to the relationships among the three persons. It is John who seems to be most fully aware of what we might term trinitarian issues. Thus, this Gospel promises to be the most helpful to us of any of the Gospels, and for that matter, of any of the books of the Bible.

Yet there is something about the Gospel of John that seems to militate against our use of it. For this is the Gospel that has been regarded with the greatest amount of skepticism by New Testament critics. Its historicity has been called into question for several reasons. One is the historical references found in it. John spends much of his time on the events of the final week of Christ's life prior to the crucifixion. His selection of materials is quite different in other respects as well. Certain important events, such as the commissioning of the twelve apostles, the transfiguration, the institution of the Lord's Supper, the exorcisms, and the parables, do not appear. On the other hand, John includes a number of items that do not appear in any of the other Gospels, such as the transformation of water into wine, the raising of Lazarus, Jesus' early ministry in Judea and Samaria, and Jesus' extended discourses, both in public and in private. There are theological differences as well. John is the only evangelist who identifies Jesus as divine. There are major chronological differences, such as the length of Jesus' ministry and the chronology of the final twenty-four hours of Jesus' life. There seem to be historical discrepancies, such as John being apparently unaware of the birth in Bethlehem. Finally, a stylistic difference is to be found in the difficulty of distinguishing Jesus' words from John's interpretation thereof.

The Reliability of John's Gospel

I have discussed elsewhere the issue of the reliability of the Gospel of John, so I will not go in depth into those matters here.[1] We do, however, need to note that since about 1960 there has been a real change in attitude toward the Fourth Gospel. John A. T. Robinson notes that even the use of that designation was something of an effectation. Matthew's Gospel is not generally referred to as the first Gospel, nor are the two other Synoptic Gospels referred to by number rather than by traditionally assigned author, even though there is no greater agreement that Matthew wrote the first Gospel than that John wrote the Fourth Gospel, and in fact probably less.[2]

This skepticism with regard to John's Gospel began to change in the 1960s, however. Robinson presented a paper in which he referred to "The New Look on the Fourth Gospel," contrasted with what he termed "critical orthodoxy" or "the old look."[3] The "old look" rested on five presuppositions:

1. The author depends on sources, including, for the most part, one or more of the Synoptics.
2. His background is different from that of the events and teachings that he professes to be recording.
3. His witness is to the Christ of faith, not to the Jesus of history.
4. His writing represents the end-point of theological development in first-century Christianity.

1. *The Word Became Flesh* (Grand Rapids: Baker, 1991), pp. 409–29.
2. John A. T. Robinson, *Can We Trust the New Testament Documents?* (Grand Rapids: Eerdmans, 1977), p. 26.
3. John A. T. Robinson, *Twelve New Testament Studies* (Naperville, Ill.: Allenson, 1962), pp. 94–106.

5. He is neither the apostle John, nor an eyewitness of the events that he claims to report.[4]

Robinson saw a change, a "new look," coming into being, however. Percival Gardner-Smith had anticipated this new look in several ways in 1938.[5] The first real indication of this change was when C. H. Dodd delivered the Sarum Lectures at Oxford University in 1954–55, later expanded into a book that he published in 1963.[6] Yet it was the work of Robinson that really established the historical reliability of John's Gospel.

A number of factors have been involved in this transformation of the estimate of the historical value of John's Gospel. Some of the problems and discrepancies have turned out not to be as severe as was once thought. The alleged discrepancies, for example, do not really involve any contradictions as such; in fact, they may be viewed more as complementary than contradictory.[7] The theological differences also can be explained in terms of John making explicit what was implicit in the other Gospels.[8] Further, the apparent chronological discrepancies become less significant when one realizes that the Synoptics really show little interest in chronology and do not limit the ministry to one year; they simply do not refer to three Passovers, as does John. The more extended period fits better with the events reported as part of Jesus' ministry, thus suggesting that John's chronology is less problematic than that of the Synoptics. The seeming historical discrepancies are less serious than first appears to be the case as well. John only reports, rather than affirms, the erroneous belief that Jesus had been born in Galilee. And the stylistic differences from the Synoptics, when examined in light of John's purposes and in terms of the much larger number of stylistic differences

4. Ibid., p. 95.

5. Percival Gardner-Smith, *Saint John and the Synoptic Gospels* (Cambridge: Cambridge University Press, 1938).

6. C. H. Dodd, *Historical Tradition in the Fourth Gospel* (Cambridge: Cambridge University Press, 1963).

7. Martin Hengel, *Acts and the History of Earliest Christianity* (Philadelphia: Fortress, 1979), pp. 3–34.

8. Royce Gordon Gruenler, *New Approaches to Jesus and the Gospels: A Phenomenological and Exegetical Study of Synoptic Christology* (Grand Rapids: Baker, 1982), p. 15.

between the discourses and the narrative portions in John, become less problematic.[9]

In addition to these responses to the criticisms, there also has been a considerable amount of positive evidence for the historical dependability of John's Gospel. One element was the revised view of the background of the Gospel. It was customary to regard John as a thoroughly Hellenistic Gospel. This idea was especially advanced by Harnack,[10] as well as by Benjamin Bacon[11] and E. F. Scott.[12] The contention was that the Gospel had been written under Hellenistic influence, so that it was geographically, conceptually, and temporally far removed from the Palestinian Judaism prior to the Jewish war. It came not from the early period of the church, when the Jewish influence was great, but from the later period when the church was under Hellenistic influence. All of this argues that the Gospel does not represent a genuine tradition regarding Jesus, and that the reported sayings of Jesus are not authentic.

A number of factors have combined to undercut this supposed consensus, however. A major one was the discovery of the Dead Sea Scrolls. There are some strong parallels between the language and terminology of these documents and John's Gospel, but also and more important, between their ideas. While it would be easy to overstate the degree and the significance of these parallels, the words of F. F. Bruce are instructive here: "the affinities with Qumran certainly provide additional evidence for the Hebraic foundation of the Fourth Gospel."[13]

There has also been archaeological confirmation of a number of topographical references in John. Robinson sees these extensive references as evidence of the historical reliability of the Gospel. It is especially informative to compare John's references to those of Luke. Luke, of course, is known for very precise refer-

9. Craig Blomberg, *The Historical Reliability of the Gospels* (Downers Grove, Ill.: InterVarsity, 1987), pp. 183–84.

10. John A. T. Robinson, *The Priority of John* (London: SCM, 1985), p. 38.

11. Benjamin W. Bacon, *The Gospel of the Hellenists*, ed. Carl H. Kraehling (New York: Holt, 1933).

12. E. F. Scott, *The Fourth Gospel: Its Purpose and Theology* (Edinburgh: T. & T. Clark, 1943), p. 6.

13. F. F. Bruce, "The Dead Sea Scrolls and Early Christianity," *Bulletin of the John Rylands Library* 49 (Autumn 1966): 81.

ences when he is dealing with familiar territory, such as is involved in the Book of Acts. In the chapters of his Gospel that deal with the Galilean ministry and in the long central portion from 9:51 to 18:14, Luke is quite vague. In comparison, John is very precise in a number of instances. Note, for example, 11:1–12:1, where John names the place, tells us that it is about two miles from Jerusalem, explains why Jesus went there on two occasions and from where, and, in the second instance, exactly when—six days before the Passover. Recent archaeological study has tended to support the view that this Gospel was written by someone who knew well the places in which the story is set.[14]

It was customary to regard John's Gospel as being dependent on the Synoptics. C. H. Dodd argues both positively and negatively, however, for the independence of John. He carefully examines the passages where John refers to an incident also mentioned in the Synoptics, and compares them carefully. In each case, he concludes that it is unlikely that John would have extracted just those details and combined them in just the way that he did. Dodd also compiled a list of the types of statements one would expect to find if John had been utilizing the Synoptics as sources. Among them are references that fit well with John's symbolism, style, and purpose in writing. These include such matters in the Gospel of Mark as the darkness at the crucifixion, the rending of the temple veil, and the confession by the centurion that Jesus was the Son of God. These are present in John's account, however. For Dodd this is confirming evidence of John's independence from the Synoptics, and thus his use of a separate historical source, which may well have been as reliable as, or more reliable than, the sources of the Synoptics.[15] Robinson refers to Dodd's work as "a massive demonstration of the greater probability that the Johannine material rested on tradition independent of and more primitive than that of the Synoptic Gospels."[16]

One other factor bearing on the issue of the historical reliability of John's Gospel is the whole matter of the dating of the Gos-

14. W. F. Albright, *The Archaeology of Palestine*, rev. ed. (Baltimore: Penguin, 1956), pp. 242–49.
15. Dodd, *Historical Tradition*. For summary and conclusions, see pp. 423–32.
16. Robinson, *Priority of John*, p. 12.

pels. It was fashionable at one time to date the Fourth Gospel well into the second century. The discovery of the John Rylands fragment of that Gospel pushed the date back to the latter part of the first century, so that it became customary to date all of the Johannine literature to the 90s.

Here also, John Robinson began to raise the question of whether the Gospel of John might not date from before the Jewish revolt of 66–70. This in turn would require on the standard theory of priority that the Synoptics be dated even earlier. One major consideration for Robinson was the absence of any reference in the Gospels to the fall of Jerusalem in A.D. 70, an event of such significance that it surely should have been referred to in any Gospel accounts. In view of such items as Jesus' statement about the stones being cast down, Mark 13:1–4 does not reflect the detail that should have been present if the event had already occurred. This is peculiar, in view of form criticism's contention that the content of the narrative reflects the Sitz im Leben of the church.[17]

These considerations do not, of course, settle the issue of the historicity of John's Gospel in any definitive fashion. There are still critics who maintain the older view. To a large extent, the plausibility of a given approach depends on the presuppositions one brings to the study of the book, as Royce Gruenler has pointed out.[18] I contend, however, that the data can more easily and smoothly be accounted for when beginning with the supernatural presuppositions about the person of Christ. Thus, although presuppositions cannot initially be verified, they can, when traced out to their implications, be validated, or shown to be more adequate than competitive presuppositions.

The Prologue

John, more than any other New Testament author, appears to pay more explicit attention to the issues of the Trinity. One of the

17. John A. T. Robinson, *Redating the New Testament* (Philadelphia: Westminster, 1976), pp. 9–10; Bo Reicke, "Synoptic Problems on the Destruction of Jerusalem," in *Studies in New Testament and Early Christian Literature: Essays in Honor of Allen P. Wikgren* (supplement to *Novum Testament* 33), ed. David E. Aune (Leiden: Brill, 1972), p. 121.

18. Royce Gordon Gruenler, *The Trinity in the Gospel of John: A Thematic Commentary on the Fourth Gospel* (Grand Rapids: Baker, 1986), pp. 148–50.

most theologically pregnant of all biblical passages is of course the prologue to John's Gospel. The issue of the paradoxical relationship of the Son (or "Word") to the Father is faced immediately in 1:1: "In the beginning was the Word, and the Word was with God, and the Word was God." Here is the seeming contradiction of the Word being God and yet not being God.

The sentence, "the Word was with God, and the Word was God," has been the subject of a great deal of exegetical debate.[19] Translated literally, it must be rendered in the above fashion. The real issue here, however, goes beyond mere translation to interpretation. To put it another way, what it means versus what it says may need to be determined on more broadly logical terms, rather than merely grammatical considerations. In the first clause, θεός, God, has the definite article, while in the second the article is lacking. Several possibilities have been offered as to the meaning of this. Some have argued that this anarthrous construction means, "of the quality of." Others have appealed to Colwell's Rule, which says that in a predicate-first construction, the predicate ordinarily appears without the article, to distinguish it from the subject.[20]

If we take this latter approach, then the actual reading, had not the writer put the predicate first, presumably for emphasis, would have been, ὁ λόγος ἦν τὸν θεόν. That could then be interpreted in several ways.

1. As a statement of identity. The Word is the same as the one who is God. The meaning would be something like this (to reverse the two clauses): "the Word was God and the Word was with himself."
2. As a statement of inclusion. The Word is being described as being with God and being God himself. The rendering then would be something like, "The Word was with God, and the Word was himself also God." This would leave the door open to something like bitheism.

19. For a summary of much of this discussion, see Murray J. Harris, *Jesus as God: The New Testament Use of* Theos *in Reference to Jesus* (Grand Rapids: Baker, 1992), pp. 57–71, 301–13.
20. E. C. Colwell, "A Definite Rule for the Use of the Article in the Greek New Testament," *Journal of Biblical Literature* 52 (1933):12–21.

It seems better to take the statement as one of predication or quality. The same quality of deity is true of the Word as is true of the one, God, with whom he is present. The rendering would then be, "The Word was with God, and the Word was of the same quality of deity as is God." This may, but need not, treat the anarthrous condition of the second θεός as qualitative. In other words, if the normal word order had been followed, it would have read, ὁ λόγος ἦν θεός. Note that Colwell's Rule does not preclude this; it merely states that it does not necessarily follow and that the anarthrous construction may simply identify the predicate. The rule does not take into consideration a qualitative meaning. Even in the research done by Colwell, approximately 13 percent of the definite predicate nouns before the verb have the article. Further, this is not to say that in 87 percent of the anarthrous predicate first clauses the predicate noun, if it were second, would have had the article. Colwell's data cannot tell us that.

Some commentators seem to think that Colwell's Rule settles the issue. We should note the logical structure of such an argument, however. It appears to be something like this:

> If a sentence is merely a predicate-first sentence, the noun is anarthrous to distinguish the predicate from the subject.
> In this sentence the noun is anarthrous.
> Therefore, this sentence is merely a predicate-first sentence.

This constitutes the fallacy of affirming the consequent. There could be other explanations of the anarthrous construction. And in a predicate-first sentence in which the noun is used qualitatively, it will also be anarthrous. Thus, Colwell's Rule, if valid, does not remove the possibility of the qualitative interpretation—only its necessity.

This interpretation adopted here seems to have the benefit of removing what was something of a redundancy in the case of the identity interpretation above. It also removes the difficulty John's Jewish readers would have had understanding what seems to be a polytheistic (or at least, bitheistic) view, on the inclusion interpretation. The question is sometimes raised, "But if this is what John meant to say, why didn't he use a more unambiguous word, θειός, which was available to him?" It is, of course, very difficult to say why a writer chose one way of saying something, rather than another that seems to say the same thing, but more clearly. Nor is it helpful to say, "If John wanted to convey the idea of quality, why did he not use the normal word order, so that the anarthrous construction would have been unambiguous?" In this case, it may be that the repetition of the two words is intended to emphasize the identity of nature of the two, as if to say, "The Word was with God, and was of the same nature as God," and the word order placed emphasis on the deity of the Word. Note, however, that this predication interpretation does not require the hypothesis that if in normal word order, the predicate would be anarthrous. The interpretation, if not the translation, would be the same regardless.

The preposition, πρός, used here is one rich with meaning. It does not mean mere physical proximity; indeed that dimension of meaning is really not present at all. Rather, it speaks of sharing, of having in common. It emphasizes the interaction with, the communion with, and yet, of course, the separateness from, the one who is the object of the preposition. We would seem to have in this one verse possibly the strongest intimation of the Trinity found anywhere in Scripture.

Equivalence of Relationship or Action of Son and Father

In addition to this potent verse, however, there are several other places where at least subconsciously John appears to be wrestling with issues that eventually led the church to formulate the doctrine of the Trinity. One group of passages is those in which John seems to make clear (ordinarily presenting the statement as that of Jesus) that to be related to the Son is to be related to the Father as well or in which an action is said to be that of both the Son and the Father. One of these is John 14:23: "Jesus replied, 'If anyone loves me, he will obey my teaching. My Father will love him, and we will come to him and make our home with him. He who does not love me will not obey my teaching. These words you hear are not my own; they belong to the Father who sent me.'" Not only does obedience to Jesus' words bring a relationship to both the Father and the Son; the words are not even simply the Son's words, but belong to the Father. The relationship between the Father and the Son is such that to be related to one is to be related to the other, but they are not simply different names for the same person. They are two closely related persons, whose actions are very much intertwined.

Another passage of this type is 1 John 2:24: "See that what you have heard from the beginning remains in you. If it does, you also will remain in the Son and in the Father." While John does not here make explicit what this is that they have heard from the beginning, the remaining of this in his hearers will have the same effect described in John 14:23: they will remain in both the Son and the Father. The same close relationship between the two is also involved here.

Closely connected with this last reference is 14:20. Here John affirms that he is in the Father, they are in him, and he is in them. The one who has his commandments and keeps them is the one who loves him, and "he who loves me will be loved by my Father, and I too will love him and show myself to him" (v. 21). As we shall see below, it may well be that this relationship with both the Father and the Son results from obedience to the commands of both the Father and the Son.

The other passage is one in which the relationship to the Father is seen to involve the other persons as well. John writes: "No one has ever seen God; but if we love each other, God lives in us and his love is made complete in us. We know that we live in him and he in us, because he has given us of his Spirit. And we have seen and testify that the Father has sent his Son to be the Savior of the world. If anyone acknowledges that Jesus is the Son of God, God lives in him and he in God. And so we know and rely on the love God has for us" (1 John 4:12–16). Being in God is dependent on acknowledging the Son whom he has sent, and is known because of the Spirit whom he has sent. Thus again, the relationship to one member of the Trinity turns out to involve relationships with the others, who in turn are related to one another.

This same type of phenomenon is found in a number of other passages as well. In John 5 Jesus gives several indications of ways in which being related to him affects the relationship to the Father. Whoever hears Jesus' words and does them has eternal life and is not condemned (v. 24). In the future, the dead will hear the voice of the Son of God and will live (v. 25) because the Father has granted the Son the power to judge (vv. 26–27). Those he addresses do not have the Father's word dwelling in them, because they do not believe the one he sent (v. 38). When his hearers ask what they must do to do the works God requires (6:28), Jesus replies that the work of God is to believe in the one he has sent (v. 29). In John 8, when Jesus tells his audience of his Father who sent him, they ask, "Where is your father?" His reply is, "You do not know me or my Father. If you knew me, you would know my Father also" (v. 19). Later in the chapter he says, "If God were your Father, you would love me, for I came from God and now am here. I have not come on my own; but he sent me" (v. 42).

One of Jesus' explicit statements about this matter is found in John 12:44–45. He says, "When a man believes in me, he does not believe in me only, but in the one who sent me. When he looks at me, he sees the one who sent me." This is a clear indication that being related to Jesus also involves a relationship with the Father. In John 14:7 Jesus says, "If you really knew me, you would know my Father as well. From now on, you do know him and have seen him." The same idea, that knowing the Son involves knowing the Father as well, is repeated in verse 9. The converse is found in Jesus' statements in 15:23–24: "He who hates me hates my Father as well. . . . But now they have seen these miracles, and yet they have hated both me and my Father." A few verses later, he comments regarding those who will kill his followers: "They will do such things because they have not known the Father or me" (16:3).

Unity of the Father and the Son

A second group of passages consists of those that emphasize the unity of the Father and the Son. Some of these statements come in the context of statements of Christ's inferiority to the Father. One is John 10:28–29. Here Jesus says, "I give them [his sheep] eternal life, and they shall never perish; no one can snatch them out of my hand. My Father, who has given them to me, is greater than all; no one can snatch them out of my Father's hand. I and the Father are one." Here Jesus seems to affirm the superiority of the Father by declaring that the Father has given them to him, and that the Father is greater than all, including, presumably in this context, the Son himself. Yet there is a parallel between the inability of anyone to snatch them out of his hand and to snatch them out of the Father's hand. And Jesus ends by explicitly stating that he and the Father are one.

A similar passage is John 17:11–23, which is part of Jesus' prayer for his followers. Jesus prays four times for the unity of the believers (vv. 11, 21, 22, 23). In verses 11 and 22 he explicitly says, "that they may be one as we are one." The unity of Father and Son is implied in the two other instances. In verse 21 he says, "that all of them may be one, Father, just as you are in me and I am in you." In verse 23 he prays, "May they be brought to complete unity to let the world know that you sent me and have loved them even as you have loved me." There is here an expression of the Son's dependence on the Father, since he receives his glory and the glory that he gives to his followers from the Father. There is also the element of the believer being related to both in being related to one, since receiving the glory from the Son is indirectly also receiving it from the Father (v. 22); Jesus states, "I in them and you in me" (v. 23).

This idea of the Father being in the Son and the Son being in the Father is also found in John 10:38. Another very interesting verse is 13:31: "When he was gone, Jesus said, 'Now is the Son of Man glorified and God is glorified in him. If God is glorified in him, then God will glorify the Son in himself, and will glorify him at once.'" Here the glorification of the Father and the Son seem virtually inseparable. In 14:9–11 Jesus replies to Philip's request that he show them the Father. He says, "Don't you know me, Philip, even after I have been among you such a long time? Anyone who has seen me has seen the Father. How can you say, 'Show us the Father'? Don't you believe that I am in the Father, and that the Father is in me? The words I say to you are not just my own. Rather, it is the Father, living in me, who is doing his work. Believe me when I say that I am in the Father and the Father is in me; or at least believe on the evidence of the miracles themselves." Here Jesus makes a series of amazing statements: he is in the Father, and the Father is in him; the words he says are not just his own; the Father, living in him, is doing his work. Again the relationship between the two is so close as to argue that they are virtually identical, and yet they are distinguished from one another, being able to relate to each other.

One other passage of significance is John 16:28, 32. Jesus states that he had come from the Father and entered the world. Now he is leaving the world and going back to the Father (v. 28). In verse 32 he says, "I am not alone, for my Father is with me."

Sonship of Jesus and Fatherhood of God

A third consideration is the strong emphasis on the Sonship of Jesus and the Fatherhood of God. It can be safely said that there is a stronger emphasis on this aspect of the relationship of the two to one another than is found anywhere else in the New Testament. This statement can easily be verified statistically. Vincent Taylor calculates that the title "Father" occurs 121 times in John's Gospel and 16 times in his letters, compared with 123 times in the rest of the New Testament.[21] Thus, John's usage of the term exceeds that of all other New Testament writers combined. The statistics are only somewhat less impressive with respect to the use of the word "Son," which appears 28 times in John's Gospel, 24 times in the Johannine epistles, and 67 times in the rest of the New Testament.[22] This certainly suggests that for John the Father-Son relationship was the dominant category for a description of the relationship.

Father, Son, and Holy Spirit Mentioned Together

We should also note the large number of passages where the Father, the Son, and the Holy Spirit are mentioned together. The first of these is John 1:33–34, which records John the Baptist's report of the circumstances of the baptism of Jesus, although the baptism is not mentioned as such. He says, "I would not have known him, except that the one who sent me to baptize with water told me, 'The man on whom you see the Spirit come down and remain is he who will baptize with the Holy Spirit.' I have seen and I testify that this is the Son of God." Of all the Gospel accounts, only John's has John the Baptist testifying to having

21. Vincent Taylor, *The Person of Christ* (London: Macmillan, 1958), p. 150.
22. Ibid., p. 147.

seen the descent of the dove. Presumably, the Baptist's reference to "the one who sent me to baptize with water" refers to God the Father, much like the testimony of the Old Testament prophets. If this is the case, then we have a collocation of these three. Indeed, even so, the "Son of God" reference brings the three together in one context.

Another passage of this type is John 14:26: "But the Counselor, the Holy Spirit, whom the Father will send in my name, will teach you all things and will remind you of everything I have said to you." Here something of the inner relationships within the Trinity is revealed. The Father does the sending of the Holy Spirit, but does so in the name of the Son. The Spirit will remind Jesus' followers of the words of Jesus.

This verse is significant for a number of reasons. The first is that Jesus identifies the Counselor as the Holy Spirit. Thus, when he mentions the Counselor elsewhere, it is clear to whom he is referring. Further, Jesus refers elsewhere in this discourse to the sending of the Spirit in a different fashion than he does here. In 15:26 he refers to "the Counselor . . . whom I will send to you from the Father, the Spirit of truth who goes out from the Father, he will testify about me." In 16:7 he says, "It is for your good that I am going away. Unless I go away, the Counselor will not come to you; but if I go, I will send him to you." Not only does Jesus say that the Father will send the Spirit, but that he also will send the Spirit. The Spirit whom Jesus sends goes out from the Father. The Father sends the Spirit in Jesus' name. Jesus sends the Spirit, who goes out from the Father. The Spirit will testify about Jesus and will remind them of everything Jesus has said to them. Jesus also says that the Spirit will not speak on his own; he will speak only what he hears (16:13). Yet Jesus' words of which presumably the Spirit will remind them are not his own words. Rather, they belong to the Father who sent him (14:24). Conversely, however, everything that belongs to the Father is his (16:15).

When looked at in light of these several considerations, John seems to be affirming or at least assuming or implying a number of tenets. The sending of the Spirit is by both the Father and the Son, or at least can be described in either of these fashions. Even when referred to as the agency of one of these persons, there is reference or at least allusion to the other. There evidently is a close relationship between the actions of the Father and the Son, and presumably also between them as persons. Further, the ministry of the Spirit is not independent of the other persons. It involves bringing to remembrance the teaching that Jesus has given. Yet in a sense these are not just Jesus' words, for he has received them from the Father. And one may deduce that this is why both the Father and the Son will make their home with the one who obeys these teachings, for they are the teachings of both the Father and the Son. It is notable that the Spirit also will be in the believers (14:17), and it may be inferred that this is because the teachings that they obey are also his as the end point of the transmission process. Further, the designation of the Spirit as "another [ἄλλος—another of the same kind][23] Counselor" (14:16) suggests a commonality of ministry of the Spirit and of the Son. This also is implied in the fact that the Spirit can come to begin his ministry in the fullest sense only if and when the Son goes away (16:7).

Three other passages deserve our attention. One is the commissioning and enspiriting of the disciples in John 20:21–22. Jesus links the three persons together in the commission: "'As the Father has sent me, I am sending you.' And with that he breathed on them and said, 'Receive the Holy Spirit.'" Their ministry is an enactment of the sending by the Son, in a fashion similar to the Son's sending by the Father, and involves the giving of the Holy Spirit. All three persons are intimately involved, in one way or another, in the ministry that these believers will carry out.

There are also significant references in John's first epistle. In urging his readers to be discriminating regarding the spirits, he says, "This is how you can recognize the Spirit of God: Every spirit that acknowledges that Jesus Christ has come in the flesh is from God, but every spirit that does not acknowledge Jesus is not from God" (4:2–3). Those spirits (and only those spirits) that come from God (presumably the Father) will acknowledge that Jesus Christ has come in the flesh. Those who do not do this have not come from the Father.

---

23. Walter Bauer, *A Greek-English Lexicon of the New Testament and Early Christian Literature,* trans. William F. Arndt and F. Wilbur Gingrich (Chicago: University of Chicago Press, 1979), pp. 39–40, 315.

Action of One Member of Trinity
Treated as Action of Others

Yet another group of passages is those in which the action of one member of the Trinity is treated as the action of one or more of the others. Some of these references have already been cited in another connection. In John 3:34 Jesus says, "For the one whom God has sent speaks the words of God; to him God gives the Spirit without limit." Jesus' words are God's words, for the speaking is done by the Spirit. Indeed, it could also be contended from this statement that the words of the Son are the words of the Spirit, as well as of the Father. In chapter 5 Jesus indicates that both the Father and the Son are working (v. 17), and that whatever the Father does the Son does also (v. 19). This latter statement could, of course, simply indicate that the Son does things similar to what the Father does, and that they are separate, but similar, workings. The context, however, especially with respect to statements about the Father delegating judgment to the Son (v. 22), seems to indicate that the Son's work is not simply supplementary to that of the Father, but is the Father's doing also. Jesus also indicates that his teachings and his words are not his, but those of the Father, who sent him (John 7:16, 18; 12:49–50). One of the clearest statements of the cooperative working of the Father through the Son is found in 14:10–11: "Don't you believe that I am in the Father, and that the Father is in me? The words I say to you are not just my own. Rather, it is the Father, living in me, who is doing my work." Finally, an issue of possession is discussed by Jesus in John 17:9–10. He prays: "I am not praying for the world, but for those you have given me, for they are yours. All I have is yours, and all you have is mine."

The Son's Close Contact with,
or Knowledge of, the Father

One additional group of passages needs to be noted. These are passages that indicate a very close contact with, or knowledge of, the Father by the Son. Two statements of this type are found in the prologue of John's Gospel. In verse 14 John says, "The Word became flesh and lived for a while among us. We have seen his glory, the glory of the One and Only, who came from the Father, full of grace and truth." In verse 18 John writes, "No one has ever seen God, but God the One and Only, who is at the Father's side, has made him known." While this translation lacks the color of the earlier "Father's bosom," it speaks of an intimacy of presence and knowledge. The reading, "one and only God" (or "only-begotten God") appears to have better textual basis than does the reading, "only-begotten Son." Jesus makes a similar statement in John 6:46: "No one has seen the Father except the one who is from God; only he has seen the Father." John 8, the report of Jesus' discussion with the Jews, contains three references of this general type. In verse 42 Jesus claims to have come from God: "If God were your Father, you would love me, for I came from God and now am here. I have not come on my own; but he sent me." In verse 55 he claims knowledge of the Father that they do not have, and in verse 58 he makes the boldest of his claims: "I tell you the truth, before Abraham was born, I am!" This statement identified him as being before Abraham, and was apparently regarded as a claim to deity, constituting blasphemy, because the Jews took up stones to stone him.

The "I" Passages

One consideration that has frequently been appealed to in evaluating the bearing of John's witness on the doctrine of the Trinity is the "I" statements of Jesus: "I am the Good Shepherd"; "I am the way, the truth, and the life." On this basis, the argument is constructed that these are references back to God's statement in Exodus 3, where he answered Moses' question about his name by saying, "I am," or "I will be." If this is the case, then all of these statements constitute claims to deity.

In my judgment, this argument as a whole is invalid and should not be utilized. It fails to recognize distinctions among the four uses of the copula, "to be." This is confusing the "is of predication" (or possibly the "is of inclusion") for the "is of existence." This is a logical distinction that is not unique to the Indo-European languages. Even Hebrews certainly knew the difference between describing something as having a particular quality and declaring its existence (see, for example, the contrast between Exod. 3:14

and 6:2). The one statement that could be used in a valid fashion is that found in John 8:58, "Before Abraham was born, I am!"

Summary

1. We have in John's Gospel, and to a lesser extent in his first letter, a clear statement of the deity of the Son. It is, indeed, the clearest, most frequent, and most consistent of any of the biblical authors. He is, for example, the only Gospel writer to clearly identify the Son as divine.

2. There are indications in the Gospel of an interaction among the members of the Trinity. This is especially the case of the relationship between the Father and the Son. A definite distinction is present between the two, indicated both by the narratives involving dialogue between Father and Son and the discussions of the nature of that relationship. This is also true of the Son and the Spirit. It is necessary for the former to leave before the latter can come. Yet the Holy Spirit descends on the Son at his baptism, and he is the one who will baptize with the Spirit. Near the end of the book the Son conveys the Spirit to his followers by breathing on them.

3. The categories of Father and Son are especially prominent in this Gospel. Indeed, these terms appear approximately as many times as in all the non-Johannine books of the New Testament. The categories involve depiction of a warm, intimate relationship between the two.

4. There is a closeness among the various members of the Trinity, especially between the Father and the Son. This unity is presented by several statements by Jesus, "I and the Father are one." It is also seen in the fact of the love between the two, the glory each gives to the other, and the lack of any indications of conflict between the two.

5. There is a very close coordination of what each person does. So it is that the working of one can be spoken of as the working of the other. Jesus indicates that his words are the words of the Father, and yet they are given by the Spirit.

6. The relationship of Father and Son is such that to be related to one is to be in the same relationship with the other. One cannot have the one without the other. This is true both with respect to salvation and punishment.

10

The Metaphysical Basis
of Trinitarian Theology

We have seen that the Christian faith involves some metaphysical conceptions. Its doctrines deal with the ultimate nature of things, and go beyond merely what happens to ask about what is and what things are like. We have also seen, however, that these metaphysical doctrines can be expressed in several forms. Another way of putting this is that there are several varieties of specific metaphysics within which the general metaphysical truths can be expressed. We have also observed that the specific metaphysical vehicle used to express the classical doctrine of the Trinity as originally formulated was a Greek metaphysics that was viable in that time but no longer makes a great deal of sense to most persons today. Consequently, we must now attempt to find a contemporary set of categories that can be used to express this crucial doctrine.

The Altered Status of Metaphysics

Later twentieth-century philosophy has increasingly recognized both the possibility and necessity of metaphysics. Christian philosophers have made some major efforts to deal with the doctrinal issues of the Christian faith philosophically, and especially, metaphysically. Examples of this would be Stephen T. Davis's, *Logic and the Nature of God*[1] and *Philosophy and the*

1. Stephen T. Davis, *Logic and the Nature of God* (Grand Rapids: Eerdmans, 1983).

Christian Faith, the symposium edited by Thomas Morris.[2] The conclusion of increasing numbers of philosophers of religion and metaphysicians is that worldviews, as broad syntheses of understanding of reality, can be tested, graded, or assessed. Thus, in terms of the criteria of pragmatic viability, logical consistency and coherence, and external applicability and adequacy, both meaningfulness and probability of truth can be vindicated. As long ago as 1961 Frederick Ferré asked, "Are any criteria in principle derivable for the extraordinarily inclusive conceptual syntheses of metaphysics?" and then answered his own question: "Despite widespread negative answers to this question, it appears to be more and more likely that criteria can be found by which metaphysical systems can be graded."[3] He elaborates the criteria listed above.

But what of the challenge of process philosophy? It has claimed to be the proper reconstruction of metaphysics. We noted in chapter 6 its construction of the Trinity. It has derived much of its force from the alleged unsuitability of the traditional or classical view of God to the nature of the universe as presently understood. Is the process objection to traditional theism fair, however? That theism may sometimes have been vulnerable to the charge that it depicts God as static, unchanging, and even unresponsive to the activities going on in the world—even among its highest creatures, humans—by rather uncritically adopting certain aspects of Greek thought.

This is not inherently necessary in the orthodox conception, however. On the contrary, the picture of God found in Scripture is of a very dynamic being. He is alive and active. He is aware of what is going on in the world, and is actively involved in it. The picture of God the Father given by Jesus is of one who knows all and takes the initiative. God knows the very number of the hairs of our heads; not even a bird can fall to the earth without the Father's will (Matt. 10:29–30). God seeks the lost sheep, searches for the lost coin, waits watchfully for the lost son (Luke 15). Indeed, he is the primary force behind all that is, that which derives

2. *Philosophy and the Christian Faith,* ed. Thomas V. Morris (Notre Dame, Ind.: University of Notre Dame Press, 1988).

3. Frederick Ferré, *Language, Logic, and God* (New York: Harper & Row, 1961), p. 162.

its vitality and energy from him; he is the one who is himself the ultimate determiner of what happens, both in terms of planning and executing that plan. Yet he does not change, in what he is. The psalmist wrote, "They will perish, but you remain; they will all wear out like a garment. Like clothing you will change them and they will all be discarded. But you remain the same, and your years will never end" (Ps. 102:26–27). God's expectations of his people are unchanging, because "I the LORD do not change" (Mal. 3:6). There is no indication, in statements of the infinite attributes of God, such as his omnipotence (e.g., Gen. 18:14; Matt. 19:26), of a time when he ever lacked or will ever lose these perfections. For it is not only possible but also desirable to separate activity or lack of it from change or lack of it.

Process philosophy seems to assume that to be dynamic is to change; it really has no place for any type of essence. The contradictory of this would be the static. Yet there is no real proof, only an assumption, that there cannot be an intermediate condition, namely, stable dynamism, or dynamism that follows a regular pattern, neither diminishing nor increasing in what it is. We may distinguish stable and unstable motion. A crude example of the difference between the two is that between riding a bicycle at a steady rate on a straight course, and falling off a bicycle. As Royce Gruenler puts it, "The biblical God is not static but inexhaustibly dynamic, *on his own terms, not ours.*"[4] Process theology seems to regard the essence of the dynamic as being unstable, or at least requiring acceleration or deceleration. But that is an assumption, not a proof.

There is another dimension to this issue. The assumption of process philosophy, and hence of process theology, is that all parts of the whole are so interrelated, and of one basic kind of reality, that what is true of one part must inevitably be true of other parts as well. Thus, God must participate in the same sort of change as all other parts. This, however, assumes a virtually totally immanent God, versus a God at least sufficiently transcendent that he may not be bound by all of the laws of the created universe. The possibility of the latter never really seems to enter into consideration. What we appear to have here is, if not a natu-

---

4. Royce Gruenler, *The Inexhaustible God: Biblical Faith and the Challenge of Process Theism* (Grand Rapids: Baker, 1983), p. 126.

ralistic, at least a naturalizing, presupposition. It should be borne in mind that in its earlier form, before becoming popular as process theology, this view was known as "naturalistic theism." The test for these two competing views will be the presence of the genuinely supernatural. The place and possibility of miracles are quite different in the two views. The historical evidences for some of the miracles, particularly the miraculous resurrection of Christ, become an unassimilable piece of data for process theology. This is not the place to argue the case for the resurrection. We have undertaken that in another place.[5] In our judgment, however, the orthodox view of God, understood as dynamically stable, fits with a current scientific understanding of the phenomena of the universe, but without the necessity of being bound by the same limitations of the created universe, including change.

While limitations of space preclude our spelling out the shortcomings of process philosophy and theology, two basic criticisms have effectively been leveled against it. On the one hand, it results in a major distortion of the Christian categories, transforming persons into abstractions. On the other hand, the philosophy itself contains numerous and serious internal contradictions.[6] In light of those problems, we must continue to look further for the appropriate and adequate categories with which to construct our doctrine of the Trinity. First, however, we wish to examine one recent attempt by a conservative theologian to adapt and revise process philosophy sufficiently to make it the basis of a traditional view of the Trinity—in other words, to obviate the first criticism.

A Conservative Process View of the Trinity

We noted in an earlier chapter that in process philosophy and hence in process theology, everything is interrelated. God in this scheme of things is understood as essentially and necessarily related to the remainder of reality, rather than ontologically independent. In the traditional Christian view of the Trinity, on the

---

5. Millard J. Erickson, *The Word Became Flesh* (Grand Rapids: Baker, 1991), pp. 481–505.

6. For an extensive and perceptive critique of process thought, see Gruenler, *Inexhaustible God.*

other hand, the relationship of God to the world is one of grace; he does not need the world but reaches out to it. Seemingly, therefore, process metaphysics and the doctrine of the Trinity are incompatible.

We observed in chapter 6 some attempts to redefine the Trinity in process terms, most notably the effort of Lewis Ford. These endeavors, however, appear to result in a view of the Trinity that scarcely can be considered the Trinity as usually understood. Recently, however, a proposal has come from an evangelical, Gregory Boyd, for a construction that ostensibly combines a process metaphysic with a genuinely triune view of God as a self-sufficient being.

Boyd is clear about his acceptance of process metaphysics: "Reality is an interrelated process. Though this insight has a long history in the East, it has not been until our present century that it has become a dominant accepted truth in the West. The traditional Aristotelian world view, supported by Newtonian physics and embraced by the Church's traditional theology, is fast becoming a piece of history."[7] He further says, "It is our conviction that the fundamental vision of the process world view, especially as espoused by Charles Hartshorne, is correct."[8] Although he disagrees with Hartshorne on a number of points, his own thinking has been influenced more by him than any other philosopher. Consequently, the question is not whether to embrace that view of reality. It is how the understanding of God as triune and as "antecedently actual within Godself," which he also is convinced is true, is to be integrated with this view. Whereas Hartshorne's metaphysic is usually thought to be incompatible with the trinitarian understanding of God, Boyd contends that, when certain tendencies within that metaphysic are corrected, it not only permits, but requires something like the trinitarian conception of God for completeness and consistency.[9]

The argument advanced by Boyd for this alternative view is too extensive to be examined within the bounds of this work. Ba-

---

7. Gregory Boyd, *Trinity and Process: A Critical Evaluation and Reconstruction of Hartshorne's Di-polar Theism Towards a Trinitarian Metaphysics* (New York: Peter Lang, 1992), preface.
8. Ibid.
9. Ibid.

sically, he accepts the validity of Hartshorne's arguments for the existence of God and the epistemology that underlies them, but makes certain modifications in what he feels are not essential aspects of the process thought. So, for example, he contends that "it is necessary to postulate the antecedent actuality of God in order to satisfy the requirements of God's necessity as the ontological and cosmological arguments purport to demonstrate."[10] Further, he accepts Hartshorne's contention that being is necessarily relational. If, however, the necessary being is necessarily actual but all nondivine beings are only contingently actual, then God's actuality must be self-sufficient. God's essential being must include relationality within itself.[11]

The point of Boyd's argument is that Hartshorne's view, when purged of some of its unnecessary and even inaccurate features, requires the idea of the triune being of God for its fulfillment. Actually, Boyd does not present arguments for why this must be triune, rather than a less complete or complex multiplicity producing relationality. His view would seem to combine the best features of two supposedly incompatible traditions: the dynamic view of reality presented by process thought and Einsteinian physics, and the trinitarian theology of the orthodox, biblically based tradition.

Is this marriage a satisfactory solution to the problem of a metaphysically responsible contemporary view of the Trinity, however? It appears that certain problems still lurk within this combination. For while some portions of the orthodox tradition are retained, certain other features, rejected as the "classical view of God," based on a substance metaphysic, may be more intricately bound up with the biblical revelation than Boyd acknowledges. While no treatment of a few pages can do justice to a dissertation of four hundred pages, we may examine one area of the divine attributes, the omniscience of God, to assess Boyd's effort.

Boyd states that until the time of the Socinians, the view that God's omniscience included knowledge of all future events was not challenged. The classical view he states as being that "God knew all things, including the future, 'perfectly.'"[12] God's knowl-

---

10. Ibid., p. 227.
11. Ibid.
12. Ibid., p. 297.

edge of the world was not contingent on the world, but God does have a necessary knowledge of all things, appropriate to their nature. He necessarily knows necessary things as necessary, and he necessarily knows contingent things as contingent.[13]

A whole host of problems attach to this view. Some are true of the idea of divine perfection generally, while others relate specifically to the concept of omniscience. One problem is that if God knew reality in a timeless mode, he would not know what time it was, for he would experience all events as in the present time.[14] A second major problem is that this view seems to conflict with human freedom. Complete knowledge of all events entails that the future is actual, relative to God's standpoint. Related to this is that if God has perfect knowledge, then we have no ability to render definite what was previously indefinite. Boyd sees, as most Arminians do not, that true divine omniscience is incompatible with human freedom as they define it.[15] Take, for example, the question of Boyd's place of residence on March 3, 1999. He says, "Now if my place of residence on the 3rd of March in 1999 is now, and has forever, been perfectly known to God, known with exhaustive definiteness, then there is no further definiteness for me to add to this fact. Hence, my self now has no say—no power to render definite—where I shall live in the 3rd of March, 1999."[16] A number of efforts have been made by Christian philosophers to obviate the difficulties produced by this dilemma. Boyd examines two of these, proposed by Alvin Plantinga and by Bruce Reichenbach, and finds each wanting in certain respects. He concludes that "the notion of an unalterable content of definite future knowledge, which is logically contingent upon an open, undetermined, and non-existent future, is internally incoherent."[17]

Boyd's final criticism of the timeless understanding of God's omniscience derives from the biblical view of God's temporality.

---

13. Ibid.
14. Ibid., p. 298.
15. Ibid., pp. 300–301. Clark Pinnock is an exception to this usual tendency of Arminians. See his "God Limits His Knowledge," in *Predestination and Free Will: Four Views of Divine Sovereignty and Human Freedom*, ed. David Basinger and Randall Basinger (Downers Grove, Ill.: InterVarsity, 1986), pp. 141–73.
16. Ibid., p. 301.
17. Ibid., p. 314.

He says, "Aside from a questionable interpretation of a few questionable passages, the Bible consistently portrays God as One who experiences time, who is immanent within the flow of the temporal process, and who thus faces the future largely as an unsettled matter. It is not, in other words, only the creatures of God who change with the flow of time. God too (within limits) changes as this One adapts Godself to new situations."[18] He contends that God repeatedly alters his plans in the light of new circumstances, such as in Jonah 3. He makes conditional statements regarding the future, such as in Jeremiah 38:13. He insists that the "if" in this and similar passages must be taken seriously. He says, "There are simply no cogent grounds for taking verses such as these as mere anthropomorphacisms [sic], as has traditionally been done."[19]

In particular, Boyd rejects Norman Geisler's contention that "God's nontemporal nature is supported by numerous passages of Scripture (for example, Ex. 3:14, Jn. 8:58)."[20] Boyd professes not to know what other numerous passages Geisler has in mind, but says of the two that are cited that most scholars agree that the second is quoting the first and that "the meaning of the first is itself notoriously difficult to pin-down [sic]. But in any case, the fundamental issue from a Christian perspective is not resolved in this or that proof text, but in the overall portrait of God in the Bible."[21] This response appears inadequate, for several reasons. One is that just because a text is problematic does not justify ignoring it. One would hope for some genuine wrestling with the meaning of the text by Boyd. The second is that the "overall portrait of God in the Bible" deserves some elaboration as well. For if something is biblical in the sense of the broad sweep of Scripture, then it ought to be biblical in some specific places. Those specific places have been very scarce in Boyd's treatment. Rather, what we have is primarily an exercise in philosophical, rather than biblical theology. He spends the major portion of the dissertation discussing and interacting with Hart-

---

18. Ibid.
19. Ibid., p. 315. Parenthetically, this spelling error is not isolated. The book contains literally several hundred spelling, grammatical, and punctuation mistakes.
20. Norman Geisler, "God Knows All Things," in *Predestination*, ed. Basinger, p. 73.
21. Boyd, *Trinity and Process*, p. 314, n. 202.

shorne's philosophical understanding of God. This in itself is fine, but it appears that we are now getting the results of that philosophic endeavor represented as "the overall portrait of God in the Bible." One would like to see him substantiate that claim, and in the process wrestle with some of the texts traditionally adduced in support of divine omniscience, such as Psalm 139:2–10; Psalm 147:5; Proverbs 15:3; Jeremiah 38:17–18; Daniel 2:28; Matthew 10:29–30; John 21:17; Hebrew 4:30; and 1 John 3:20.

Basically, Boyd's contention seems to be that the traditional way of understanding the omniscience of God is simply an Aristotelian or Thomistic philosophical conception. While Geisler is a self-declared Thomist,[22] it seems that Boyd should have given us a process-based or philosophically neutral exegesis and interpretation of those passages. It appears rather that there are enough passages teaching or implying clearly enough the idea of God's knowledge of everything, both actual and contingent, that Boyd's process-based view has led him to a position that conflicts not only with the classical view, but with the biblical view. Thus his solution, appealing as it may be in general conceptual terms, simply cannot be followed, given our commitment to the view of Scripture that we hold. While we have not the space here to engage in a full-fledged critique of process philosophy, we must at least offer a responsible metaphysical alternative.

The Spiritual as Metaphysically Basic

The orthodox interpretation of the Christian faith leads us to some definite conclusions. One is that the spiritual is most real. There is one eternal, uncreated reality: God. All other things that exist have derived from him through his act of creation. Further, Scripture makes quite clear that God is spirit, not matter (John 4:24). It is also implied by references to God's invisibility (John 1:18; 1 Tim. 1:17; 6:15–16). Carl Henry says, "All theistic schools, however they may disagree in relating the nature of God to his activity, affirm the priority of mind in the universe of being. Christian theology, whether realistic or personalistic, agrees on this principle. The starting point of any theology worthy of the

22. See his *Thomas Aquinas: An Evangelical Appraisal* (Grand Rapids: Baker, 1991).

name Christian is the denial of any nonmental ultimate, and the insistence that the living God originates and sustains the universe of men and things."[23]

The material is derived from this ultimate reality, God, by creation. This is not to deny the reality of the material in the present creation, but its independent or ultimate or eternal character. This is, in other words, rejection of both a metaphysical dualism and a material character of God. To fail to recognize this dependent or derivative or contingent nature of the reality of the material universe would lead to metaphysical dualism.[24] It is important that we think through the implications of this conception. Some objections to this concept stem from implicitly materialistic assumptions. So, for example, the widely held idea of the unity of the human often fails to ask what that single nature is. In many cases, the idea has been borrowed from behaviorism, which is a thoroughly materialistic view.

The Universe as Personal

Beyond this, however, the fundamental characteristic of the universe is personal. This is not to say that there is not a major segment of reality that is impersonal; it is rather to deny the ultimacy of the impersonal. The spiritual or nonmaterial character of ultimate reality is not an impersonal set of ideas or concepts, as was true of Platonic idealism. Nor is the fundamental reality one great mind or self, all-encompassing in nature, as was held by Georg Hegel and the absolute idealism that derived from his thought. The supreme person is indeed a person, with identity, thought, will, and personality, with whom it is possible to have a relationship, conscious to both parties.

This supreme being, however, was not content to remain solitary. He acted to create reality external to himself. This involved the creation of the material universe and all physical objects within it. It also involved bringing into existence other selves be-

---

23. Carl F. H. Henry, *God, Revelation and Authority* (Waco, Tex.: Word, 1982), 5:105.

24. Michael Williams, if his statement is taken literally, seems to hold such a view: "I would suggest that Scripture assumes that the material universe is as real, as ontologically fundamental as mind." Review of *The Word Became Flesh, Pro Rege* 21.1 (September 1992): 27. The quotation does, however, appear in a very imprecise writing.

sides himself. These persons, to a large extent, exist for relationship with the creating and originating God.

Reality as Primarily Social

If, then, the most significant members of the creation are persons in relationship, then reality is primarily social. This means that the most powerful binding force in the universe is love. If material is the basic element of reality, then physical forces, such as electromagnetic forces, are the binding power that unites and controls what is. Here, however, it is love. Love is the attractive force of unselfish concern for the other person.

Love, expressed, experienced, and appropriated, is necessary to the proper existence and functioning of persons. When love is not accepted or returned, it easily becomes hatred. Or, love that is not reciprocated, or which is not genuinely unselfish, quickly and easily becomes narcissism. Both reactions are fundamentally negative in a world based on love.

The Trinity as a Society of Persons

In light of these considerations, the Trinity must be understood as fundamentally a society. The Godhead is a complex of persons. Love exists within the Godhead as a binding relationship of each of the persons to each of the others. Indeed, the attribute of love is more than just another attribute. The statement "God is love" in 1 John is a very basic characterization of God, which cannot be understood simply as a definition or an equation, but is more than merely, "God is loving." The Trinity is three persons so closely bound together that they are actually one.

In a sense, God being love virtually requires that he be more than one person. Love, to be love, must have both a subject and an object. Thus, if there were not multiplicity in the person of the Godhead, God could not really be love prior to this creation of other subjects. For love to be genuine, there must be someone whom God could love, and this would necessarily be more than mere narcissism. The Father loves the Son; the Son loves the Father; the Father loves the Holy Spirit; the Holy Spirit loves the Father; the Son loves the Holy Spirit; the Holy Spirit loves the

Son. The fact that God is three persons rather than merely two also is a demonstration of the character of love. There is an old statement, "Two's company; three's a crowd." It is possible for two human persons to have a relationship of love for one another that is much more difficult for three persons to have among themselves. Two persons may simply reciprocate love, not having to share the other person's love with anyone else. With three persons, there must be a greater quality of selflessness, of genuine *agapē*. Thus the Trinity founded upon love is a demonstration of the full nature of *agapē*.

Love, among human persons, always involves some measure of incompleteness or imperfection. This is not true of the love within the Trinity. The factors that separate or isolate human beings from one another simply are not present within the Trinity.

One of these factors is the possession of physical bodies. These effectively keep people "outside of" each other. Two physical objects cannot occupy the same space, a phenomenon that can be confirmed by observing the collision of two automobiles or two football players. This separation serves to distinguish entities, including human beings, from one another. This separation, however, means that communication must be through some medium. Physical contact makes the sense of touch the most complete and direct form of communication.

A second factor that separates persons is differing experiences. This means that we are unable to identify with the thoughts and experiences of the other person, not having had those ourselves. This factor also leads to faulty communication. Having had different experiences than others, we understand and interpret the symbols used in communication differently than others. Thus, we think we agree when we really do not. Or, we think we disagree, when we simply misunderstand. We may be agreeing with something different than the other person is agreeing with, or may be disagreeing with something different than the other person is agreeing with.

A third separating or isolating factor with human persons is preoccupation with one's self, with one's own needs and problems, which makes it difficult to focus on, understand, or empathize with other persons. The ability to understand the other in any genuine sense involves the ability to place oneself in the other's situation. If, however, one is dominated by and preoccupied with one's own concerns, this is simply impossible. One cannot get outside of oneself, to reach out to another.

Let us now observe how these separating or isolating factors do not apply to the three persons of the Godhead. The first is obviously negated simply by virtue of the fact that God, being spiritual, does not have a body, and that none of the three persons has a body. Thus, there is no spatial separation and there can consequently be a degree of intercommunication not experienced by any other trio of persons.

There is, however, one apparent exception to this fact, namely, the incarnation of Christ. One of the members of the Trinity took on a physical body as part of assuming human nature. It is also the belief of the Christian church that the incarnation is a continuing matter, so that Jesus still possesses a full human nature, including a body, albeit a resurrected and glorified body.

We should note that the incarnation did involve certain limitations. Christ did not, apparently, have quite the direct access to the consciousness of the Father (and of the Spirit) that he had possessed previously. Thus, for example, he did not seem able consciously to access without aid the infinite knowledge of the Father. The most prominent example of this is found in his statement in response to the disciples' question about the time of the second coming: "No one knows about that day or hour, not even the angels in heaven, nor the Son, but only the Father" (Matt. 24:36). Further, it was necessary for him to pray, as he demonstrated numerous times during his earthly ministry. He needed to express to the Father that which he was thinking and feeling.

This degree of separation should be understood as part of the earthly abode of Christ, as part of the state of humiliation, as it is sometimes called. The Father was in heaven, the Son was on the earth. At the ascension, however, he returned to the presence of the Father. He is now pictured as being at the right hand of the Father, making intercession for us (Matt. 26:64; Rom. 8:34; Eph. 1:20, etc.). There is now a closeness of relationship that was precluded by the physical absence of the Son during the time of his earthly life and ministry. Further, however, although the incarnation continues, the body Christ now possesses is his glorified body, or what Paul terms the "spiritual body" (1 Cor. 15:42–49).

This body presumably does not have the limitations of space and time associated with the created physical universe. One's conception of the nature of heaven, whether it is a place physically and geographically located or not, will of course affect this understanding. If space and time came into being with the creation of the physical universe, then God is not located in some place that could be geographically plotted on a sort of celestial globe, or to which one could travel with a sufficiently powerful rocket ship or something of that type. The limiting restrictions of the physical body will no longer be present to inhibit communication among the members of the Trinity. This is of course related to the fact that all are deity and are a unified being; we will never have such direct access to God's consciousness, even in the glorified future state of possession of spiritual bodies.

Further, there is not the separating effect of different experiences. If each person of the Trinity shares the consciousness of each of the others, thinks the others' thoughts, or at least is conscious of those thoughts, then there really are no such things as separate experiences. For example, by virtue of his incarnation, the second person of the Trinity has had experiences, such as temptation, which the Father and the Spirit have not. Yet while they have not experienced temptation, they have experienced Christ experiencing temptation. The point is that there are no experiences of one member of the Trinity that the others cannot understand, and thus the barriers to perfect love that such varying experiences present do not occur here.

Finally, there is not the preoccupation with oneself, and the self-centeredness related to that, which we find with human persons. This is *agapē*, the unselfish love that is concerned for the welfare of the other. This is the love exemplified by Christ in Philippians 2:1–11. And in a situation where each of the other persons is similarly motivated, there is no need for anything other than this altruistic love.

But what of the question being raised in our day about the importance of self-love? Loving oneself for the sake of the other has two dimensions. One is that I love myself because someone whom I love loves me. In such a close relationship of love, one would love that which the other loves, in this case, oneself. Further, loving oneself, concern for oneself, would bring joy to the other, the one who is concerned for one. Thus a husband would be concerned for his health because a loss of that health would bring sorrow to his wife, which he would not want to see. Similarly, there must be altruistic self-interest in some larger situations. If the United States were under attack, it would be in the national interest for the president to be concerned for his security, for his safety is important to the safety and welfare of the country's citizens. It would not be ultimately unselfish or loving for him to give up his place of safety to private citizens, if their lives were saved and his were lost. Regardless of the competency of the president involved, the breakdown in continuity of government at a time of crisis would be unfortunate, and would no doubt result in the loss of many more lives. It would not result in the greatest good for the greatest number. So in the case of the Triune God, each of the persons loves himself through the others loving him.

Mutual Communion and Accessibility of the Three Persons

Each of these three persons then has close access, direct access, to the consciousness of the others. As one thinks or experiences, the others are also directly aware of this. They think the other's thoughts, feel the other's feelings. It is an extreme, perhaps we might say, infinite case of the type of empathy sometimes experienced by two human persons. Probably all of us have had times when we know exactly what another person is experiencing, and feel just what he or she is feeling. In many cases, this grows over time, as we get to know the other person and know what each facial expression, each bodily movement or posture, means. This is especially true of persons who are close to each other, such as good friends or family members. Think, however, what it means to have been with another, not for only a few years, but for all eternity. Identical twins are especially able to empathize with one another. In the case of the Father, Son, and Holy Spirit, they are of the same nature, deity, and it is a type of nature of which they are the only instances. In addition, persons vary greatly in their suggestibility. Some persons can be made to think or feel or imagine something with the slightest of sugges-

tions. Such persons are also frequently relatively more susceptible to hypnosis than are others. In the case of the three members
of the Trinity, we should think of them as extremely suggestible
with respect to one another.

The closeness of these three is accentuated through the fact
that the goals, intentions, values, and objectives of each of the
three is the same as those of each of the others. There is no difference in these respects that would tend to draw any of the three
away from either of the others. The example of the early church,
the members of which were "one in heart and mind" (Acts 4:32),
is a small-scale approximation to this. These Christians also did
not consider any of their property the exclusive possession of that
one person or family, instead sharing freely with one another.

There also is a closeness to this relationship due to the fact that
each knows that there is no option of separation. Sometimes love
among humans becomes tentative because there is the fear that
the other will somehow turn away from the relationship or
against the person himself/herself. This cannot be in the case of
the three members of the Trinity, however. They are eternally
and permanently one with the others.

The conception we have been employing in this construction
tends to emphasize the uniqueness and distinctness of the three
persons more than do some theologies. Indeed, there is a fairly
general agreement that what was meant by the concept of person
in the ancient trinitarian theologies was quite different from the
modern understanding of person and did not involve separate
self-consciousnesses as such. Rather, the concept of person was
related to the prosopa or masks, so that one person was revealed
in three modes of existence. Yet this consensus may need some
reexamination, both in light of the biblical witness and of the understanding of the dynamics of social interrelationships.

Wolfhart Pannenberg points out that Jesus distinguished himself from the Father. His whole message was that the name of
God should be hallowed by accepting and living by his lordship.
He said that the Father was greater than he (John 14:28), and
that his words were not his own but the Father's who sent him
(v. 24). He would not allow himself to be called "good teacher"
because "no one is good—but God alone" (Mark 10:18). While
the Arians and the Socinians drew from this the conclusion that

the Son was not fully divine, this is taking the sayings further than one should. These statements do, however, argue for the distinctness of personhood or of consciousness of the Son from the Father. The Son is only Son because of his distinction from the Father. Similarly, however, the handing over of rule by the Father to the Son and the handing back of this by the Son to the Father constitute the distinction of the Father from the Son. Pannenberg means by self-distinction that the one who distinguishes himself from another defines himself as also dependent on that other. Similarly, there is a self-distinction that constitutes the Spirit a separate person from the Father and the Son and relates them to both. From these teachings of Scripture, Pannenberg then derives the understanding of the nature of persons. He says,

> If the trinitarian relations among the Father, Son, and Spirit have the form of mutual self-distinction, they must be understood not merely as different modes of being of the one divine subject but as living realizations of separate centers of action. Whether we must also view these centers of action as centers of consciousness depends on whether and in what sense we can apply the idea of consciousness, which derives from human experience, to the divine life.[25]

It does seem, from the considerations that Pannenberg adduces, as well as from others that we have noted above in the biblical text, that there is a distinctness of consciousness capable of originating thoughts and relationships among the members of the Trinity. The way in which each refers to the other, and interacts with the other, suggests a greater multiplicity of identity than has sometimes been thought of in trinitarian theology. In particular, the parallel drawn between the oneness of the Father and the Son on the one hand and the believer to believer, and husband and wife to one another on the other hand, suggests something of this relationship. Not that these latter relationships are by any means of the same degree as the relationship of the Father and Son to one another, but there must at least be some univocal element present, for such an analogy even to be sug-

25. Wolfhart Pannenberg, *Systematic Theology* (Grand Rapids: Eerdmans, 1991), 1:319.

gested. Note also the reference to the Father and the Son being in one another. This chapter is then followed by Jesus' teaching about the vine and the branches: his followers are to remain in him and he will remain in them (John 15:5). And in the seventeenth chapter, after praying that his disciples will be one as he and the Father are one, he then adds immediately, "I in them and you in me." There is apparently an interpenetration and closeness in the relationship of Father and Son like that of Christ to the believer and of believer to believer, except taken to the infinite degree.

This oneness and interpenetration is not spoken of in Scripture only as being between Father and Son, but also is attributed to the relationship of the Spirit to the Son. It was by the Holy Spirit that Mary conceived a child, although she was a virgin (Matt. 1:18, 20; Luke 1:35). The Spirit also descended on Jesus at his baptism (Matt. 3:16; Mark 1:10; Luke 3:22; John 1:32). It was the Spirit who then thrust him out into the desert to be tempted (Matt. 4:1; Mark 1:12; Luke 4:1). Jesus claimed that the Spirit of the Lord was upon him, anointing him to preach (Luke 4:18). He also claimed to be driving out demons by the Spirit of God (Matt. 12:28). He breathed out the Holy Spirit upon his followers (John 20:22). The Spirit who is to carry on his work after his departure is another counselor of the same (ἄλλος) kind (John 14:16). This also accounts for the apparent paradox of the indwelling Holy Spirit (v. 17) and of Christ in us (Gal. 2:20; Col. 1:27). They are not really as opposed as might be thought, for they are together, intimately linked and functioning together.

Perichoresis as the Guard Against Tritheism

In this type of approach there is a danger of falling into tritheism. The guarantee against that, which would be three separate, distinct, and independent individuals, is in the closeness and interaction among them that we have described above. Moltmann seeks to guard against this by saying that we are not to think of the three persons as three individuals that then enter into relationship with each other.[26] What we have been describing in the inti-

---

26. Jürgen Moltmann, *The Trinity and the Kingdom: The Doctrine of God* (San Francisco: Harper & Row, 1981), p. 175.

mate relationship of the three is the doctrine traditionally referred to as *perichoresis*. It is also referred to at times as *circumincessio*, the Latin equivalent. It means that each of the three persons shares the life of the others, that each lives in the others. It involves what Moltmann calls the "circulatory character of the eternal divine life." According to this concept, "an eternal life process takes place in the triune God through the exchange of energies."[27]

While the concept of interpenetration or mutual communion of the three persons with one another goes back quite a bit further, it appears that the first person to use the term "perichoresis" of the relationships of the three persons of the Trinity to one another may well have been Pseudo-Dionysius.[28] It was, however, John of Damascus who really adopted the term and developed it most fully with respect to the Trinity. He said, for example,

> For the subsistences dwell in one another, in no wise confused by cleaving together, according to the word of the Lord, *I am in the Father, and the Father in Me* . . . they are made one not so as to commingle, but so as to cleave to each other, and they have their being in each other without any coalescence or commingling. . . . For the Deity is undivided amongst things divided, to put it concisely: and it is just like three suns cleaving to each other without separation and giving out light mingled and conjoined in one.[29]

Later he elaborates on this concept:

> The subsistences dwell and are established firmly in one another. For they are inseparable and cannot part from one another, but keep to their separate courses within one another, without coalescing or mingling, but cleaving to one another. For the Son is in the Father and the Spirit: and the Spirit in the Father and the Son: and the Father in the Son and the Spirit, but there is no coalescence or commingling or confusion.[30]

In Latin, the term came to be translated by two words, which represent two different understandings of the nature of persons,

27. Ibid., p. 174.
28. Pseudo-Dionysius the Areopagite, *On the Divine Names* 2.4.
29. John of Damascus, *Exposition of the Orthodox Faith* 1.8.
30. Ibid., 1.14.

and which together capture the full meaning of the Greek. The word, *circuminsessio,* means literally "to be seated in." It conveys the more static conception of being located within one another. The word, *circumincessio,* is a more dynamic concept. It comes from a word meaning to permeate or to interpenetrate. Together, these ideas as found in *perichoresis,* mean both permanence of location with respect to another and ongoing interchange or sharing.

There were basically two different approaches to the three-ness and oneness of God in ancient theology. The Greek approach began with the emphasis on the monarchy of the Father, and with him as the source of the Trinity, and of the deity of the other persons. The Latin approach was different, and for definite reasons that can be discerned within its context. In the Roman Empire, the danger of polytheism was very present and real. Consequently, the unity of the Godhead was necessarily strongly emphasized. So the beginning point of thinking for Western theologians was the substance of God, differentiated in three persons. A third approach, which began to come to expression in the Cappadocians and has gained considerable popularity in recent years, emphasizes the three persons intimately linked to one another by perichoresis. Its emergence was in large part a means of countering the tritheism into which some tended to fall.[31]

There are a number of reasons for our adoption of this option. The first is the description of the relationships among the three persons found in Scripture. While the earthly incarnate life of Jesus introduces some dimensions into the relationships that perhaps were not previously present, it gives us the most complete revelation both into the nature of those relationships during the time of that earthly existence and also in the eternal interaction of the three. So, for example, Jesus' communion with the Father is obvious, becoming most explicit in the prayer in the Garden of Gethsemane (John 17). It seems apparent from that prayer that some sort of multiplicity of persons enabled Jesus to choose that the will of the Father be done. Note, however, the reference to the oneness between the two of them. Jesus has given

---

31. Leonardo Boff, *Trinity and Society: Theology and Liberation* (Maryknoll, N.Y.: Orbis, 1988), pp. 77–85.

his followers the glory that the Father had given him, so that they may be one as he and the Father are one (v. 22). The nature of this oneness is also spelled out in verse 21, where his prayer is "that all of them may be one, Father, just as you are in me and I am in you." Earlier he had said to the disciples, in his farewell address before his capture, trial, and crucifixion: "Don't you believe that I am in the Father, and that the Father is in me? The words that I say to you are not just my own. Rather, it is the Father, living in me, who is doing his work. Believe me when I say that I am in the Father and that the Father is in me" (John 14:10–11). Here is the perichoresis, or interpenetration: "as you are in me and I am in you."

Note, as well, the nature of this oneness. It appears that this oneness of God is not simplicity or numerical singleness. Rather, it is true unity, union of those that are more than one. The word for one in the Shema in Deuteronomy 6:4 (אֶחָד) is the same as that used for the man and woman becoming "one flesh," as described in Genesis 2:24. In other words, the unity is more like that of a married couple than like that of a single person. In impersonal terms, it is more like a molecule, made up of atoms of two different elements, than like the unity of an atom (although, of course, the atom is in turn made up of differing components, such as electrons, neutrons, positrons, etc.). It is more like the unity of water than the unity of oxygen. It is in light of biblical data such as these that the concept of the perichoresis of three persons seems more adequate than either of the two other approaches.

Some special attention needs to be given here to the concept of persons within this context. There is currently much confusion about the meaning or definition of persons. Thus, Karl Barth avoids the use of the term "person," stating that the theologian's task would be hopeless if it involved saying what is really meant by "person" in the doctrine of the Trinity. He feels that the idea of three self-consciousnesses or a threefold individuality is scarcely possible without falling into tritheism. He quotes with approval F. Diekamp's statement, "In God, as there is one nature, so there is one knowledge, one self-consciousness."[32] He prefers

---

32. Karl Barth, *Church Dogmatics* (Edinburgh: T. & T. Clark, 1975), I/1, p. 358.

to speak of God existing in three modes of being,[33] or of a repetition in God.[34]

Wolfhart Pannenberg, on the other hand, argues that the trinitarian relations among the Father, Son, and Spirit must be understood "not merely as different modes of being of the one divine subject but as living realizations of separate centers of action."[35] Whether one would also attach the expression "centers of consciousness" to such a concept depends on whether the idea of consciousness can really be applied to God at all. It would appear, however, from the biblical narratives, that Pannenberg's view more adequately fits the data of those accounts than does that of Barth. This is particularly true of passages in which there is interaction and conversation among the several persons of the Trinity.

Leonardo Boff points out three meanings that the word "person" has had at various periods in the life of the church and the history of Christian thought. It has meant simply an existing subject distinct from others. This idea successfully preserved the Christian belief against the unitarian monotheism that denied any plurality of persons in God, but it was susceptible to tritheism. The difficulty with this concept, however, as Augustine saw it, was that it really did not give any content or specific qualities to any of the persons.[36] He also objected that if each of these persons is so distinct from each other, why do we give them a common and generic name, "person"? Should we not perhaps give each its own name?[37]

The second meaning of person in the discussion of the Trinity has been *"a subsistent relationship or the individual and incommunicable subsistence of a rational nature."*[38] Here, within the Trinity, everything possible is placed in common, entering into the play of relationships and completing the communion. Thus, the Father bestows everything on the Son and the Holy Spirit, except the fact of being Father; the Son bestows everything on the Spirit and the Father except the fact of being the begotten Son; the Spirit bestows everything on the Father and the Son except

33. Ibid., pp. 359–60.
34. Ibid., p. 350.
35. Pannenberg, *Systematic Theology*, 1:319.
36. Augustine, *On the Trinity* 5.9.10.
37. Ibid., 7.4.7.
38. Boff, *Trinity and Society*, p. 88.

the fact of being the Spirit breathed out by the Father and the Son. This view, says Boff, has the advantage over the first of stressing the relationship among the three divine persons, but unfortunately emphasizes that which cannot enter into relationship, the condition that makes the relationship possible: the incommunicability of each in the act of communicating.[39]

The third definition, which Boff thinks most suitable and which is also adopted in this work, is the idea of a person as "a *being-for,* a *knot of relationships,* an identity formed and completed on the basis of relationships with others."[40] Persons are, in the first place, conscious beings, and in the second place, so structured as always to be oriented toward others. Thus, says Boff, interiority (or consciousness in its ontological aspect) and openness to the other (freedom and the ethical dimension) constitute the mode of being proper to a person.[41] This definition seems to fit with and integrate the biblical data that we have been examining.

In the chapter on the logic of the Trinity, we will note several analogies that will help us grasp the profound meaning of the three in one and one in three. We need to examine one of those and pursue another in light of the meaning given to the metaphysics developed in this chapter. We suggest the idea of the human organism, consisting, for our purposes, specifically, of the heart, brain, and lungs. Each organ is distinct from the other, but not separable, or at least not separable without each of the other organs ceasing to be. Each is dependent for its existence on the shared life, supplied in turn by itself and each of the others. The organism that is that person would not be a human organism without each of these organs, and none of them would be a living human organ without each of the others. Each, in its own way, supplies life to the others and is dependent on the others in order to live and to continue to supply life. Similarly, the linkage and interdependence within the Trinity are such that there could not be a living God, nor could there be a Father, Son, or Spirit, without each of the others.

Another model that embodies some of the qualities we are trying to expound would be Siamese twins. These twins are formed

39. Ibid., pp. 88–89.
40. Ibid., p. 89.
41. Ibid.

when a single fertilized egg fails to divide properly; the two fetuses are joined to one another, in varying degrees, as "conjoined twins." They are unable to function separately, and may even share some vital organs.

A rather recent example is the Holton twins, Katie and Eilish, who were born to parents living just outside Dublin, Ireland. They were conjoined from the shoulder to the hip, and shared one liver and one intestinal system. They had two legs and two arms in roughly the normal place, with two additional arms protruding from the middle of their back. They had two hearts, and the remainder of the normal organs in approximately the usual fashion, although their torso was larger and heavier than that of a single child. The parents had to make the agonizing decision whether to approve the surgery attempting to separate them. They were determined that under no conditions would they decide to sacrifice the life of one child to preserve the life of the other. Finally the decision was made to proceed with the operation, which was attempted in May 1992. Eilish survived, but Katie died after a few days. An autopsy revealed that her heart was weak and underdeveloped, and that she had been relying on Eilish's heart to supply her part of their body with blood. Eilish showed strong indications of missing Katie. Here was a case in which not only the bodies but the lives of the two sisters were so intertwined that one literally depended on the other for physical survival, and the latter depended very heavily on the former psychologically. Whereas the personalities of the twins had been quite different, Mr. and Mrs. Holton testified that Eilish, who had been the more serious of the two, now took on some of the personality qualities of Katie, especially her playfulness, so that, in the parents' words, "It is as if a part of Katie lives on, as well."[42]

Inadequate as this illustration is, it does convey a bit of the nature of the internal life of the Trinity.[43] The Father, Son, and Holy

42. "Katie and Eilish," *Discovery Journal* (the Discovery television channel), February 1993.

43. To illustrate the perichoresis of the Trinity, these should of course be triplets rather than twins. While there are genetically identical triplets, there is a bit of asymmetry involved, for the egg does not split three ways. In the case of identical triplets, then, there is an initial split of the egg into two, one of which then in turn splits again. Because conjoined twins constitute only about one in one hundred thousand births, the possibility of conjoined triplets would be extremely rare.

Spirit are so intimately interlinked and intertwined that they are unable to live apart from one another. Each supplies life to the others. What they do, although it may be primarily the work of one of them, is done together. In this respect the Holton twins also illustrate the cooperative working of the members of the Trinity. With just two functional arms, each of which was apparently controlled by one of the twins, they would work together. For example, when opening a bottle, Eilish would hold it and Katie would turn the lid.

This leads us to one final aspect of the nature of the Triune God. Perichoresis means that not only do the three members of the Trinity interpenetrate one another, but all three are involved in all the works of God. While certain works are primarily or more centrally the doing of one of these rather than the others, all participate to some degree in what is done. Thus, while redemption is obviously the work of the incarnate Son, the Father and the Spirit are also involved. Similarly, sanctification is primarily the work of the Holy Spirit, but the Father and the Son are involved as well.

This can most clearly be seen by examining the biblical teaching regarding creation. This is generally, and correctly, thought of as most properly the work of the Father. It is difficult to isolate the roles of the respective persons from the Old Testament materials, since there had not yet been much more than hints or intimations of plurality in the nature of God, as we have seen in an earlier chapter. Creation is simply attributed to God. In the New Testament, however, we find more detailed information, helping us distinguish among the roles of the several persons. Probably the best single text capturing the variegated roles is found in 1 Corinthians 8:6. Paul is dealing with the question of food offered to idols. He does so by drawing on Psalm 96:5; Isaiah 37:16; and Jeremiah 10:11–12, which affirm that God has created everything that is, whereas idols are incapable of creating anything. He then goes beyond those passages, saying, "yet for us there is but one God, the Father, from whom all things came and for whom we live; and there is but one Lord, Jesus Christ, through whom all things came and through whom we live." Other texts also give clear indication that the Son had a major role in creation. John 1:3 says, "Through him all things were made; without him nothing was made that has been made." The writer to the Hebrews cites God as saying to the Son, "In the beginning, O Lord, you laid the foundations of the earth, and the heavens are the work of your hands" (1:10). The Old Testament seems to attribute a part in the creative work to the Spirit of God. While there are some difficulties in demonstrating conclusively the equivalence of the Spirit of God with the Holy Spirit, these texts collectively probably can be used of the Holy Spirit, whom Peter identified with the Old Testament Spirit of God in Acts 2:28. Among these texts are Genesis 1:2; Job 26:13; 33:4; Psalm 104:30; Isaiah 40:12–13.

It may not be possible to determine with precision the exact role played by each of these three persons in the events of creation. It should not be difficult for us to conceive of multiple aspects of creation or multiple participants in it, since we can see parallels to this in other "creative" occurrences. Thus the cause of a house may well be the architect, the general contractor, the materials suppliers, the workers who do the actual construction, and the mortgage company. So, Paul's use of the preposition ἐκ of the Father and διά of the Son in 1 Corinthians 8:6 is probably indicative of different roles, perhaps of origin or source and of agency.

While less clearly seen in Scripture, there are also indications of the three persons' participation in the works of redemption and sanctification. Clearly, the Son died in a way in which the Father and the Spirit did not, for only the Son had been incarnate. Yet Scripture has numerous indications of the part of the Father in sending the Son. John 3:16 says, "For God so loved the world that he gave his one and only Son, that whoever believes in him shall not perish but have eternal life." In 1 John 4:10 John writes, "This is love: not that we loved God, but that he loved us and sent his Son as an atoning sacrifice for our sins." Paul writes, "God presented him as a sacrifice of atonement, through faith in his blood" (Rom. 3:25). Both the act of the Father in sending the Son and in receiving the sacrifice were part of the total picture of redemption. And although only the Son actually died personally and physically on the cross, any loving parent can testify that the parent is not unaffected when the child suffers. Given the closeness of the Father and Son—they are "in" one another, and can be said to be "one"—that effect would be accentuated, if anything. This, then, is the sense in which "patripassianism" is true—not that the Father was the Son, but that he felt what the Son was feeling. It should be noted, also, that the Spirit was involved in this redemptive work. As we noted above, the Spirit came on Jesus and indwelt and empowered his ministry. Even his emotions were in the Spirit, so that we read in Luke that "in that hour he rejoiced in the Spirit." It is therefore safe to conclude it was by the Spirit within him that Jesus was able to offer his life as a sacrifice.

This triadic work is also indicated with respect to sanctification. It appears to be the Father to whom Paul is referring when he writes, "May God himself, the God of peace, sanctify you through and through. May your whole spirit, soul and body be kept blameless at the coming of our Lord Jesus Christ" (1 Thess. 5:23). This is even clearer in Hebrews 13:20–21: "May the God of peace, who through the blood of the eternal covenant brought back from the dead our Lord Jesus, that great Shepherd of the sheep, equip you with everything good for doing his will, and may he work in us what is pleasing to him, through Jesus Christ, to whom be glory for ever and ever. Amen." There is also clear statement of the role of the Son in sanctification. Paul says that Christ gave himself for the church, "to make her holy, cleansing her by the washing with water through the word, and to present her to himself as a radiant church, without stain or wrinkle or any other blemish, but holy and blameless" (Eph. 5:26). In Titus 2:14 Paul writes of Christ, "who gave himself for us to redeem us from all wickedness and to purify for himself a people that are his very own, eager to do what is good." That the Spirit works sanctification is apparent from numerous references, including Galatians 5:16, 25, and the reference to the "fruit of the Spirit," in verses 22 and 23. In Romans 8 Paul gives extensive attention to the relationship between the believer and the Holy Spirit, indicating the sanctifying work of the Spirit in such references as verses 4, 5, 9, 14, 16, and 26–27.

One other way of conceiving of this relationship of the three persons of the Trinity is in terms of the categories of immanence and transcendence, usually reserved for discussion of God's relationship to the created world. The three persons of the Trinity are thoroughly immanent within each other, interpenetrating one another. There is, however, also an element of transcendence, a degree to which each is to be distinguished from the other, allowing the ability to interact with one another as distinct subjects. While total immanence would lead to a unitarian monotheism, possibly of a modalistic type, total transcendence would produce a tritheism of some sort. The combination of both, rather than the exclusion of either aspect, governs here.

11

The Logical Structure of the Doctrine of the Trinity

The logical problem of the Trinity has been stated quite thoroughly in chapter 6. There we noted that there is both a narrow and a broad meaning of the term "logic." The narrow meaning concerns the logical status of the propositions that express the doctrine of the Trinity. Quite simply, the doctrine maintains that God is one and that God is three. Yet on the surface of it, these are contradictory statements. The first part of this chapter will therefore concern itself with that formal problem. The broader sense of logic is the whole status of the doctrine with respect to meaningfulness. In what way can we explicate the meaning of a doctrine such as this? We turn to the first of these problems, the problem of the seemingly contradictory character of the doctrine, and will begin our examination by noting several attempted solutions to the problem.

William Power

William Power, in an article entitled "Symbolic Logic and the Doctrine of the Trinity," offers one solution.[1] He begins by citing Alfred North Whitehead's statement, "Today there is but one religious dogma in debate: What do you mean by 'God'?"[2] Power

1. William L. Power, "Symbolic Logic and the Doctrine of the Trinity" *The Illiff Review* 32.1 (Winter 1975): 35–43.
2. Alfred North Whitehead, *Religion in the Making* (New York: Macmillan, 1926), p. 67.

notes that a number of heuristic devices have been used in attempting to explicate this meaning, but that very little has been done by way of employing symbolic logic and semiotics, two of the most powerful tools ever devised as aids in clarification and understanding. He proposes to apply first-order logic and first-order semiotics to the problem at hand. He hopes to show how the trinitarian problem can be understood in terms of a semantical theory of the identification of unique individuals.[3]

Power notes that in Judaism and Christianity, the terms "God" and "Yahweh" (or their vernacular equivalents in other languages) have been used to designate or refer to one and only one object, entity, or individual. They function as proper names rather than common names, singular terms, or general terms or predicates.[4] When God is spelled with a lowercase initial letter it becomes a predicate. Now usually a predicate is considered to designate a property or a relation and to denote the several members of the class having that predicate or being ordered by the relation designated by the predicate. In Judaism and Christianity, however, it is generally maintained that God is the only member of the class of gods, and that there cannot be any other members of the class. Thus, the name "God" has the same denotation as the predicate "god," and the latter cannot have any other denotation than that of the name, "God."

This means that the name "God" is not much different from that of other individuals. Here one gives a name and lists certain property and relation expressions with that name. Power illustrates this point with his wife, "Amburn," who, he says, is "the only daughter of Mildred and Jay Huskins of Statesville, North Carolina, a cute thing, a graduate of Duke, a puppeteer, and a mother of four sons."[5]

When the question is put, "Who is God?" we do not know in our age what to say. The answer given by trinitarian orthodoxy is that God is the Father, the Son, and the Holy Spirit, or the Creator, the Revealer, and the Sanctifier. These three identifying descriptions are "the linguistic expressions which present the three eternal and distinct modes of the divine being." The three hy-

---

3. Ibid., p. 35.
4. Ibid., pp. 37.
5. Ibid., pp. 37–38.

postases are "distinct expressions of a single divine reality," or "objective presentations of the one divine being." To put it somewhat differently, "the three hypostases of God constitute the set of eternal attributes which enable a person to identify God as distinct from all other objects."[6]

Ordinarily, when one speaks of properties, relations, or attributes, one is treating them as common to the class of those individuals or objects possessing these qualities. When, however, one identifies an object as unique and distinct from all other objects, one must specify a set of unique attributes only that object has. The church fathers found individual uniqueness difficult to deal with.[7] Now, however, Power believes that the doctrine that God is the Father, the Son, and the Holy Spirit, or the Creator, the Revealer, and the Sanctifier can be summed up quite nicely in quantification theory with identity. He believes that what the fathers seem to be saying is: "There exists an x such that x is a creator and x is a revealer and x is a sanctifier, and given any y if y is a creator and y is a revealer and y is a sanctifier, then x is identical to y." Asserting that God is the one and only member of the class of Creators, Revealers, and Sanctifiers does not make it so, but if we define "Creator" as "necessary condition for all beings including itself," and "Revealer" as "necessary condition for all aims, rationality and order including its own" and "Sanctifier" as "necessary condition for all value including its own" then it would be analytically true that there could not be more than one member of the class of Creators, Revealers, and Sanctifiers.[8]

Power believes that he has protected himself from one of the accusations that could brand him as a modalist, for he has asserted that these unique identifying attributes of God are eternal or necessary attributes, attributes that could not be otherwise. They are modes of presentation of the eternal rather than the temporal economy of God. What, however, is the distinction between "being the creator of," "being the revealer of," and "being the sanctifier of"? And what of the unbegotten characteristic of the Father, the begotten characteristic of the Son, and the

6. Ibid., p. 38.
7. Ibid.
8. Ibid., p. 39.

processional characteristic of the Holy Spirit? Power grants that these metaphors are extremely difficult to unpack, but quotes with apparent approval J. N. D. Kelly's assertions that "the distinction of the Persons is grounded in their origin and mutual relation" and that "the divine action begins from the Father, proceeds through the Son, and is completed in the Holy Spirit."[9]

While Power develops this concept further, this is the major thrust of his thought. How, then, shall we evaluate what he has done? It must be said that there is real benefit from his attempt to relate the logic of the Trinity to the category of individuals who are unique, that is, who are the sole members of the class that they occupy. This is a fundamentally correct insight, and one that should not be overlooked. If God is the sole member of the class, then linguistically his name will behave something like the name "Amburn Huskins Power" or any other distinctive and unique name. There are, however, problems with carrying through on the analogy as a solution to the logical puzzle.

The first problem is that whereas "Amburn Huskins Power" is the sole member of the class bearing her name, and that by virtue of being the sole member of the class combining the specific set of attributes or predicates that she does, she is not the sole individual possessing each of those attributes, only the combination of them. Another way of putting this is that while she is the sole member of the class of "Amburn Huskins Powers," she is, in each case, part of a larger class, such as human beings, puppeteers, mothers of four sons, and so forth. But God is the only member of the class of Creators, Revealers, Sanctifiers. He is utterly unique, whereas Amburn is only unique in a way comparable to the uniqueness of many other human beings.

There is another problem: God is unique as God, not necessarily as Triune God. The uniqueness applies to his monotheistic nature, not necessarily to his triunity. Power has escaped the charge of modalism in one of its forms, namely, that God is successively Father, Son, and Holy Spirit (or Creator, Revealer, and Sanctifier). He has not, however, escaped the charge of modalism in the sense that his God might eternally exist as Creator, Re-

9. Ibid., p. 40.

vealer, and Sanctifier. In other words, these three attributes might simply refer to three actions of the one God. They may be merely adjectives applied to the one subject, God. In that case, while he has solved the problem of the logic of the Trinity, he has actually simply solved the problem of monotheism rather than polytheism. He has done so, however, in a way that does not necessarily preserve the divine triunity.

There is yet another difficulty with Power's solution. It appears in his discussion of unbegottenness, begottenness, and procession. These seem to be predicates that apply to each of the three, Father, Son, and Spirit, respectively, but not to all of them collectively. Here, however, we have a problem. If Creator, Revealer, and Sanctifier are predicates, then what is the logical status of these predicates? To put it another way, if each of these has a predicate that neither of the others has, what is their logical status? Do we have one set, one class of which there is only one member, or three such sets? This is an unclarified issue in Power's thought, and one which by virtue of its ambiguous character seems to reopen, albeit in a somewhat modified form, the old logical problem of the Trinity.

Karl Rahner

A second suggested solution is that of Karl Rahner in his major work, *The Trinity*. He begins by acknowledging that we are here dealing with an absolute, eternal mystery. We do not understand such mysteries even after they have been revealed to us. Compared to the ideal of modern science this may appear to be a negative, but we are not dealing with an object within a neutral horizon of knowledge. Indeed, the knowledge of the Trinity may actually deepen the very concept of mystery, for in such a theology God's incomprehensibility might, as a positive predicate of our knowledge, be brought into inner proximity to the mystery of the Trinity.[10]

As a Roman Catholic theologian, Rahner is working with the church's pronouncements on this subject. There are basic concepts in terms of which the doctrine has been stated, namely, "es-

10. Karl Rahner, *The Trinity* (New York: Herder & Herder, 1970), pp. 50–51.

sence" (which he treats as identical with "substance" and "nature") and "person." The church, however, has never really defined or explained these terms. It is presupposed that these concepts are intelligible in themselves. There may be any one of three reasons for this presupposition. It may be based on their having a general, stable sense, ascertainable from everyday experience. The use of the terms "bread" and "wine" in the doctrine of the Eucharist would be an example of such a case. A second reason for this presupposition would be if the church had already developed these concepts in its ordinary teaching to the point where they have a certain accepted meaning. The third reason would be if the meaning of the concepts employed is clear from their total context, at least in a first approximation. Rahner says, however, that the first possibility is excluded in this case and the second is reducible to the third and does not allow us to arrive at a definition.[11]

Rahner distinguishes between two types of explanation, which he terms logical explanation and ontic explanation. A logical explanation is an explanation of something that makes a statement clear, that is, more precise, less liable to be misunderstood. It explains the statement in light of itself, not by the use of another. All the concepts used to explain that statement can be derived from it. Even if the verbal terminology used is obtained elsewhere, it is understood that the terminology employed is meant only in the sense and scope of what is explained, rather than in that more general sense. An ontic explanation, on the other hand, is one that uses another state of affairs to help understand what is to be explained. It functions by giving the cause of something, the way in which it comes about.[12]

It is the former type of explanation, the logical explanation, which Rahner is attempting to give in this treatise, at least insofar as these concepts belong to the dogma of the Roman Catholic Church. It will remain to be seen, however, whether it is possible to invest even more speculative content into the concepts, so that the logical explanation becomes an ontic explanation, a theological explanation, not one proposed by the magisterium.[13]

---

11. Ibid., pp. 51–52.
12. Ibid., p. 53.
13. Ibid., pp. 54–55.

Rahner feels that the concept of person is problematic for doing trinitarian theology today. It has had a continuing history after its introduction into dogmatic thought and the church's dogma. This has taken its meaning beyond that which it had in the original usage. When we now hear of "three persons," it is almost impossible not to connect the term with three centers of consciousness and activity, resulting in a heretical tritheism. In light of this, the theologian must consider carefully whether the term should not be replaced with another whose meaning more closely approximates the meaning "person" had when first introduced into the church's dogma.[14]

The next move in his effort to alleviate the problem comes in Rahner's concept of relative distinctness. The Father, the Son, and the Holy Spirit are only "relatively" distinct, according to Rahner. By that he means that they should not in their distinction "be conceived as constituted by something which would mean a distinction previous to their mutual relations and serving as their foundation."[15] What he seems to be attempting to avoid is the idea of some sort of separate entities, existing independently of each other, and thus distinct. What he apparently maintains is that what makes them distinct is their relations to one another. Thus, he insists that the concept of "relation" is, at least initially, a logical, rather than an ontological explanation. In other words, the concept is not something more general, drawn from any general ontology. Whether it is possible to pass from such a logical explanation to an ontological one will have to be discussed.[16]

Does this concept of relationality of the divine persons give us any help with the difficult question of how there can be three distinct persons in God if each is identical to the same essence? Rahner believes that it does. This concept does not solve the difficulty positively, but shows negatively and defensively that the present difficulty, namely, how two things that are identical with a third are not identical with each other, can be shown not to be insuperable.[17]

14. Ibid., pp. 56–57.
15. Ibid., p. 68.
16. Ibid., p. 69.
17. Ibid., p. 70.

It is obvious, says Rahner, that two absolute realities cannot be identical with a third without being identical with each other. This is not true, however, when dealing with two "mere" and opposed relations, which are really identical with an abstract reality, namely, God's essence. It is not sufficient to say that the relations are "virtually" distinct from the essence and that this makes them not identical with each other, even though they are really identical with the essence. For either this "virtual" distinction is a mental one, in which case the difficulty is not dispelled, or it is a real distinction, however that is understood, in that it posits two distinct realities in the thing itself. In that latter case, however, the basic trinitarian axiom of the Council of Florence must be given up, and a heretical "Quaternity" in God cannot be avoided. To put it another way, the virtual distinction between person and essence is of help in avoiding the logical difficulty only if it is not a distinction between two absolute realities, but between an absolute and a relative identity.[18]

Rahner distinguishes between that which is absolute and that which is relative. The former has its content in itself, whereas the latter has it constituted only by its relatedness to another. So, while the Father, Son, and Spirit are identical with the one Godhead, they are "relatively" distinct from one another.[19] Rahner strongly desires to avoid tritheism. This appears in his discussion of person, a term he feels currently causes much confusion through the current popular understanding of the word. There is self-awareness, but not uniquely by each person. There is one power, one will, one self-presence, a unique activity, a unique beatitude. Self-awareness is "not a moment which distinguishes the divine 'persons' one from the other, even though each divine 'person,' as concrete, possesses a self-consciousness. Whatever would mean three 'subjectivities' must be carefully kept away from the concept of persons in the present context."[20] While this statement is far from clear, what Rahner seems to be saying in this context is that each of the three persons is self-conscious, but there is not a different or unique self-consciousness possessed by

18. Ibid.
19. Ibid., pp. 71–72.
20. Ibid., pp. 75–76.

each. There is one self-consciousness possessed by each of the three, or perhaps more accurately, by all three, not three self-consciousnesses. Rahner adds that there is only one outward activity of God. When in ecclesiastical usage such activity is attributed to one of the persons, it is also implicitly attributed to the other two persons as well, and in this sense only "appropriated" to the one person.[21]

Rahner indicates that he is consciously not dealing with many of the more convoluted issues that textbook theology has customarily addressed. He feels that many of these do not really bring one much closer to the solution of the problems. He also takes it for granted that modern man does not find it especially difficult to accept from the start the fact that there may be statements that do not admit of a positive (as contrasted with a merely verbal) synthesis and that may nevertheless stand very solidly. This allows the neglect of some of those metaphysical subtleties that previously had to be dealt with by theology.[22]

The concept of relations is not as clear as we might wish. Rahner states that relationality should not be considered first of all as a means of solving the apparent contradictions involved in the doctrine of the Trinity. To the extent that relations are understood to be the most unreal of realities, they are unsuitable for understanding a Trinity that is most real. Yet relations are as real as other determinations.[23]

As noted earlier, Rahner feels that contemporary misunderstanding of the concept of persons contributes to much of the confusion about the nature of the Trinity. In the doctrine of the Trinity, this concept involves aspects not found in any other concept. It attempts to generalize that which is absolutely unique. When we say "there are three persons in God, God subsists in three persons," we are adding up that which cannot be added up. What alone is in common to Father, Son, and Spirit is the one and only Godhead. There is no higher point of view from which the three can be added as Father, Son, and Spirit. In other cases of individuals the several of them can be added up, but not here. In our experience elsewhere, what exists as distinct cannot be

21. Ibid., p. 76.
22. Ibid., pp. 80–81.
23. Ibid., p. 103.

multiplied without a multiplication of natures as well, but with respect to the Trinity, this is not the case.[24]

In speaking of three persons in this context, we must always return to the original experience of salvation history. What we find there is that we experience the Spirit as God, the Son as God, and the Father as God. When, however, we generalize and say that we experience three persons, we are doing this subsequent to experience. This is, at least at first, a logical explanation, not some new extra knowledge, which was not included in the original explanation.[25] We must always bear in mind that there are not several spiritual centers of activity in God, several subjectivities and liberties. It fact, there is properly no mutual love between Father and Son, which would presuppose two acts. Rather, there is loving self-acceptance of the Father and of the Son, which rise to the distinction. There is in God a knowledge of these three persons, and thus in each person a knowledge about himself and about the two other persons. There are not three consciousnesses; rather, the one consciousness subsists in a threefold way.[26]

Rahner wants to make clear that the expression, "distinct manner of subsisting" should not be understood as something subsequent, without which the substantially real might also exist. It is impossible to conceive of a Godhead that would, as real, be previous to these matters.[27] These manners of subsisting are distinct as relations of opposition; they are real through their identity with the divine essence. God as subsisting in one determined manner (as Father, Son, or Spirit) is "somebody else" *(ein anderer)* than God subsisting in another manner of subsisting, but he is not "something else" *(etwas anderes)*.[28]

How shall we respond to Rahner's effort to alleviate the logical difficulty? I share the assessment made by Stephen Davis: "A reader confused by the doctrine of the Trinity would, I believe, be all the more confused by Rahner's explanations."[29] We may have here a classic case of explaining the obscure by the even more ob-

---

24. Ibid., pp. 104–5.

25. Ibid., p. 106.

26. Ibid., pp. 106–7.

27. Ibid., p. 112.

28. Ibid., pp. 113–14.

29. Stephen T. Davis, *Logic and the Nature of God* (Grand Rapids: Eerdmans, 1983), p. 139.

scure. It is not at all clear what Rahner means by "relative realities." He wants to avoid giving them such a status of reality that they would have to equal each other if each were equal to a third entity, the essence. The persons do not have separate existence from one another, and their distinctness consists only in their relative opposition, that is, in their being related to each other. Yet Rahner does not want this relatedness thought of as something subsequent, as if the persons could somehow exist independently of the relatedness. Then, however, the question becomes, What is the status of relations? Is it possible for relations to exist without some things that are related to each other? There seems to be a dilemma between making them so real that the contradiction appears, and making them so unreal that the concept becomes unintelligible. This problem does not seem to be helped at all by Rahner's statements that relations are the most unreal of realities and that they are as absolutely real as other determinations.

It would appear on the surface of things that there is a contradiction for Rahner, not within the concept of the oneness and threeness of God, but within the concept of relations. Undoubtedly, there exists a distinction in his mind that would preclude this apparent contradiction, but his failure to clarify such a distinction leaves us with a puzzle. He claims not to solve the problem in a positive way, but only in a negative or defensive way, showing how the problem is not insuperable, yet that way appears to be unintelligible. Perhaps he has merely relocated and relabeled the problem.

Relative Identity Theory

The relative identity approach uses a particular type of reasoning and analysis known as relative identity logic, especially developed by Peter Geach, who, although he had not specifically applied his analysis to the problem of the Trinity, had become involved in the question of the oneness and threeness of God in a discussion of the virtues.[30] Probably the first thinker to utilize this conceptuality systematically in treating the logical problem of the Trinity was A. P. Martinich in a 1978 article.[31] Peter van Inwagen has more recently developed the concept independently.[32] For our purposes we will especially rely on a second article by Martinich, both because it incorporates his more mature reflection on the subject and because its contents are relatively more accessible to readers not trained in symbolic logic.[33]

Martinich states that the orthodox doctrine of the Trinity includes four propositions:

(1) There is only one God.
(2) The Father is God.
(3) The Son is God.
(4) The Father is not the Son.

If identity is understood in the usual way, it is easy to show that (1)–(4) form an inconsistent set. (1)–(3) entail

(4′) The Father is the Son

which Sabellius in effect defended and which contradicts (4). In addition, (1), (2), and (4) entail

(3′) The Son is not God

which Arius in effect defended and which contradicts (3). If, however, as Geach says, identity is always relative to a general term, then (4) and (4′) are both incomplete sentences, expressing incomplete thoughts, and therefore not having truth-values. When properly expanded they become, respectively,

(5) The Father is not the same person as the Son

and

30. P. T. Geach, "Aristotle," in *Three Philosophers*, by G. E. M. Anscombe and P. T. Geach (Ithaca, N.Y.: Cornell University Press, 1961), pp. 118–20; *Logic Matters* (Berkeley: University of California Press, 1972), pp. 238–49; "Ontological Relativity and Relative Identity," in *Logic and Ontology*, ed. Milton K. Munitz (New York: New York University Press, 1973), pp. 287–302; *The Virtues: The Stanton Lectures 1973–74* (Cambridge: Cambridge University Press, 1977), pp. 72–81.

31. A. P. Martinich, "Identity and Trinity," *The Journal of Religion* 58.2 (April 1978): 169–81.

32. Peter van Inwagen, "And Yet They Are Not Three Gods But One God," in *Philosophy and the Christian Faith*, ed. Thomas V. Morris (Notre Dame, Ind.: University of Notre Dame Press, 1988), pp. 241–78.

33. A. P. Martinich, "God, Emperor and Relative Identity," *Franciscan Studies* 39 annual 17 (1979): 180–91.

(6) The Father is the same God as the Son.

When thus interpreted, the contradictions dissolve and the positions of Arius and Sabellius can be rejected. (3′) does not follow from (1), (2), and (5); and (5) and (6) are not contradictory.[34]

Some philosophers, however, have claimed that this use of relative identity logic is merely a delaying tactic. Even when identity is construed relatively the doctrine of the Trinity can be seen to be inconsistent with the addition of two semantic postulates:

(P1) Whatever is God is a person.
(P2) If x and y are the same God and whatever is God is a person, then x is the same person as y.

For (1)–(3), (P1) and (P2) entail

(5′) The Father is the same person as the Son.[35]

The argument to (5′) is valid, and Martinich is already committed to (1)–(3) and (P1), so unless (P2) is false, (5′) follows. It, however, appears to be true. It is an instance of what appears to be a true and more general semantic proposition. This proposition can be symbolized with relative identity predicates:

(SP) For any properties Φ and Ψ and any objects x and y, if x is the same Φ as y and every Φ is a Ψ, then x is the same Ψ as y.

This seems to be true, because there are some instances of it which are clearly true, such as:

If Whiskers is the same cat as Tabitha and every cat is an animal, then Whiskers is the same animal as Tabitha.
If Cicero is the same orator as Tully and every orator is a person, then Cicero is the same person as Tully.

(P2) must be false, given the commitment to (1)–(3), (5), (6), and (P1), if contradiction is to be avoided. Fortunately, (P2) can be rejected without contradiction.[36]

---

34. Ibid., p. 181.
35. Ibid., p. 183.
36. Ibid., pp. 184–85.

Martinich's final move is to show that this claim that there is no contradiction in denying (P2) is plausible, or at least, not implausible, by showing that there is some other concept, which like the concept of the Trinity, would show that (SP) is not true in general. He does this with the concept of emperor, which Tertullian claimed was such a concept.[37]

Tertullian apparently had in mind the Roman Empire under the Antonines. Without dividing the empire, Hadrian adopted as his son Antoninus Pius, who in turn adopted Marcus Aurelius and Ceionius Commodus (Lucius Verus). When Marcus became emperor, he gave Lucius Verus equal rights as emperor. A century later, the Roman Empire had become so unwieldy that it was in danger of collapse or bifurcation. Diocletian appointed Maximian to rule the one empire with him, Diocletian in the East and Maximian in the West. Both men possessed the full power of emperor. Both had absolute power over every person in the empire other than the emperor himself, and each had absolute power over every part of the territory, even though each restricted his actual exercise of power to certain citizens and certain parts of the empire. In this case, Diocletian and Maximian are the same emperor, since there is only one empire and there can be only one emperor for each empire, yet they are not the same person. The analogy with the Trinity is obvious. Martinich states it as follows: "There is a single rule of the universe and a single ruler, God. But there are three persons who possess that rule, the Father, the Son and the unmentioned Holy Spirit. Each person has the full power of rule even though each is a different person."[38]

Martinich is aware of a number of possible objections to his position, and states and responds to three of these. The first is that if two persons are simultaneously emperor, then there are two emperors, for otherwise the distinction between persons is lost. This is hardly a decisive objection, however, for the converse is equally arguable, namely, that if two persons are simultaneously emperor, there are two empires, since the emperor gives unity to the empire. However, since there was only one Roman Empire, there must have been only one emperor; therefore, Diocletian was Maximian. The problem with both the objection and

37. Ibid., p. 185.
38. Ibid., p. 186.

its converse is that both refuse to separate the arithmetic of persons from that of emperors.[39]

A second objection could be that the idea of two persons who are one emperor is incoherent since it gives rise to the possibility of contradictory edicts. If, however, this objection possessed any force, it would apply equally against the view that there could be two emperors at one time, since two emperors could issue contradictory edicts as easily as two persons. The difficulty does not apply only to the possibility of two persons being the same emperor, but also to the possibility of any emperor who can contradict himself.[40] And so, as well, although Martinich does not explicitly say so, if valid it would preclude one person being one emperor.

A third possible objection is that as a matter of fact during the reign of Diocletian there was one empire and two emperors because there were two persons who ruled the empire. Martinich's response is that it is incorrect to say that the two were one emperor, because this is an abuse of the word "emperor." He is not about to dispute the ordinary uses of the words "emperor" and "person," because what is really at issue is whether it is coherent to say that two somethings are one and the same something else. If not allowed to use the word "emperor," he will then coin the word "memperor," defining it such that "something is a memperor just in case it is a person and has absolute rule over all humans within the territory of the empire; and x is the same memperor as y just in case x has absolute rule over all the humans within the territory of the empire and x and y are persons."[41]

Martinich then applies this last point to the question of God. He says we can truly assert the following:

(P2′) For any x and y, if x and y are the same God and every God is a person, then x is a person and y is a person.

But (P2′) in conjunction with (1)–(3) and (P1) does not entail

(5′) The Father is the same person as the Son

39. Ibid., p. 187.
40. Ibid., p. 188.
41. Ibid.

but

(7) The Father is a person and the Son is a person.

This, Martinich insists, is what orthodoxy wants to say.[42]

His final point is that although he has been comparing part of the logic of "God" by comparing it to the logic of "emperor," and the meanings of both involve an office, he is not claiming that the logic of "God" is like the logic of "emperor." This does not mean that both terms in fact mean an office. They might still mean a being, substance, nature, or "whatever you like."[43]

What shall we say in response to this proposed solution to the logical problem? On the one hand, it is certainly the case that identity frequently is relative. In many cases, one thing is the same as another thing in some respect, but not in another. This may therefore be giving us a clue as to the direction in which this endeavor may effectively go. As such, of course, it may simply be a very sophisticated version of the statement that God is one and God is three but that he is not one in the same way or the same respect as he is three.

There are, however, some problems with this. Take the following examples of what presumably would qualify as instances of relative-identity logic:

"The house is the same color as the garage, but it is not the same building."
"Rover is the same species as Sport, but it is not the same animal."
"This church is the same architectural type as that church, but it is not the same structure."
"Juan is the same nationality as Carlos, but he is not the same man."

What these examples show is that the two are members of the same class, but are not identical. Suppose now, we apply this to the case at hand:

"The Father is the same God as the Son, but he is not the same person."

42. Ibid., p. 189.
43. Ibid.

What is to prevent this formula from saying that God is a class, of which the Father and the Son are both members? Perhaps relative-identity logic has succeeded in avoiding Sabellianism and Arianism, but at the cost of losing monotheism.

The problem is also that, as Davis has pointed out, we do not know enough about the logic of the terms "person" and "God" to evaluate the coherence of the statement, "The Father is not the same person as the Son but is the same God as the Son." As he says, the statement, "Ronald Reagan is the same *person* as the president of the United States [which was true when Davis wrote] but is not the same *name* as 'The President of the United States'" is coherent. But the statement, "Ronald Reagan is the same *person* as the president of the United States but is not the same *man* as the president of the United States" is not coherent. The reason we know this is that we know the meaning of the terms "name," "person" (referring to a human person), and "man." We do not, however, understand the logic of the terms "name" and "person" (when applied to God) so as to know whether Martinich's claims are coherent.[44] If Davis's analysis is correct (and I believe it is), then this is the same problem as saying that God is one and God is three but without knowing just what is being referred to in each of these references.

When we look more closely at the example of the two who are the same emperor, the difficulty becomes more sharply focused. Can we really say that the two are one emperor? Or, to put it differently, is it really possible to say of two persons that both have absolute rule over all persons in the empire? Can two persons have absolute rule over the same person? Specifically, can two persons have absolute rule each over himself and each over the other? In what sense is absolute rule absolute, if it is shared with someone else, who presumably could rule differently? There is quite a difference, Martinich notwithstanding, between contradicting oneself and contradicting someone else who also is thought to be an emperor.

Martinich offers some help here, but in the final analysis it does not appear that his position will resolve the difficulty. On the one hand, his view does not preclude tritheism. Each of the per-

44. Davis, *Logic and the Nature of God,* p. 138.

sons is capable of being God without the other, just as each of the emperors would be capable of being emperor without the other. In this respect, there is a difference from the thought of Rahner, for whom being (a mode of being of) God required for each of the persons the relational opposition from the other. It is in this latter issue that we may find a clue to a more adequate logical analysis.

Stephen Davis

A fourth approach is that of Stephen Davis, to whose thought we have already alluded. Davis feels that the treatments by Power, Rahner, and Martinich do not adequately resolve the problem of the relationship between the threeness and the oneness of God. He concludes the discussion of these three attempted resolutions of the problem by saying, "It appears, then, that the doctrine is still mysterious." Although he does not dogmatically hold that the doctrine can never be shown to be coherent, he claims that this has not yet been achieved.[45]

It is not surprising, says Davis, that we find mysteries in the Christian doctrine of God, for we are dealing with a transcendent being who has revealed himself to us. Divine transcendence does not mean that God cannot be coherently described in human language, but that we never fully understand even the true statements that may be made about him. Since we are not ourselves transcendent or infinitely wise, it is obvious that we will not be able to comprehend God with the same skill or insight with which we comprehend rats or pencils or triangles. If God in his essence is unknowable, then perhaps mysteries will inevitably appear even when he reveals himself to us.[46]

The question to which we must now turn, Davis believes, is this: Is there ever any good reason to believe a mystery, such as, in this case, the mystery of the Trinity? That requires first that the term "mystery" be defined. Mystery must be distinguished from contradiction. A contradiction is "an inconsistent statement of the form 'p and not-p,' where there is no suggested or available amplification of the terms in the statement that removes the contradition [sic] or shows that it is only apparent." By contrast, a

45. Ibid., p. 140.
46. Ibid., pp. 140–41.

mystery is "an apparent contradiction which there is good reason to believe." Religious mysteries then are paradoxical religious claims that stretch the mind and are difficult to comprehend, but which (it is claimed) there is good reason to believe.[47]

Is there ever a good reason to believe a mystery? Davis suggests two criteria to apply. First, it is rational to believe a mysterious doctrine only if there is good reason to believe that its contradictory character is only apparent. This means that on amplification one would see that it may be coherent and that its subject matter is something we would expect to be puzzled about, such as God. Second, it is rational to believe a mysterious doctrine only if apart from the question of its coherence we have strong reasons to believe it. This would mean, for example, that there is good reason to believe it was revealed by God, or that it makes the best available sense of other statements that one has good reason to believe.[48]

What then about the doctrine of the Trinity? How does it measure against these criteria? In terms of the first, Davis insists that although we do not have apt categories for explaining how God can be three-and-one, we can legitimately describe God as being one when considered as a certain sort of thing and three when considered as another sort of thing. This is enough to believe that what we are dealing with here is not a contradiction but a mystery.[49]

In terms of the second criterion, people may rationally believe a mystery if the mysterious doctrine makes the best available sense of other statements that they have good reason to believe, or if they have reason to believe that the doctrine was revealed by God. Davis believes this criterion is satisfied in the case of the Trinity. Christians have good reason, namely, the belief that God has revealed them, for believing that the Father is God, the Son is God, the Holy Spirit is God; the Father is not the Son, and the Son is not the Holy Spirit, and the Holy Spirit is not the Father; and there is one and only one God. So, unless they can find a better way of understanding God's self-revelation, they have no choice but to affirm these propositions and thus the doctrine of

47. Ibid., p. 141.
48. Ibid., pp. 142–43.
49. Ibid., p. 143.

the Trinity. In terms of the part about revelation, Christians claim to have good reason to believe that God is three-in-one because they believe that God has revealed that he is three-in-one. While it may be debated whether the Bible and the Christian tradition are correct, Christians believe that this has been revealed, and this is enough for them to be judged rational.[50]

Davis has examined the major contemporary explanations, and, having found them not to accomplish what they claim to do, has been honest in acknowledging that he feels he is dealing with a mystery. In so doing, he has perhaps been more candid than many of us, who when pressed may have to admit that we really do not know in what way God is one and in what different way he is three. Davis's distinction between contradiction and mystery is a helpful one. And his contention that something is not mysterious if it makes the best sense of other tenets that we have good reason for believing is a suggestion that may well stand us in good stead later.

There, are, however, some points of reservation. Davis is not dogmatic when he affirms simply that the attempts he has examined do not remove the mysterious element, not that no possible attempt could do so. Nonetheless, one would hope that he would endeavor to formulate some alternative approach. In other words, perhaps he has not yet exhausted the various alternatives and so has opted for mystery prematurely. Even if we cannot possibly understand God fully, have we yet understood all that might be understood?

Another point of concern deals with Davis's contention that the three-in-oneness of God has been revealed. If what he is saying is that the elements from which the doctrine is inferred, or even from which it is constructed, have been revealed, that is one thing. To say that the doctrine has been revealed is a bit too strong, however, at least with respect to the biblical revelation. This is a point at which Davis really should offer some specific indication of the locus of that revelation.

Catherine LaCugna

One more stance on the issue is found in the thought of Catherine LaCugna. Although she has concentrated on the doc-

50. Ibid., pp. 143–44.

trine of the Trinity and has authored a major work on the Trinity, her primary contribution to the discussion of the logic of the Trinity is found in a 1986 journal article.[51] Her major purpose in the article is to show how philosophers and theologians might be brought into a mutually beneficial conversation regarding the Trinity. This she proposes to do through a systematic theologian's critique of the recent philosophical literature on the Trinity.[52]

LaCugna believes she detects two basic variations on the analytic approach to the doctrine of the Trinity in the existing literature. The first is represented by Michael Durrant, who proceeds by analyzing Augustine's statement that God is three persons of (or in) one substance.[53] While it is customary to assume that the major philosophical influence on the Greek fathers was Plato and the Stoics, Durrant believes the influence of Aristotle should not be overlooked. He considers their use of Aristotle illegitimate. By a *reductio ad absurdum* he shows that God cannot be a substance in Aristotle's sense. Thus, statements such as "of one substance" are nonsensical and can have no place in trinitarian discussion. Nor will it help to take "substance" to be an analogical term, and then rely on the univocal/analogical distinction to safeguard the discourse. Analogy applies only to ordinary first-order predicates, not to predicates signifying categories, which is what substance is. Consequently, Durrant concludes that "no intelligible account can be offered of the Trinitarian formula and hence of the doctrine of the trinity."[54]

As the second variety, LaCugna considers together the thought of Stephen Davis and A. P. Martinich. She sees both attempting to defend the doctrine of the Trinity on the basis of first-order predicate logic. Martinich employs the concept of relative identity, while Davis contends that the doctrine of the Trinity is a mystery, but one that we are justified in believing.[55]

LaCugna's first response is that logical analysis of the types

---

51. Catherine Mowry LaCugna, "Philosophers and Theologians on the Trinity," *Modern Theology* 2.3 (April 1986): 169-81.
52. Ibid., p. 169.
53. Michael Durrant, *Theology and Intelligibility* (Boston: Routledge & Kegan Paul, 1973).
54. Ibid., p. 195.
55. LaCugna, "Philosophers and Theologians," pp. 170–71.

she is examining fails to take account of the historical nature of human statements and theological doctrines. The passages these philosophers have chosen to deal with have been taken out of their historical context. So Durrant, collapsing the entire trinitarian tradition into its Augustinian form, is quite unjustified in his statement that "no intelligible account can be offered of the doctrine of the Trinity."[56]

At least Durrant has taken a specific historical formulation of the doctrine. Davis and Martinich, on the other hand, have taken a paragraph of Augustine's and represented it formally. La-Cugna, however, doubts whether these philosophers have succeeded in capturing the logical form of Augustine's statement. This is especially true of Davis's formulation, which is probably not Augustine's or anyone else's theological position. Her criticism of these two statements follows much the same contour as that of Durrant's view: that these fail to understand that the exegesis of dogmatic or theological statements requires setting them within their own particular history. This would require understanding that Augustine wrote his *De Trinitate* over a sixteen-year span, as well as understanding the polemical tone of the time. Further, there should be some appreciation shown for the fact that Augustine does not comprise the entire trinitarian tradition or orthodoxy.[57]

There is, however, another sense in which history is important. The original subject matter of trinitarian theology was the acts of God in history, not ontology. This, of course, fits well with LaCugna's identification of the immanent and the economic Trinities. It is here that the analyses of Davis and Martinich fail to capture the logical form of trinitarian statements, for historicity is one of the logical entailments of trinitarian assertions. Whereas some other kinds of statements, such as the Liar Paradox, can be understood without knowledge of context or of its history, this simply is not true of trinitarian statements.[58]

LaCugna also sees "a kind of naive theological fideism" underlying Davis's argument. His definition of mystery is better a definition of paradox. Mystery means to theologians the compre-

---

56. Ibid., p. 172.
57. Ibid., pp. 172–73.
58. Ibid., p. 173.

hensibility of God. Doctrines therefore are not mysteries, but simply doctrines, that is, human formulations meant to shed light on religious experience. Christians, strictly speaking, do not "believe in" doctrines, only in God. They merely assent to doctrines, insofar as they elucidate and helpfully articulate experience. This equivocation then also leads Davis to state inaccurately that Christians believe that the doctrine was revealed and therefore should be believed. This, however, reveals a lack of sufficient sensitivity to the essential historicity of all human statements, including biblical ones. Even if one appeals to divine assistance, such as through biblical inspiration or ecclesiastical indefectibility, this amounts to special pleading, exempting one class of statements from historical conditioning.[59]

LaCugna's final criticism of these philosophical analyses is that they fail to take full account of the unique nature of doctrinal statements. In particular, they often overlook the fact that theological language, arising as it does out of religious language, often retains the very images, metaphors, and symbols employed by the religion. The more poetic language is often "wrenched from its narrative context" and carefully qualified in order to be utilized in theological theorizing. An example would be the use of the New Testament metaphor of divine fatherhood.[60]

By way of concluding, LaCugna indicates two areas where she thinks the conversation between theology and philosophy might most fruitfully be conducted. She states initially, however, that there can be no real advance in understanding so long as the doctrine of the Trinity is reduced to a puzzle of the sort, "How can three be one?" Rather, there must be an understanding that relation has priority over person. The very nature of God is to be related, and it is only in this sense appropriate to add that God is personal. The second point is that in the final analysis, theology is not merely analytical, but constructive. Therefore the conversation between philosophers and theologians that she advocates could be a forum for entertaining new constructive proposals developed in both fields.[61]

Theologians and philosophers, then, have quite a bit to say to

59. Ibid., p. 175.
60. Ibid., p. 176.
61. Ibid., pp. 177–78.

each other, LaCugna concludes. Theologians can counterbalance the philosophers' discourse that tends toward the ahistorical by an emphasis on soteriological rootedness and historical conscientiousness. Philosophers can challenge theologians to be more precise in their formulations, and more consistent in the systematization of history, exegesis, doctrine, and theology. Such a joint dialogue might even have the effect of restoration of a doctrine that "for too long has only been collecting dust on the shelves of church history."[62]

How, then, shall we respond to LaCugna's statement? There is certainly benefit in her observation regarding the historical context of any doctrinal formulation, and of the fact that an entire tradition cannot be evaluated by examining one instance of it. Yet, having said this, there are certain reservations that need to be expressed.

First, there seems to be here something of one of the very characteristics and actions that LaCugna criticizes. Just as the philosophers mentioned may be guilty of treating one theological formulation, that of Augustine, as representative of all trinitarian thinking, so LaCugna speaks for theology without showing sensitivity to its variegated character. The tenets that she advances, such as the priority of history over ontology and of relation over person, are not universally held among theologians, to say the least. Yet she proceeds without really justifying the particular stance that she takes and advocates.

Second, there seems to be a lack of regard for true theological dialogue. LaCugna rejects the approach of treating the doctrine of the Trinity as some sort of puzzle over how God can be both three and one. This may be satisfactory if the doctrine is intended only for theologians, or even only for Christians. In the wider intellectual world, the issue of the Trinity most certainly is the logical puzzle. Unless theology is to be a monological activity rather than truly dialogical, unless it is to be pure didache rather than also kerygma, it must grapple with these issues that those outside the context are raising. To fail to do so will be to concede by default the charges that those outside level against Christian theology.

62. Ibid., pp. 178–79.

This is seen in LaCugna's own theology. Although she rejects the purely analytical approach to problems, arguing that theology must be constructive as well, she does not really contribute much to the constructive treatment of the problem raised here. She has, in her major work, given considerable attention to the question of relations. The constructive dimension of the relationship of the one to the three is largely bypassed, however.

Finally, this tendency is seen in the article itself. If the purpose of the article is to show how philosophers and theologians can be brought into a constructive dialogue, there should probably be a more extensive statement about what theology can learn from philosophy. There seems to be a striking absence of listening, or of indication of listening, to the criticisms of theology some philosophers offer. Rather, because of the extended criticisms of the philosophers and the statements about what they could derive from theology, one gains the impression that the interchange is a one-way street, that in practice LaCugna has not really learned much from philosophy.

This in itself is a form of begging the question. For the issue seems to be whether entities like the doctrine of the Trinity are the exclusive possession of theology or of philosophy, or whether they fall into a domain that is common to the two endeavors. Virtually by stipulation LaCugna seems to feel that her discipline is better equipped to deal with the doctrine. An example is her rejection of Davis's use of the term "mystery," even though he has disavowed any claim that his analysis of mystery reflects the use of the term in ordinary language or even all uses of the term in theology.[63] The issue actually is which usage is to be followed in such a discussion. And closely related to that is the question of whether there can be translation from the categories of one discipline to those of another. Is there indeed something lost or distorted in translating from the language of religion to that of theology or philosophy, or may something be gained thereby? And should the language of theology be closer to that of religion than to that of philosophy? These are questions that can only be settled by careful analysis and argumentation, not by stipulation.

---

63. Davis, *Logic and the Nature of God*, p. 141.

An Alternative Approach

We have now examined five different approaches to the logic of the Trinity. While each has had certain points to commend it to us, we have also found significant shortcomings in each. It is not enough, however, to survey these options. We must now offer some alternative, which exceeds in its efficacy the five that we have examined and at least partially rejected.

As we noted in the chapter on metaphysics, it is most helpful to think of God as being like an organism. The Godhead is to be thought of less as a unity, in the sense of oneness of simplicity, than as a union, involving three persons, Father, Son, and Holy Spirit. Without each of these, God would not be. Each is essential to the life of the whole. God could not exist simply as Father, or as Son, or as Holy Spirit. Nor could he exist as Father and Son, as Father and Spirit, or as Son and Spirit, without the third of these persons in that given case. Further, none of these could exist without being part of the Trinity. There would be no basis of life, apart from this union. Thus, in speaking of union, there should be no inference combining that which antecedently existed, prior to coming together. None has the power of life within itself alone. Each can only exist as part of the Triune God.

This means that each of the persons of the Trinity is essential to the whole. Beyond that, each is essential to each of the others. It is not simply that each would not be what it is without the other, as if it (he) could exist without the others, but would be different from what it is. It simply could not be, without being part of this. Another way of putting it is that God could not be and not be triune. The triune nature of God is essential to his very being. He could not exist as something other than the Trinity. He could not be God, and could not even be, without being triune.

How then shall we express the grammar of this concept? It is important to note some of the different uses of the copula, "to be," which in the third person singular is, "is." There is the "is" of identity. This is used to express terms or concepts that are equivalent. To put it another way, they are members of one-member classes, which are then linked together. They are invertible sentences. An example would be, "Mr. Bill Clinton is the president of the United States." That sentence is invertible: "The president of the United States is Mr. Bill Clinton." Each of these is unique.

There is only one Bill Clinton (at least this one, as sufficiently defined and delimited). And there is, at any given time, only one president of the United States. This would not, however, be true of the usage of "is" in a sentence like, "The president of the United States is a man." That cannot be inverted to, "A man is the president of the United States." In one sense of the sentence, of course, it is true, as saying that some male human being, rather than a female, or some other kind of being or object, is president. In the more general sense, however, it is not true that a man is president of the United States, for there are innumerable men who are not president of the United States. This use is therefore, an instance of the "is" of inclusion. The president of the United States is a member of the class of objects known as "man."

There is a third use of "is," that of predication or attribution. When we say, "That car is blue," we are not stating the "is" of identity, for blue is a color, not an automobile. Nor are we including it in a class of things, for the same reason. "Blue" is not a noun; it is an adjective. If, of course, one happens to be a Platonist, then there is no difference between predication and instantiation, or inclusion in a class, and the distinction breaks down, but Platonism is not the intellectual underpinning of most ordinary language conversation. Rather, we are predicating some quality of the subject. In effect, we are saying, "That car is bluish."

Now let us apply this logic to the question of the Trinity. We may say, "God is God," using the "is" of identity. It will be more apparent, if we use another term, such as "Jehovah." When we say, "Jehovah is God," as the people of Israel did after the demonstration of his power at Mount Carmel (1 Kings 18:39), we are doing something of this type. What we are saying is, "Jehovah is the true and living God." This statement is invertible: "The true and living God is Jehovah." We may also speak of the three persons together by use of this "is" of identity. We may say, "The Father, the Son, and the Holy Spirit are God." This is an invertible proposition: "God is the Father, the Son, and the Holy Spirit."

When, however, we speak of the individual members of the Trinity we are working with a different use of "is." When we say, for example, "The Father is God," we are not using the "is" of identity. If that were the case, we would be saying, "The Father equals God." It is not invertible to say, "God is (or equals) the Father." For if that were true, then when we say, "The Son is God," and "The Holy Spirit is God," we would be saying, "The Son equals God," and "The Holy Spirit equals God." When we invert them, we would have "God is the Father," "God is the Son," and "God is the Holy Spirit," which would clearly lead us into the type of contradiction that the doctrine of the Trinity is thought to represent.

Rather, when we speak of each of these persons individually and use the predicate "God," we are using the "is" of predication. What we are actually saying, then, is "The Father is divine," "the Son is divine," and "the Holy Spirit is divine." Because of the rather diffused meaning of "divine" in the English language, and in theology where it has been used in a weaker sense than "deity," the preferred statements may be "The Father is deity," and so forth, so long as one understands that this is the "is" of predication, rather than identity or inclusion. As we noted in an earlier chapter, in terms of the interpretation, as contrasted with the translation, of the clause "the Word was God" in John 1:1, this is not asserting an identity of "Word" and "God," any more than we are asserting the identity of "the car" and "blue" when we say, "that car is blue."

But what of the other dimension of logic, the more general question of the usage of language? Here we should set the question of meaning within a semiotic or general theory of signs. The layout of this developed by Charles Morris, which is actually something of an adaptation of the view of Charles Saunders Pierce,[64] is quite helpful. This has also been adopted and used, with some modifications, by Frederick Ferré.[65] According to this scheme, there are three dimensions of meaning. The pragmatic dimension is the relationship of a sign to a knower. It affects the person relating to it. The syntactic dimension is the relationship of one sign to another within a set of signs. The semantic dimension is the relationship of a sign to its referent or object. There are criteria for assessing the efficacy of each of these dimensions.

64. Charles Morris, *Signification and Significance: A Study of the Relations of Signs and Values* (Cambridge, Mass.: MIT Press, 1964).
65. Frederick Ferré, *Language Logic and God* (New York: Harper, 1961); and *Basic Modern Philosophy of Religion* (New York: Scribners, 1967).

For example, with respect to the syntactic dimension, the criteria are internal to the set or system of signs. These include consistency, or the absence of any formal contradiction between the signs. The other major internal criterion is coherence, or the positive relatedness between signs or even the implication of one sign by another. The criteria of the semantic dimension are applicability and adequacy. Applicability is the degree to which a sign or set of signs "rings true" to experience, or to some other source of knowledge. Adequacy is the degree to which the set of signs integrates the largest possible set of data within the sphere of relevant data, and with the least distortion, or more positively, with the most accurate rendition.

This means that there need not necessarily in every case be a demonstration of the reality or veridical nature of the semantic dimension. Thus, for example, in a worldview it may not be possible to show the empirical correspondence of each tenet or element of that view to a protocol sense experience. It should however be logically connected, as by inference, with data that are so demonstrable, so that the worldview as a whole fits the sense data better than any competitor.

The status of the propositions forming the doctrine of the Trinity is not that they can be shown directly, either from Scripture or from experience. They are, however, a part of a coherent whole, which can be shown to fit well and integrate and explain well the data that it is called on to tie together. As a necessary (or at least the best available) explanation of the data of biblical revelation, this doctrine is meaningful. It has this meaningfulness in much the same way as the tenets of a broad scientific synthesis. The content of that theory, general as it is, cannot be verified or explicated by direct correlation with sensory data, on a one-to-one basis. The overarching synthesis, however, best integrates and explains the specific data, whose protocol sentences make up the synthesis or theory.

But what of the matter of understanding the referent of these concepts? We have said, for example, that God is three and that he is one, and that his threeness is with respect to a different aspect than his oneness. How can we grasp the referents of these terms? How can we ascertain that they really refer to anything objective?

It is the contention of the view of religious language with which we are working that the assertions of its declarative sentences do indeed refer to something objective. That is to say, they are not merely expressions of some inward state or attitude of the speaker, but are actually referring to some objective state of affairs in the nature of things. How, however, can we explicate this?

While the propositions of theology refer to actual dimensions of the nature of God, those are not dimensions that can be "unpacked" empirically, in some straightforward, one-to-one fashion. Rather, the role of religious language is to evoke discernment, and here as well, the use of symbols, figures of speech, analogies, and other devices is needed to help bring about the discernment of what is objectively present.

This role of language can be seen in other areas. The symbols employed in algebra and other branches of mathematics refer to actual reality, relationships among signs that actually obtain. Yet it is not easy to make that meaning clear in a simple fashion. The discernment of the pattern has to take place. Thus, some students understand and are able to solve an algebra problem relatively easily. They can discern the relationships that are present. Others, however, do not recognize those genuine relationships so easily. There is relatively little that can be done in a direct way to explain the problem to them. Attempted explanations are offered, with the hope that somehow they will "see." Once understanding takes place, once the pupil learns to solve the problem, it is apparent to him or her that this is real meaning that has been obtained. The meaning is there, but it is not readily obvious on the surface.

So it is with the objects of religious language, and for our purposes specifically, with the meaning of the Trinity. It simply is not possible to explain it unequivocally. What must be done is to offer a series, a whole assortment of illustrations and analogies, with the hope that some discernment will take place. We must approach the matter from various angles, "nibbling at the meaning" of the doctrine, as it were. To do that goes beyond the scope of this chapter, so that this discussion must be supplemented by that in the chapter on metaphysics, but we wish to offer at least a couple of analogies that should provide some minimal degree of insight into the formal structure of the doctrine.

Let us think first of a human person. His body is made up of many parts, but for our purposes here, we shall think of those as just three: the brain, the heart, and the lungs. Without any one of these, of course, he would not live. He would not be a human; he would simply be a cadaver, assuming one of the attributes of a human being is life. We could say that he is human being. He is a member of that class, but suppose that there had been a nuclear holocaust of which he is the sole survivor, so that he were the only human being, the only member of that class. We could then say that it was an identity statement. "Bill is human being" could be inverted to be "Human being is Bill." Each of the three organs mentioned, brain, heart, and lungs, is also human, for they are not organs belonging to or derived from any other species. Yet they are not human in the same sense, for they are not individually a human being. They are human adjectivally or predicatively. "This brain is human" is to predicate a quality of it. Collectively they form an organism, a composite of parts that is more than a collection. Each depends on the other, and each is essential to the life of the other and of the organism. Apart from the organism, this is not a human heart. It is a dead organ, which used to be a heart. Without each of the other organs, none of these organs would really be such an organ. Each is essential to the other two and each is dependent on the other two. Each is human, so long as in union with the other two, but together the three, the organism, is a human, a human being. Note that I said the three is, rather than the three are, for together they constitute a new entity, a single being, which is more than the sum of the parts.

Now let us think of another example, drawn from human relations. A couple, Hans and Bertha, fall in love. In this relationship, something happens to them, changing their personalities when they are together. Whereas each was rather shy and introverted, the joy of their love draws them out of themselves. In relationship to each other and even to other persons when they are together, they are happy, sociable, and outgoing. When they marry, rather than retaining the name of one or of compounding their names into one, they choose to take a new name, indicating that a new entity, a new reality, has come into existence. They call themselves the "Zweieinigers." They are the only persons in the world with such a name. They are unique. There is a remark-able quality of their love, their joy when together, their unselfish concern for one another. Over the years of their marriage, the name "Zweieiniger" comes to stand for a virtual quality of the re-lationship of the two to each other. People in their village say of married couples who are to some degree of this same closeness, "Sie sind fast zweieinigerlich" ("They are almost zweieiniger-ish"). It is an expression of the fact that these two people emulate the quality of being one flesh that the Bible speaks about with re-spect to husband and wife. Hans and Bertha together can be said to be Zweieiniger. That is an identity statement, for they are the only such couple in the world. They may each also be said to be zweieinigerlich. Yet each is that only because of the other, and the unique entity known as Zweieiniger only exists because of both of them. Were one of them to die, the other would presum-ably continue to bear that name, but the reality of Zweieiniger, that entity that consisted of the two of them, would cease to exist, and the one remaining person would no longer be zweieiniger-lich, for that quality is only present when there are the two of them, in relationship with each other.

It may also be necessary, in order to convey the unusual mean-ing involved in this doctrine, to utilize what analytical philoso-phers would term "logically odd language." This means using language in such a way as intentionally to commit grammatical errors. Thus, I have sometimes said of the Trinity, "He are three," or "They is one." For we have here a being whose nature falls out-side our usual understanding of persons, and that nature can per-haps only be adequately expressed by using language that calls attention to the almost paradoxical character of the concepts.

12

The Triune God
of All People

We have noted in a previous chapter the problem that the doctrine of the Trinity creates for persons of a feminist bent. Because the Trinity is composed of three persons, at least two of whom are identified as masculine in nature, women have no one to identify with. The spiritual qualities set up as ideals are those of the masculine gender. Furthermore, the Trinity has frequently been used to justify patriarchalism and hierarchicalism. Women have been made to feel that they are inherently less than men. So, for many feminists, both women and men, the Trinity seems incompatible with their fundamental experience.

There are other persons, however, who do not see the problem as quite this intractable. While the doctrine of the Trinity as traditionally construed creates difficulty for the feminist consciousness, that is not the only way that the doctrine can be approached. There are ways of understanding or of stating the doctrine that enable it to coexist with the basic feminist outlook. It is to these persons that we now turn, to see whether the problem is insuperable.

Desexing the Persons

The first group of persons is those who seek to desex (or degender) the persons of the Trinity. These individuals decline to use the usual terms of Father, Son, and Holy Spirit, or at least to use them as they have usually been used. Rather, if employed, they must be used in connection with other balancing terms, such as God as Father combined with God as Mother, or sometimes simply, "Father-Mother God." The images evoked by these terms are thus frequently quite different from those that have traditionally been evoked by the names for the Trinity. Among the most common are God the Creator, God the Redeemer (or Revealer), and God the Sanctifier (or Sustainer). These names are gender-neutral, and thus do not cause the sort of offense that the earlier terms do.

One who has given some concerted attention to this problem and to the solution to the problem is Sally McFague. Her approach must be set within the context of her understanding of theology as metaphorical. She thus rejects the approach of fundamentalism, which identifies the Word of God with human words, specifically, the words of the canonical Scriptures of the church. The essence of metaphorical theology, however, is the refusal to identify human constructions with divine reality.[1] Since a metaphor is a word or phrase drawn from one context but used in another, it cannot be applied univocally, that is, in the form of identity. To say, then, "God is mother," is not to identify God with mother, but to see him as having some of the characteristics associated with mothering. It would be preferable to say, "God *as* mother," viewing God in the role, capacity, or character of mother.[2]

On the opposite extreme we find deconstruction, which insists that there is nothing but metaphor. McFague notes Jacques Derrida's statement that "there is nothing outside the text," which also includes author and referent. There is only the play of words, interpretation upon interpretation, referring to nothing but other words, an endless spiral with no beginning or end. There is, in deconstruction, nothing but metaphor, for there is no conventional or literal context for a word or phrase.[3]

The major correct point that the deconstructionists are making, says McFague, is that all constructions are metaphorical,

1. Sally McFague, *Models of God: Theology for an Ecological, Nuclear Age* (Philadelphia: Fortress, 1987), p. 22.
2. Ibid., pp. 22–23.
3. Ibid., pp. 23–24.

that we never experience reality "raw." There is no way behind our constructions to test them for correspondence with the reality they claim to represent. She does believe, however, that constructions have a twofold relationship with reality, which deconstruction ignores. They are productive of reality, that is, they are redescriptions of what lies outside of them, in place of old or conventional descriptions or readings. They also are intended to be better than those that they replace or refute.[4] To say this is a very difficult thing, for how does one assess such adequacy? The most one can do is to "live within" a construction, testing it for "its disclosive power, its ability to address and cope with the most pressing issues of one's day, its comprehensiveness and coherence, its potential for dealing with anomalies, and so forth."[5]

McFague then proposes to seek for constructions that one may live within and that meet these tests she has enumerated. In so doing, one must always keep in mind the metaphorical character of all such constructions. And, one must understand the nature of the sources. The Bible is not to be taken as some literal rendition of God's communication to us. It is a case study, a prototype, or a prime Christian classic. It is composed of a number of persons and communities witnessing to the transforming power of God in their lives, interpreted in terms of their own time rather than some past time.[6]

As she examines the paradigmatic story of Jesus of Nazareth, McFague finds a distinctive feature in the appearance stories. She follows those scholars who understand the resurrection primarily in terms of a promise of the continued presence of God with us. The resurrection is a way of saying that God continues to be present in Jesus in the world.[7]

The traditional view of the resurrection does not fulfill the criterion of God being present to everyone. It is only the elect who will be resurrected in the future. The idea of a bodily translation of some persons to another world is a mythology that is no longer credible to us. Suppose, however, that instead of taking it in this literal fashion we were to speak of it as "the promise of God to be

4. Ibid., p. 26.
5. Ibid., p. 27.
6. Ibid., p. 43.
7. Ibid., p. 59.

permanently present, 'bodily' present to us, in all places and times in our world." What if we experimented with the metaphor of the universe as God's "body"? This would allow for a palpable presence of God in all space and time.[8]

McFague suggests that the older metaphor of the world as the realm of King God be replaced. This metaphor carries royalist, triumphalist images, such as God as king, lord, ruler, and patriarch, which are inappropriate. Other metaphors that suggest mutuality, interdependence, caring, and responsiveness will be needed. Thinking of the world as God's body means that it is not something foreign or alien to him. If it is expressive of God's very being, then how would he respond to it, and how should we? The metaphors of parents, lovers, and friends are suggestive, carrying the implications of creation, nurture, passionate concern, attraction, respect, support, cooperation, and mutuality.[9] Rejecting the metaphor of God as king, McFague explores the models of mother, lover, and friend.

When McFague concludes her endeavor she notes that she has used exactly three models for God, and that they conveniently fall into the categories of creator, savior, and sustainer. Thus, they take the place of the most ancient and revered names of the trinitarian God, namely, Father, Son, and Holy Spirit. This, she acknowledges, is no mere coincidence but a deliberate attempt to show that the older terms can be replaced with other terms, even though this is a byproduct rather than the primary goal of the endeavor. This, however, is not an attempt to set up a new Trinity. That would make the mistake of failing to see that all constructions are metaphorical.[10] In light of the nature of theology as McFague has depicted it here, "a trinity is not necessary nor should the divine nature be in any way circumscribed by it."[11] She does see a trinity fitting well with the models of her experiment, and finds a pattern of three as expressing appropriately the unity, separation, and reunification that have been the central theme of her experiment. Here she recognizes and admits the presence in her thought of similarities to the views of

8. Ibid., p. 60.
9. Ibid., pp. 61–62.
10. Ibid., pp. 181–82.
11. Ibid., p. 184.

Hegel and Tillich, although for more modest reasons than theirs.[12]

It becomes immediately apparent that McFague's proposal really will not serve our purposes. Any Trinity in the older ontological sense has been lost. There may be an economic Trinity of sorts, but there really is no immanent Trinity. Thus, McFague's discussion so redefines Trinity as to become subject to the same problems as the Hegelian view.

Is this, however, too severe an assessment to level at all efforts to refer to God by other names than Father, Son, and Holy Spirit? What of those who wish to maintain basically a trinitarian conception, but want to replace the names, Father, Son, and Holy Spirit with more genderless ones, such as Creator, Redeemer, and Sanctifier? Is this a viable possibility? Did not, after all, even such a champion of an ontological Trinity as Augustine use language of this type? Among his most well known terms were that of the Trinity as love, lover, and object of love; of sun, light, and ray. And Karl Barth used images of Revealer, Revelation, and Revealedness. One difference that immediately comes to mind is that Augustine was using these images as illustrations of what God is like, rather than as actual qualities or names for God.

Donald Bloesch has undertaken a major treatment of this type of approach in his book, *The Battle for the Trinity*.[13] The immediate occasion of his treatise was the proposals by a number of denominations of inclusive language lectionaries, but the topic treated in his book is considerably broader. He notes that some of this concern comes from the simple desire to avoid use of masculine pronouns for God. For example, he had written in a manuscript, "God reveals himself," which the copy editor changed to "God is revealed." Here is an example of a change that does not merely alter the gender, but by changing the expression from a reflexive to a passive use of the verb, "reveal," makes a much larger theological change in the bargain.[14] Other terms, seeking to avoid the gender-linked "Father" and "Son," either intention-

12. Ibid., pp. 184, 224, n. 6.
13. Donald G. Bloesch, *The Battle for the Trinity: The Debate over Inclusive God Language* (Ann Arbor, Mich.: Servant, 1985).
14. Ibid., p. 45.

ally or unwittingly fall into the error of making God overly transcendent or exclusively immanent, using respectively the terminology of deism (Divine Providence, Source of Sustenance, and
Cosmic Benefactor); or of process theology (Creative Process, Divine Eros, Creativity, Directive of History, Absolute Relatedness,
Creative Transformation, Creative Event, Principle of Concre-
tion, and Growth in Qualitative Meaning). In either case, the effect is that of depersonalization.[15] Depersonalization, it should
be noted, can come from either excessive transcendence or excessive immanence. God may be so far removed that we cannot
relate to him, or so involved and present within everything that
we cannot relate to him in any distinct fashion, apart from
merely relating to everything that is.

There are further problems with such an approach. One is that
in addition to changes such as that involved in "God reveals himself" there are other alterations of the status of one or more members of the Trinity. For example, by substituting "the Human One"
for "the Son of Man," the National Council of Churches' lectionary
changes from an honorific title, Jesus' favorite title for himself,
which, based on the background of Daniel, indicates a supernatural being, one that is a model of authentic selfhood.[16] The nature
or quality of divine acts is affected by this type of change in terminology as well. Letty Russell has suggested use of the terms "Creator, Christ, and Spirit." Lutheran theologian Martha Stortz, however, responds that "It would be easy for a 'Creator' to sacrifice a
'Christ.' Perhaps the category of 'sacrifice' would not even apply.
It would not be so easy for a Father to sacrifice a Son."[17]

Some of the terminology seriously obscures the relationship of
humans to God. In the desire to do away with terminology that
suggests domination, some have brought God into a relationship
basically of equality. Virginia Mollenkott, for example, who at
one time identified herself as an evangelical, says that the relationship is to be characterized by "mutuality," "reciprocity," and
"parallelism."[18] This, however, comments Bloesch, "denies that

15. Ibid.
16. Ibid., p. 46.
17. Martha E. Stortz, "The Mother, the Son, and the Bulrushes: The Church and Feminist Theology," *Dialog* 23 (Winter 1984): 25.
18. Virginia Ramey Mollenkott, *The Divine Feminine: The Biblical Imagery of God as
Female* (New York: Crossroad, 1983), p. 37.

God is over us before he is with us and for us. God is friend, to be sure, but he is Master before he is friend."[19]

Some types of language not only do not include enough about God; they also do not exclude enough. So, for example, some of the language about God as mother fails to exclude sufficiently Goddess religion. Even as staunch a feminist as Paul King Jewett reminded us that the doctrine of the virgin birth not only affirmed that Jesus had no earthly father, but also that he had no heavenly mother (in contrast to the surrounding pagan religion of the time).[20]

Probably the most serious danger of this type of language, even when used by those who hold to an ontological Trinity, is that it tends to substitute what God does for what he is. The traditional formula of Father, Son, and Holy Spirit refers to the persons of God, or who he is. Such terms as Creator, Redeemer, and Sanctifier, on the other hand, describe activities of God. Thus we have the substitution of functional language for language of ontology, or references to the economic Trinity rather than the immanent Trinity. But this is language of three activities, not three relationships within the Godhead. As such, it lays itself open to the danger of modalism, although it would diligently avoid the monarchianism that motivated Sabellius and others.[21] Although the more conservative persons who choose to use this language are careful to correlate these names with specific persons of the Trinity, the transition from three persons, each of which has this distinctive role, to one person who performs three roles is fairly easily done, and there seem to be inadequate safeguards against that in this nomenclature.

This can also lead to the opposite error. If a given work is identified with one person and not the others, an excessive separation of the three persons may occur. To be sure, these works are primarily the activity of one of these persons, but not exclusively so. The Father is the primary agent in creation, but the Son and the Spirit were also involved (e.g., Gen. 1:2; John 1:3). If the work of creation is restricted to the first person of the Trinity, we may have a type of separation that denies any sort of perichoresis.

19. Bloesch, *Battle*, p. 53.
20. Paul King Jewett, *The Ordination of Women* (Grand Rapids: Eerdmans, 1980), p. 53.
21. Bloesch, *Battle*, pp. 50–51.

There also is a tendency toward depersonalization here. "The one who creates" is considerably less personal and intimate than "Father" or "Daddy." And "Divine Parent," being less concrete and specific than "Heavenly Father," also tends to lose some of the warmth and intimacy of that name.

In short, then, while the approach of substituting nongender names for those of Father and Son has certain values, when properly used, there are both implicit and inherent dangers. While this is preferable to Goddess religion and the Quaternity, it solves the problem at potentially too great a cost. In this respect, it is like modalism, which solved the logical problem of the Trinity but at the cost of denying or at least ignoring major portions of Scripture that showed two or more persons of the Trinity simultaneously present, acting and interacting with one another. While we are somewhat closer to the solution of the problem, we must look still further.

God as Neither Male Nor Female

The best help will come from recognizing that God is neither male nor female, and that the qualities of femininity as well as masculinity apply to him. This, however, requires some discussion of the meaning of sex and gender. Sex is a function of a biological character. This, presumably, God as a spirit, does not have. There is some indication that redeemed and glorified human beings will not have such, either, in the resurrection. Jesus was approached by the Sadducees, a group of Jews who believed that there was to be no resurrection. They sought to engage him in a *reductio ad absurdum*, about a woman whose husband had died. In keeping with the best tradition of levirate marriage, the next brother married her, then died, and so on, until a total of seven brothers had married her. "Now," asked the Sadducees, "whose wife will she be in the resurrection?" Jesus answered, "Those who are considered worthy of taking part in that age and in the resurrection from the dead will neither marry nor be given in marriage, and they can no longer die; for they are like the angels" (Luke 20:35–36). Jesus may, of course, simply have been saying that there will not be such institutions as marriage in heaven. It seems quite likely that he was alluding to much more radical discontinuities in heaven than some would think. It may be that the biological phenomenon of sex is completely left behind.

Gender, however, is a set of characteristics or qualities. These may be a function of physical factors or of conditioning. There is some evidence that hormones have considerable influence on gender. Masculine and feminine gender characteristics are not mutually exclusive, in terms of their presence in a person, being more a matter of degree or of relative presence. Rather, in any given individual they are like two overlapping bell-shaped curves.

In the strict sense, neither sex nor gender applies to God. Yet some of the qualities of personality that are associated with one gender or the other are both found in him. The imagery of both the masculine and the feminine is represented in him.

We may examine the data found in both the Old and New Testaments that shed light on this matter. In the Old Testament, the dominant imagery is of God as Father, with the accompanying masculine qualities ordinarily associated with fathers. Yet pictures of the feminine are also found. For example, in Isaiah 66:13 God is described as the mother of Israel whose comfort never ceases. In Deuteronomy 32:18 God is pictured both as the rock, who fathered them, and the God who gave them birth, certainly a maternal image. In the psalms, God is frequently described as sheltering and protecting his children in the shadow of his wings, or covering them with his feathers (17:8; 36:7; 57:1; 91:1, 4). In all likelihood this is an allusion to a mother bird, sheltering her young. The same imagery is found in Deuteronomy 32:11–12 and Isaiah 31:5.

In the New Testament, Jesus develops one of his three parables of lostness and foundness with the story of a woman who had lost her coin, a representation of God. Although the other two parables picture God as a father and a shepherd, they also refer to more feminine qualities of care, intimacy, and tenderness. Jesus even used such feminine characteristics to describe himself: "O Jerusalem, Jerusalem, you who kill the prophets and stone those sent to you, how often I have longed to gather your children together, as a hen gathers her chicks under her wings, but you were not willing" (Matt. 23:37).

We may also take note of the way in which Jesus related to women. He taught them as he did his other disciples, although apparently not as extensively. In this regard, he did what no rabbi would have done, namely, treated women as pupils. This in itself, of course, does not signify anything directly about the gender of God. If, however, the argument is made that women should not be teachers or leaders because such should be male, representing a masculine deity, then either Jesus was wasting his time giving this sort of teaching to women, who instead should be taught by their husbands or other male disciples, or, by *modus tollens,* God is not to be thought of as masculine.

What, however, of the Holy Spirit? Some have made much of the fact that the Hebrew word for spirit, *ruah,* is feminine, and the Greek word, *pneuma,* is neuter. This may not, however, be significant, since as is well known, gender is not always correlated with sex in most languages. Another way of putting it is that linguistic gender is not to be equated with personal or cultural gender. Perhaps more significant, however, is that the Spirit is often associated with feminine functions such as nurturance, consolation, eschatological groaning in childbirth, and emotional warmth and inspiration. L. I. Sweet cautions against envisioning the Holy Spirit as totally feminine, as that contention is really without adequate biblical support. He also thinks it inadvisable to conceive of the Spirit as the only feminine persona in the Trinity, as that would leave the Trinity two-thirds masculine and only one-third feminine, thus further reinforcing the inferior position of women in Christianity. He believes it would be wiser to understand the Spirit (like the other members of the Trinity) as having both feminine and masculine aspects.[22]

Other considerations must be noted and evaluated as well. One is the doctrine of the image of God. Probably the primary passage for understanding this doctrine is Genesis 1:27, "So God created man in his own image, in the image of God he created him; male and female he created them." Here we are faced with a rather clear case of the type of parallelism typical of Hebrew poetry. The debate with respect to this passage is whether this should be understood as a two-strophe or a three-strophe paral-

22. L. I. Sweet, *New Life in the Spirit* (Philadelphia: Westminster, 1982), pp. 40–41.

lelism. Karl Barth saw this as involving all three strophes, so that "male and female he created them" is simply another way of saying "God created man in his own image." In other words, the fact that man is male and female is the image of God. From this Barth does not deduce the bisexuality (or bigenderity?) of God, but rather that this contrast and complementarity, with the consequent social interaction, is the image of God.[23] God is social, that is, triune. If one takes the passage as involving only two strophes in direct and primary parallelism, then what we have here is an elaboration of what was said in the first two strophes. In other words, God not only tells us (twice) that he made man in his image and likeness, but that he made both the male and the female in this image. In either event, both male and female bear the image of God; both are able to resemble God. Thus, God must presumably possess both feminine and masculine qualities, as do men and women, albeit in them the respective qualities may vary in degree.

One other point needs to be made, which will be considerably elaborated, in the section on the interrelationships among the members of the Trinity. If the Fatherhood of God is thought to imply the hierarchicalism and subordination sometimes associated with that concept, then if we find that such ordering of the persons is not true, we would have to conclude that the Fatherhood of God and the Sonship of Christ are not to be understood in the patriarchal fashion sometimes found. This would mean that the domination sometimes associated with masculinity (especially of the macho type) is not the exclusive way in which the Father relates to the other members of the Trinity. If those relationships are also characterized by what are usually thought of as feminine characteristics, then women need not feel excluded from fellowship with God.

If our argument in this preceding section has been cogent, then it is not necessary to think of God in exclusively masculine terms and images. He is not really bound by gender and sex; he transcends both. It is also quite possible that the patriarchal depiction of God that we find in much of Christian theology is an illicit development of the masculine motifs in isolation from the

23. Karl Barth, *Church Dogmatics* (Edinburgh: T. & T. Clark, 1958), vol. 3, part 1, pp. 184–87.

other qualities and from the biblical contexts in which they were originally given. The picture of God is not one to which only men can relate, or which only men can emulate. The Triune God is, in other words, the God of all people. Just as Paul declared this with respect to the doctrine of justification (Gal. 3:28), it is also true of all areas of the Christian life.

God as Necessarily Lord

One additional point must be made, however. Rebecca Pentz has argued that Christ can be the savior of women, just as of men, but not on their own terms.[24] Those who would become Christians must be prepared to surrender to Christ's lordship, irrespective of gender. If anyone, male or female, refuses to submit to Christ and requires that he in effect submit himself to them, then there can really be no relationship. For Christ to have to accommodate himself to the beliefs and will of human beings would in the final analysis be a denial of the very character of Christianity. It would be to put the human in the position of authority, of lordship, rather than God. Humans must change, not God.

A somewhat different problem arises with the comparative religions objection. There, it is not so much an objection to the concept of the Trinity, but rather, simply to the exclusivity of the Christian version of it. The strategy is to demonstrate that the concept of the Trinity, if not universal, is at least to be found in a number of other world religions. Thus, this view universalizes Christianity by removing the seeming differences between it and other religions. We must now ask about the adequacy of this approach.

It appears that this removal of differences has been accomplished, at least from the perspective of Christianity, by a considerable redefinition or reinterpretation of Christianity, at least as it has traditionally been understood. In so doing, however, it appears that a considerable amount of question begging has been engaged in.

First, there is a change of understanding of the means by which the essence of Christianity is determined. The conserva-

24. Rebecca D. Pentz, "Can Christ Save Women?" in *Encountering Jesus*, ed. Stephen T. Davis (Atlanta: John Knox, 1988), pp. 78–82.

tive approach has been that there is an original essence of Christianity, defined by certain sources that are considered revelatory of the essence. This is to say that there is a pure type or ideal of what Christianity is, and that this is timeless. One then measures various forms of expression of Christianity against this pure type. Somewhat more liberal approaches define Christianity through historical or descriptive means. Christianity is what it is, whatever may be the differences among varieties of it at different times. Such approaches may even include the idea that there must inevitably be changes, that evolution, development, progress are necessary for real value to be present. Otherwise it is static and maladaptive.

There is a parallel here to the differences between liberals and conservatives in other realms, including politics. Strict constructionists with respect to the United States Constitution hold that it defines the values by which the Republic was and still is to function. Thus, the question is frequently asked of laws and actions whether they are constitutional, that is, whether they are in agreement with the constitution in terms of what the constitutional fathers are believed to have meant by what they wrote. Others, of a more liberal persuasion, believe in a "living constitution," to be interpreted in line with current understandings. These interpretations may be quite different than those held at an earlier time, particularly at the time of the document's composition. While both hold at least formally to the authority of the Constitution, neither group would want to set it aside officially. What is done instead, in the case of the latter group, is to change the definition, so that what the Constitution really says is different.

It is this latter type of approach that Raimundo Panikkar follows. Indeed, he makes quite clear that to be faithful to the tradition is never simply to repeat it but to give it the evolving meaning that it deserves. Now, of course, what he might be saying is simply that the expression of the unchanging truth requires a continuing updating, since even the meaning of words changes with time. That is not what he seems to be saying, however. It is not simply saying the same thing in more modern, and hence more easily understood, terminology. It seems to be the case that the content changes in some ways. No one form that it has taken during its history is to be absolutized. The problem becomes, however, determining the basis for continuing to refer to this as Christianity. If it is not a particular set of beliefs or practices, what is the constant, the underlying factor, which entitles us to continue to use the same nomenclature with respect to it? It must surely be more than simply the fact that these people call themselves Christians, or claim to be Christians, as did earlier persons, and thus we should also. That is essentially the position that "Christianity is that religion practiced by those persons who call themselves Christians." That would be a circular argument, with all the problems attending such arguments.

Beyond that, however, those who were in a position of authority in the early stages of the church seemed to regard the beliefs that they propounded as being important, and as having some sort of permanent significance. So, for example, Jesus said, "Heaven and earth will pass away, but my words will never pass away" (Matt. 24:35). Paul wrote to the Galatians, "But even if we or an angel from heaven should preach a gospel other than the one we preached to you, let him be eternally condemned!" (Gal. 1:8). If, then, one does not attribute any special authoritative status to the teachings of these people, one must ask how they are to be regarded. Put another way, if Jesus himself was mistaken about the permanence of his words, then what source does one follow in determining what is authentically Christian?

Further, and parallel to this problem, is that Panikkar seems to assume a development to reality itself, or, to put it differently, that there is a developmental or process view of reality. There does not seem to be nearly as much emphasis on what remains constant in the universe as on change and evolution. Yet this point also is simply asserted, rather than argued. Here, however, is a major issue, and one which, if answered in the fashion in which Panikkar does, creates additional complications. In light of this, he ought to argue and explain, but this he fails to do.

The other point from which Panikkar's willingness to find varying meanings for Christianity comes is his understanding of the nature of symbols. An earlier approach had fixed meaning in the symbol itself, as placed there by the author or the speaker. Panikkar rejects this as unduly limiting. A symbol's meaning is not just what *you* say it means, but what *I* find there as well. This is because the symbol represents not only the object to which it refers, but also the consciousness of the symbol. This more subjective approach is, of course, popular in our time. Yet there are accompanying problems.

A major difficulty for this more subjective approach, whether it is reader-response criticism, deconstruction, or milder forms, is the extent to which it can assume that there is communication, as well as its very understanding of communication. In what sense do we know that the meaning is the same for two persons, if the symbol represents its object and the consciousness of the first person, and the object and the second person's consciousness? Is it sufficient that they seem to agree with one another, or that they seem to function in harmony with one another?

What is disappointing about Panikkar's treatise is that he does not argue his position; he simply asserts it. In part, this can probably be attributed to his decision not to write a large book, complete with extensive documentation. If, however, he is going to propose such a revolutionary approach to interreligious dialogue, then he probably should have chosen to write the type of book he did not choose to write. Beyond that, he should have come to grips with the problems associated with the position that he has adopted. In particular, one must raise the question of the status of the assertions in his book. If one applies the view he advocates of the nature of symbols to the symbols that make up his book, then what does he believe he is doing in writing? If the symbols represent not only the objects (i.e., what he intends by the use of those symbols) but also the consciousness of the symbols (i.e., what the reader brings to it), then what type of communication is taking place? One obtains the impression that Panikkar believes he really is communicating an objective meaning. Is it possible to hold, for example, that the only way for advocates of two different religions to relate to one another is through the Christian attempting to win the Hindu over to agree with his view, to convert him, and maintain that one agrees with Panikkar? Is it possible while holding this view, to insist that this is what Panikkar means? Does Panikkar hold that the theory he espouses also applies to him? Does he practice what he advocates? The problem, of course, is that this would virtually preclude the type of communication he is attempting to engage in. It is quite possible that the theory he is defending applies only to religious language, as contrasted with theological language, but again it seems that he should have stated that. If not, he may be holding a view that either is internally self-contradictory or cannot be put into practice.

Panikkar also makes no real effort to evaluate the relative truth-value of the various religions. In Panikkar's case, it seems to be that there would be a breakdown of real dialogue if one partner were to attempt to persuade the other of the truthfulness of his or her view. That being the case, the benefit for the whole of the human race that Panikkar envisions resulting from true dialogue would be lost. There would be a continued encouragement of the sense of difference and of claimed superiority of one over the other, which not only would not alleviate world tensions but actually contribute to them. While John Hick also fails to evaluate the truth-value of religions, it is because of a different reason. It is also pragmatic, but in a different way. For him, there is no point in trying to establish the truth of a given religion simply because the classic methods employed, the arguments or "proofs," do not succeed. They are only the attempt to set forth what has already been believed on other grounds, those being the religious experience of the persons involved.[25] Hick's assumption seems to be, however, that these are the best and perhaps the only type of argument that can be offered. There are numerous apologists and philosophers of religion, however, who do not think the proofs are valid, or at least that they are effective, but who nonetheless believe that arguments for the truth of Christianity can be offered. Some of these involve the presupposition of the Christian revelation, preserved in Scripture, which can be tested and weighed for adequacy. Others take a different approach, such as Wolfhart Pannenberg, whose argument is from history and especially centers on the resurrection of Christ. To some, it appears that what Hick is rejecting—the type of philosophical proofs for the existence of God about which he has written—is not the best, but rather perhaps the poorest, of the arguments that can be advanced. Hick fails to explore the alternatives adequately. Nor, for that matter, does Panikkar evaluate sufficiently his own hypothesis, whether this type of dialogue does in-

25. John Hick, *God Has Many Names* (Philadelphia: Westminster, 1982), p. 23.

deed produce the results that he suggests. This sounds like many of the other solutions to human conflict that have been proposed over the years. As much as these—improving education, economic status, housing, or whatever—have been explored, there does not seem to be any real improvement in human relations.

There seems as well to be an unproven commitment to a monistic view of reality. This enables Panikkar to assimilate his view to that of Hinduism and Buddhism quite easily. The problem, however, is whether this is really the view underlying Christianity, or for that matter, the other two major religions that in part share the same root: Judaism and Islam. Certainly in the latter two, it has been theism rather than pantheism that has prevailed over the years, and I would argue, that has been true of Christianity, as well, certainly within the biblical period, when great pains were taken to distinguish the revealed faith from nature religion, fertility cults, and other types of pantheistic piety. There have certainly been pantheistic varieties of Christianity, but they have been far from the mainstream during much of its history. Here again, much of Christianity would have difficulty recognizing itself in this description, and hence of seeing real affinity with the other religions with which dialogue is proposed.

The Essence of Christianity

Since the beginning of the nineteenth century, there has been considerable debate about what the essence of Christianity is, or for that matter, wherein the essence of religion proper resides. Up until Friedrich Schleiermacher, Christianity was distinguished in terms of its beliefs. Schleiermacher changed that view, relocating religion to the realm of feeling. Albrecht Ritschl, following Immanuel Kant more closely, located the essence of religion more directly in the realm of value judgments. Yet it appears that for most of its life, there was the sense that religion, or at least the Christian religion, involved all of these areas. While the exact circumstances of the experiences might vary, there was a sense that all of these were related to the personality and cultural situation of adherents to various religions but that all had in common a certain set of doctrines or beliefs. It was primarily on the basis of different beliefs that various denominations were distinguished from one another. To move the locus of distinctiveness from belief to experience is to contradict much of the history of religion. Unless one is prepared to say that only the most recent form determines what is normative, there appears to be a difficulty here.

Panikkar does, of course, seem to be making some such value judgment. There are better and less desirable varieties of the Christian religion. In particular, those that do not further interreligious dialogue do not contribute to the good of the human race as a whole, and thus are not good. Pragmatic considerations are the criteria for such evaluation as this. What, however, are the source and the basis of these criteria? How does one conclude that these values are those that should be adopted? This is a question Panikkar really does not face.

Finally, what evidence is offered that the experiences that are singled out as the three forms of spirituality really are the same in each of these religions? Some varieties of Christianity in many ways resemble, in the experiences of their practitioners, the religious experience of Hinduism. Are these the normative variety of Christianity, however, and should they be? And is the experience of believers, within the two religions basically the same? What Hick offers as apparent evidence is basically devotional literature of different religions. If, however, the conception of the god worshiped differs, are the experiences really the same? For example, is the Muslim prayer to the god who orders things really experientially the same as that of a Christian, particularly an Arminian Christian whose understanding of divine providence may be considerably different from that of the more rigidly controlled Muslim view of God? While the language may be similar, even identical, does not the meaning of the language depend on the context, part of which is the remainder of the doctrinal framework?

On the level of doctrine, there is a distinctness and difference between the biblical picture of the Triune God, and the views of the highest power as found in any other religion. These simply do not approach that view. While there are elements within several religions that in certain respects resemble aspects of the Christian doctrine, the idea of an ontological Trinity is unique to Christianity. Indeed, Panikkar's statement virtually corroborates that, for his denial of the reality of the plurality and consequently of the equality within the Trinity is scarcely the traditional or orthodox Christian doctrine.[26]

It seems strange that a Christian theologian would attempt to show the fundamental similarity of Christianity to other religions. Throughout its history, and indeed during the period when the revelation was being given and it was attempting to establish itself, Christianity and its Old Testament predecessor made a clear and definite effort to distinguish itself from the other religions that surrounded it. In fact, its success and ability to survive in the face of a hostile world seemed to be tied up with the belief and the maintenance of the distinctiveness of its beliefs. Thus, Kenneth Scott Latourette, near the end of his seven-volume *History of the Expansion of Christianity* wrote:

> Those forms [of the church] which conformed so much to the environment that they sacrificed this timeless and placeless identity died out with the passing of the age, the society, and the climate of opinion to which they had adjusted themselves. The central core of the uniqueness of Jesus, of fidelity to his birth, life, teachings, death, and resurrection as events of history, and of belief in God's working through him for the revelation of Himself and the redemption of man proved essential to continuing life.[27]

There does seem to be an inherent contradiction between Christianity and the other religions of the world. This is something that cannot be removed without destroying Christianity proper. Just as we saw with respect to some of the views of the feminists, this may simply be one of the points that cannot be made acceptable to those outside of Christianity. One Christian scholar entitled his book years ago, *Christianity Is Christ*;[28] those who would be part of it must accept the lordship of Christ. In the final analysis, if God as revealed in the Scriptures conflicts with someone's ideas or will, it is they who must change, not he.

---

26. Raimundo Panikkar, *The Trinity and the Religious Experience of Man: Icon-Person-Mystery* (New York: Orbis, 1973), p. 45.

27. Kenneth Scott Latourette, *A History of the Expansion of Christianity* (New York: Harper & Brothers, 1945), 7:492.

28. W. H. Griffith Thomas, *Christianity Is Christ* (Grand Rapids: Eerdmans, 1955).

13

Internal Relations Between the Members of the Trinity

We now come to an issue that has both considerable theoretical or doctrinal and practical significance. It pertains to the relationships among the members of the Trinity. Another way of putting this, which more specifically gets at the fundamental issue, is the relative status of the three persons of the Trinity.

The Eastern or Greek, and the Western or Latin, theologies approached the matter in different ways. The Greek theologians saw personhood as preceding and causing existence. The principle, origin, and cause of everything is traced to one specific hypostasis, the unoriginated origin, God the Father.[1] Further, Greek theology follows the order of the economy: Father-Son-Holy Spirit. Quite a different position is taken by those recent and contemporary theologians who represent a more Latin or Western tradition. In Latin theology, nature is the principle of personhood, so that the divine nature exists as a Trinity of coequal persons. Under this approach, emphasis is placed on substance.[2]

The Greek or Eastern Approach

A recent example of the Eastern approach is Karl Rahner. Although deeply indebted to Augustine and Thomas Aquinas, both

1. Catherine Mowry LaCugna, *God for Us: The Trinity and Christian Life* (San Francisco: Harper, 1991), pp. 247–48.
2. Ibid., p. 248.

Western or Latin theologians, Rahner affirms the identity of the immanent Trinity and the economic Trinity. He says: *"The 'economic' Trinity is the 'immanent' Trinity and the 'immanent' Trinity is the 'economic' Trinity."*[3] There is no second Trinity. There not only is a connection among the immanent and the economic, but an actual identity. What we can know of the Trinity and the relationships among its members from the history of salvation is the way they actually are, in and of themselves, or itself.

This means that for Rahner there is a real or inherent nature of the relationship between the Father and the Son that corresponds to the relationship as revealed in the earthly ministry of Jesus. He says, for example,

> Jesus is not simply God in general, but the Son. The second divine person, God's Logos, is man, and only he is man. Hence there is at least *one* "mission," *one* presence in the world, *one* reality of salvation history which is not merely appropriated to some divine person, but which is proper to him. Here we are not merely *speaking* "about" this person in the world. Here something occurs "outside" the intra-divine life in the world itself, something which is not a mere effect of the efficient causality of the triune God acting as one in the world, but something which belongs to the Logos alone, which is the history of the one divine person, in contrast to the other divine persons.[4]

Thus the relationship of the Son to the Father is not merely a matter of the earthly incarnate history of the Son. It is of the eternal nature of the Son to be sent by the Father.

Rahner insists that the opposite thesis, that any one of the divine persons could have become incarnate, must be rejected. This would mean that the incarnation of the Logos reveals nothing specific about the Logos himself, that is, about his own relative specific features within the divinity.[5] It would mean that there really is no essential difference among the persons of the Trinity, that any one of them could have become incarnate as easily as the Son. Thus, our experience of the incarnation only means that God in general is a person.

3. Karl Rahner, *The Trinity* (New York: Herder & Herder, 1970), pp. 21–22.
4. Ibid., p. 23.
5. Ibid., p. 28.

Is the presupposition that every divine person might have become incarnate, rather than merely the second person, true? Rahner insists that it is not. It has not been demonstrated. It was never considered in the most ancient tradition prior to Augustine. Indeed, that tradition has always presupposed the very opposite. By definition, the Father is the Unoriginate, in principle "invisible." He reveals himself and appears precisely by sending his *Word* into the world. But, says Rahner, a revelation of the Father without the Logos and his incarnation would be like speaking without words.[6] Further, it is false. From the fact that one divine person became incarnate, one cannot deduce the same for either of the other two persons. That would presuppose two other concepts: that "hypostasis" in God is a univocal concept with respect to the three persons; and that the different ways in which each person is a person would prevent a person from entering into a hypostatic relation with a created reality, like the divine second person. The former of these two presuppositions is, however, false and the latter is undemonstrated. Nor does his contention deny any perfection of the Father.[7] It is a perfection for the Son as Son to descend from the Father, but it would be pure nonsense to conclude that the Father must also possess this perfection. "Since the hypostatic function 'outwards' *is* the corresponding divine hypostasis, we are not allowed to deduce anything for another hypostasis from the function of *this* hypostasis even when our *abstract* universal concept of subsistence shows no contradiction with the hypothesis that the Father should cause a human nature to subsist."[8]

The thesis of the virtual interchangeability of the three divine persons in their immanent or eternal state is false and must be rejected. If it were true, it would create havoc with theology. There would be no connection between "mission" and the internal life of the Trinity. Rahner sees this separation as being absolute in nature. He says: "Our sonship in grace would in fact have absolutely nothing to do with the Son's sonship, since it might equally well be brought about without any modification by another incarnate person. That which God is for us would tell us

6. Ibid., p. 29.
7. Ibid.
8. Ibid., pp. 29–30, n. 25.

absolutely nothing about that which he is in himself, as triune."[9] Such conclusions, however, go against the whole sense of holy Scripture. This would be denied only by those who do not put their theology under the norm of Scripture, but accept from it only what they have learned from textbook theology, and rationalize away the rest.

There are two major reasons Rahner is motivated to investigate this question, and why this particular conclusion to the question is important. The first is because of the apparent practical irrelevance of the doctrine of the Trinity to most Christians' living and to theology. While the Trinity appears in official creeds and liturgies, it would seem to make little difference in the practical lives of most Christians.[10] In addition, most theology is done quite independently of the doctrine of the Trinity. Christology, for example, is written in terms of what it would mean for "God" to become human.[11] This is also true of doctrinal discussions of grace. These are put in terms of the grace of God, but not of Christ or the Spirit.[12] The doctrine of creation as well is virtually unaffected by trinitarian considerations. Although the creeds speak of God creating through Christ, creation is discussed in the textbooks as if it is "God" who creates, or the divine essence. In other words, God's relationship to creation is virtually unitary, not threefold.

The traditional way of putting the doctrine is basically as follows. The Father is the ungenerated person. The Son is begotten of the Father, but in a fashion that must be thought of as eternal. There has never been a time when he did not exist, but similarly, there has never been and will never be a time when he will not exist as Son. The Holy Spirit proceeds eternally from the Father, and, if one follows the Western or Latin version of the doctrine, from the Son as well.

These relationships of begottenness and procession are not to be seen as situations of causation or subordination, however. The three persons are equal, but they are not merely identical or interchangeable. To some extent, what underlies this conception

9. Ibid., p. 30.
10. Ibid., pp. 10–11.
11. Ibid., p. 11.
12. Ibid., pp. 34–36.

is the maxim that the economic Trinity is the immanent Trinity and the immanent Trinity is the economic Trinity. Indeed, Rahner, who popularized this identity of the immanent and economic Trinities, insists on the uniqueness of the relationship of each of the persons to us.[13]

Here Rahner is taking a very different approach from that of classical scholastic theology. According to that view, any divine person could have become incarnate.[14] Then all relations of God to us would be "appropriated." The specific pattern of the economy, its taxonomy, would disclose nothing to us about God's eternal life. This view, however, must be rejected, according to Rahner, for it would create havoc with theology. He says, "There would no longer be any connection between 'mission' and the intra-Trinitarian life. . . . That which God is for us would tell us absolutely nothing about that which he is in himself, as triune. These and many similar conclusions, which would follow from this thesis, go against the whole sense of holy Scripture."[15]

What this means is that the direction of movement in doing Trinitarian theology must be from the economy of salvation to the nature of the Trinity, not the reverse. Rahner believes we must begin with the historical narratives of salvation history, rather than any speculative ideas about the nature of the Trinity. The distinctions among God, Christ, and the Holy Spirit must be understood as being the very way God is in himself.

Another contemporary theologian who has represented this more Eastern form of thinking is Catherine LaCugna. She starts with much the same sort of concern as Rahner, namely, the fact that the doctrine of the Trinity has become, for all practical purposes, irrelevant to the actual practice of Christians. Indeed, the whole thrust of her major work on the subject—that this is the case and must be reversed—is stated in her opening words: "The doctrine of the Trinity is ultimately a practical doctrine with radical consequences for the Christian life. That is the thesis of this book."[16]

13. Ibid., pp. 22, 34–38.
14. Thomas Aquinas, *Summa Theologica*, IIIa, 3, 5.
15. Rahner, *Trinity*, p. 30.
16. LaCugna, *God for Us*, p. 1.

LaCugna's guiding principle, however, is that "for Christian theology, the mystery of God can be thought of only in terms of the mystery of grace and redemption."[17] That means, specifically for the purposes of the topic under consideration here, that true statements about the triune nature of God can only be made on the basis of the economy, that is, God's self-revelation in Christ and the Spirit. We do not have any independent knowledge of God, and cannot speak from God's viewpoint. We know him only as he has communicated himself in the pattern of salvation history.

LaCugna sees a definite parallel between the methodology of the doctrine of the Trinity and that of christological studies. In the latter area a consensus has been reached in recent years regarding two points: the historical Jesus is the primary source and norm for Christology; and Christology cannot be separated from soteriology. Thus, Christology is done "from below" rather than "from above." This means ascending or functional Christology, rather than descending or metaphysical Christology.

This development is related to a broader or more general phenomenon in our culture. Prior to the Enlightenment a metaphysical statement or a statement about what something was in itself was believed to make the most true statement about something. Now, however, that status is accorded instead to historical statements, statements about what has really happened.[18] Thus, the older type of metaphysical treatment of the Trinity, in terms of what God is in and of himself, cannot really be maintained. LaCugna's principle is similar to that of Rahner: "*theologia* and *oikonomia*, the mystery of God and the mystery of salvation, are inseparable."[19]

LaCugna, however, takes a somewhat different approach than Rahner. She believes that his insistence that the economic Trinity is the immanent Trinity and the immanent Trinity is the economic Trinity is basically sound. It does, however, still perpetuate the distinction between the two. In contrast, she wants to speak simply of what she believes is the biblical and pre-Nicene concept of the economy as the dynamic movement of

17. Ibid., p. 2.
18. Ibid., p. 4.
19. Ibid.

God the Father outward, his personal self-sharing in which he is forever bending toward his "other." Economy and theology are therefore simply two aspects of one reality, the mystery of divine-human communion.[20] The very terminology of immanent Trinity and economic Trinity seems itself to be based on a framework that involves a gap between economy and theology. It should therefore be abandoned as misleading and the terms *oikonomia* and *theologia* should be clarified. The former is not the Trinity *ad extra*, but the comprehensive plan of God reaching from creation to consummation, according to which God and all creatures are to exist together in the mystery of love and communion. Similarly, the latter is not the Trinity *in se*, but simply the mystery of God. An immanent theology of God is therefore simply a summary of the one revelation of God to us in Jesus Christ.[21]

There is, from LaCugna's perspective, another reason to avoid identifying "immanent Trinity" with "inner life of God." When we cease to think of two levels of the Trinity, a life internal and a life external to the nature of God, then we see that

> there is *one* life of the Triune God, a life in which we graciously have been included as partners. Followers of Christ are made sharers in the very life of God, partakers of divinity as they are transformed and perfected by the Spirit of God. The 'motive' of God's self-communication is union with the creature through *theosis*. God's economy of salvation is the economy of divinization and glorification. To conceive trinitarian life as something belonging *only* to God, or belonging to God apart from the creature, is to miss the point entirely. To analyze the "immanent Trinity" as a purely intradivine reality also misses the point. The doctrine of the Trinity is not ultimately a teaching about "God" but a teaching about *God's life with us and our life with each other.* It is the life of communion and indwelling, God in us, we in God, all of us in each other.[22]

Since, now, there is really no distinction between the economic and immanent Trinity, the distinctions and characteris-

---

20. Ibid., p. 222.
21. Ibid., p. 225.
22. Ibid., p. 228.

tics revealed in the pattern of salvation history are the very way God is. Thus, the traditional dimensions of divine begetting and proceeding are retained in LaCugna's theology. She says, "The fecundity and dynamic life of God involves the eternal procession of love from love, of Son and Spirit from the originating person (Father). . . . The eternal processions exist in time and history as the missions of Incarnation and deification."[23] Whereas we tend to think, because it is true biologically, that begetting is an activity that takes place at a particular moment, the process of begetting and being begotten is an eternal and unceasing exchange of persons. And she says, "The fecundity of God, which originates in the Unoriginate Origin, gives rise to the Son and is completed in the Spirit."[24]

From the same considerations, however, some, particularly the Arians and their descendants, drew subordinationist conclusions. They determined that the Son really is subordinate to the Father. They held that statements made by the Son, such as, "The Father is greater than I," are to be taken as referring not merely to the economic Trinity, or the earthly life and ministry of the Son, but to the eternal or immanent Trinity.

This Eastern or Greek approach claims to be derived from Scripture. For the most part, this contention is based on certain texts that refer to the "only-begotten Son" or something similar. Among these are John 1:14, 18; 3:16, 18; Hebrews 11:7; and 1 John 4:9. Because these passages appear to refer to the eternal Word, it is concluded that the relationship of fatherhood and sonship must apply to these two from all eternity, and that this entails that the Father is ingenerate, while the Son is generated by the Father. This is to say that the term "Son" is a term, not of office, but of nature. This approach is argued for by Geoffrey Bromiley: "'Generation' makes it plain that there is a divine sonship prior to the incarnation (cf. John 1:18; I John 4:9), that there is thus a distinction of persons within the one Godhead (John 5:26), and that between these persons there is a superiority and subordination of order (cf. John 5:19; 8:28)."[25] He adds an im-

23. Ibid., p. 353.
24. Ibid., p. 354.
25. Geoffrey Bromiley, "Eternal Generation," in Evangelical Dictionary of Theology, ed. Walter A. Elwell (Grand Rapids: Baker, 1984), p. 368.

portant qualifier to his statement, however: "Nor does his subordination imply inferiority."[26]

We must ask, however, whether the traditional position is correct. May the Arians have discovered something in the application of the idea of begetting that, if held, leads logically to their conclusion? And does the biblical revelation really teach the quasi-subordination or the derivation of one person from the other? The bases used for this conclusion are quite clear. One is the use of the term "begotten," especially by John, to refer to Christ. Certainly, if one is begotten, there must be a begetter. This is an asymmetrical relationship. Jesus also uses expressions like "The Father has sent me," suggesting derivation of a type. It is also made explicit regarding the Holy Spirit while remaining merely implicit regarding the Son in Jesus' statement, "I will pray the Father, and he will send *another* comforter." The very use of the terms "Father" and "Son" contributes to this understanding. The Father is one from whom the Son has derived, just as in all earthly relationships of this type. There also is the apparent subordination of the Son and the Holy Spirit to the Father. The Father has given authority to the Son, as if the former possesses it by right, and the latter only by bestowal. The Son, when he achieves victory, turns the kingdom over to the Father. He is seated at the right hand of the Father, but this imagery suggests a continuing secondary status for the Son, rather than a coequal dividing of the authority. The Son makes intercession to the Father for us, and the Holy Spirit even intercedes currently, as if the Father is the one who ultimately is the answerer of prayers. A final indication is believed to be found in the baptismal formula given by Jesus in the great commission of his disciples, according to which they are to baptize in the name of "the Father and of the Son and of the Holy Spirit" (Matt. 28:19), presumably the proper order of reference of the three persons.

The Latin or Western Approach

One modern theologian who followed the Western approach is Benjamin B. Warfield. He notes that the traditional position

26. Ibid.

rests on a limited and rather carefully selected set of data. For one thing, we find a variation of the terminology applied to the several persons of the Trinity. While the Father-Son-Holy Spirit terminology is customary for Jesus and John (whose statements closely resemble those of Jesus), they are not so uniformly found in the writings of Paul and the other New Testament writers. For example, instead of Father, Son, and Holy Spirit, Paul prefers God, Lord Jesus Christ, and Holy Spirit. This variance can be accounted for in terms of the different relations of each of the speakers to the Trinity.[27] Jesus could not very well have referred to himself as one of the members of the Trinity by using the term "Lord." His consciousness of his close relationship to God, would, however, have been quite naturally expressed with the designation of "Son," with all that was involved in this term. While he refers to the one person as "God," the use of the term "Lord" would, for Paul who had been reared as a strict Jew, be virtually an equivalent for "God." He was Paul's Lord, and this was really his favorite name for Jesus. It had become practically a proper name for Christ. It should be observed that Paul is dealing with these issues from the standpoint of a worshiper, not a theologian. His concern with the persons is in terms of his relationship to them, rather than their relationship to one another. Having said this about the perspective from which he writes, we must nonetheless attach considerable importance to this phenomenon. As Warfield puts it, "It remains remarkable, nevertheless, if the very essence of the Trinity were thought of by him as resident in the terms 'Father,' 'Son,' that in his numerous allusions to the Trinity in the Godhead, he never betrays any sense of this."[28]

A second consideration is the order of the names. As noted above, the Father-Son-Holy Spirit order is thought to be normative, indicating the superiority or priority of the Father to the Son and of both the Father and the Son to the Holy Spirit. What is remarkable, however, is the lack of uniformity of this pattern in the New Testament. Indeed, occasionally the reverse order occurs,

27. Benjamin Breckenridge Warfield, "The Biblical Doctrine of the Trinity," in *Biblical and Theological Studies*, ed. Samuel G. Craig (Philadelphia: Presbyterian and Reformed, 1952), p. 50.
28. Ibid.

as in 1 Corinthians 12:4–6: "There are different kinds of gifts, but the same Spirit. There are different kinds of service, but the same Lord. There are different kinds of working, but the same God works all of them in all men." Another example is Ephesians 4:4–6, a passage whose content quite closely parallels the 1 Corinthians 12 passage. This may be a climactic arrangement, and thus a testimony to the order of Matthew 28:19. Yet there are passages where even the reverse order is not preserved. An instance would be the Pauline benediction in 2 Corinthians 13:14: "May the grace of the Lord Jesus Christ, and the love of God, and the fellowship of the Holy Spirit be with you all." Warfield expresses the issue well: "The question naturally suggests itself whether the order Father, Son, Spirit was especially significant to Paul and his fellow-writers of the New Testament. If in their conviction the very essence of the doctrine of the Trinity was embodied in this order, should we not anticipate that there should appear in their numerous allusions to the Trinity some suggestion of this conviction?"[29]

There is one other major issue of significance to be evaluated here: the designation of the words used in expressing the various persons. For us, living in a very different culture and nearly twenty centuries removed from New Testament times, it seems very natural to assume that the use of the term "Son" indicates subordination and derivation of being. This certainly is true of sons in relationship to fathers in our experience. All sons are born to their fathers and mothers, without whom they would not be. Warfield maintains, however, that this is not quite the meaning of the word in the Semitic consciousness that underlies the statements of Scripture. Rather, the dominant factor in scriptural speech is "likeness." Thus, whatever the father is, the son is also. When the term "Son" is applied to one of the persons of the Trinity, therefore, it is his equality with the Father, rather than his subordination to the Father, which is being affirmed. If there is any implication of derivation in the word "son," it would appear to be very distant, says Warfield.[30] That the Jews understood such of Jesus' reference to the Father is seen in John's explanation in John 5:18: "For this reason the Jews tried all the

29. Ibid.
30. Ibid., p. 52.

harder to kill him; not only was he breaking the Sabbath, but he was even calling God his own Father, making himself equal with God."

What is true of the Son is basically also true of the Spirit. Warfield holds that the expression "Spirit of God" or "Spirit of Jehovah" found in the Old Testament "certainly does not convey the idea there either of derivation or of subordination, but is just the executive name of God—the designation of God from the point of view of His activity—and imports accordingly identity with God."[31] And, Warfield believes, there is no reason to think that any change occurred from the Old Testament to the New. Just as he found specific evidence for this New Testament view regarding the meaning of the word "Son," so he also finds it with respect to the Spirit. In 1 Corinthians 2:10–11 Paul writes, "The Spirit searches all things, even the deep things of God. For who among men knows the thoughts of a man except the man's spirit within him? In the same way no one knows the thoughts of God except the Spirit of God." Warfield's interpretation of this passage is that the Spirit appears as the "substrate of the divine self-consciousness, the principle of God's knowledge of Himself . . . just God Himself in the innermost essence of His Being . . . His very life-element."[32] If this is the case, how can he be supposed to be subordinate to God, or to derive his being from God? Warfield summarizes the evidence of this set of considerations: "If, however, the subordination of the Son and Spirit to the Father in modes of subsistence and their derivation from the Father are not implicates of their designation as Son and Spirit, it will be hard to find in the New Testament compelling evidence of their subordination and derivation."[33]

There is, to be sure, a subordination of the second and third persons of the Trinity to the first person with respect to what may be termed the "modes of operation." It is apparent that the pattern is uniformly the Father first, the Son second, and the Spirit third, in the general operations as revealed to us, and especially those pertaining to the accomplishment of redemption. Whatever the Father does, he does through the Son. The Son is

31. Ibid.
32. Ibid., p. 53.
33. Ibid.

sent by the Father and does his will. Similarly, the Spirit is sent by the Son and does not speak from himself, but takes the things of Christ's and communicates them to us. Jesus himself said, "My Father is greater than I"; Paul states that Christ is God's as we are Christ's (1 Cor. 3:23), and that as Christ is the head of every man, so God is the head of Christ (1 Cor. 11:3).[34]

From this, some, Warfield alleges, have inferred a subordination in the subsistence of the three persons, that the reason why it is the Father who sends the Son and the Son who sends the Spirit is because the Son is subordinate to the Father and the Spirit to the Son. There should, however, be some definite evidence of subordination in modes of subsistence before such is assumed. There is, however, another possibility. It may be that it is due to a convention, an agreement among the persons of the Trinity, a "Covenant," as Warfield terms it. According to this, a distinct function in the work of redemption is voluntarily assumed by each of the members. The incarnation, in which the Son takes a creaturely nature into union with himself, definitely involves the Son in a consequent subordination, and this must be taken into account in interpreting passages that seem to affirm subordination. These subordinationist passages can be fully explained by the facts of the covenant of redemption, the humiliation of Christ, and the two natures of his incarnated person. Warfield's concluding summary is:

> Certainly in such circumstances it were thoroughly illegitimate to press such passages to suggest any subordination for the Son or the Spirit which would in any manner impair that complete identity with the Father in Being and that complete equality with the Father in powers which are constantly presupposed, and frequently emphatically, though only incidentally, asserted for them throughout the whole fabric of the New Testament.[35]

Another thinker who has emphasized and developed the Latin approach is liberation theologian Leonardo Boff. Boff states that reflecting on the Trinity calls all of our human concepts into question. We must therefore evaluate such expressions as "cause

34. Ibid., pp. 53–54.
35. Ibid., p. 55.

of all divinity," "begetting," "breathing-out," and "trinitarian processions." He notes that causal metaphysical concepts have been
used since the early church to explain the relationships in the
Trinity. He questions, however, the legitimacy of the idea of
"cause" in a trinitarian perspective. While it may be appropriate
to speak of origin and cause when referring to the world, what of
speaking of the Father as "origin of all humanity"? While we can
ask of a natural object where it came from and what its origin is,
can we ask such questions with respect to God, who by definition
is eternal, or without beginning and end? Even the church has
stated that the three persons of the Trinity are coeternal, equally
powerful and immense; everything in them is simultaneous and
there is nothing greater or superior, lesser or inferior, before.[36]
His interpretation of these concepts with respect to the Trinity is
that, for example, "cause" is

> not a philosophical concept but a linguistic resource for helping
> us to see the diversity in communion between the three persons.
> It is a descriptive figure of speech. In the Trinity, the "cause" (the
> Father) is not anterior to the "effects" (the Son and the Holy
> Spirit). The "effects" possess the same eternity and dignity as the
> "cause." So what is cause and what is effect here? In the same way,
> what does "begotten Son" or "procession of the Holy Spirit"
> mean?[37]

Boff suggests that instead of employing causal terminology
we should use the language of revelation and recognition, according to which the three Persons reveal themselves to themselves and to each other. His basic thesis is that the three are simultaneous in origin and coexist eternally in communion and
interpenetration.[38]

Boff insists that there is always a triadic relationship among
the Father, the Son, and the Holy Spirit. There is a complete mutuality. In eternal perichoresis, the complete intertwining of love
and communion, all three have their origin from all eternity,
none being anterior to any other. The relationship among them
is one of "reciprocal participation rather than hypostatic deriva-

36. Leonardo Boff, *Trinity and Society* (Maryknoll, N.Y.: Orbis, 1988), pp. 141–42.
37. Ibid., p. 142.
38. Ibid.

tion, of correlation and communion rather than production and procession."[39] Each person is the condition for the revelation of the others. They are what they are because of the infinite, intrinsic communion among them.

This means that in a sense each is the cause of the other or that they mutually exist as a result of the others and of the communion among them. Boff says that "everything in God is triadic, everything is *Patreque, Filioque* and *Spirituque*. The coordinate 'and' applies absolutely to the three Persons: 'and' is always and everywhere."[40]

Wolfhart Pannenberg has also drawn attention to the problem of deriving an eternal generation for the Son by the Father from the "begetting" texts, and then distinguishing between the eternal generation and the temporal sending of the Son. A similar issue attaches to the eternal procession of the Spirit and the temporal breathing out of the Spirit. While making clear that his argument does not preclude the generation, he argues that several biblical texts have been misused in this regard. He observes that in Luke 3:22, the heavenly voice at the baptism of Jesus quotes Psalm 2:7, "You are my son, today I have begotten you," but uses "today" not as the timeless "today" of divine eternity, which knows neither past nor future, but in terms of a specific event. It treats the baptism as a fulfillment of the prophecy, just as Luke 4:21 regards the coming and preaching of Jesus as a fulfillment of Isaiah 61:1–2. Pannenberg holds that Matthew 3:17 states that on the occasion of the baptism the divine sonship, based on Jesus' birth, is made manifest. By quoting Psalm 2:7 rather than Isaiah 42:1, Luke perhaps is thinking of the installation of Jesus as high priest, as in Hebrews 1:5 and 5:5, according to Pannenberg. This, however, can hardly be the case in Acts 13:33, which specifically relates Psalm 2:7 to the resurrection. Pannenberg summarizes his argument by saying:

> Always, however, the NT references to the verse find its fulfillment in the historical person of Jesus Christ. To say this is not to rule out the idea of an eternal generation. It is simply to say that we cannot base it on these passages. Nor may we appeal to the description of

39. Ibid., p. 146.
40. Ibid.

Jesus as the only-begotten Son of God in John (1:14, 18; 3:16, 18). This certainly tells us that Jesus is the only Son (cf. Luke 7:12; 8:42; 9:38) but it does not express the idea of an eternal begetting. Only when Origen combined it with Prov. 8:23 did it form an adequate biblical basis for this concept (*De princ.* 1.2.1–4).

Thus the biblical statements about the begetting of Jesus relate no less to his historical person than do those about his sending. . . . If this central thesis of the 4th-century doctrine of the Trinity is to be justified, the implied relation of Jesus to the Father has to be demonstrated. Traditional Christian theology might well have worked this matter out correctly under the guidance of the Spirit of Christ even though it cannot be adequately proved from individual biblical verses. The relations between the person of Jesus, the Father, and the Spirit might well prove to be not just historical or economic but relations which characterize the eternal divine essence. That is not to say, however, that we may reduce their description to the traditional concepts of procession, begetting, and breathing.[41]

We must now attempt to evaluate these somewhat conflicting positions. It appears that the concern of both Rahner and LaCugna stems primarily from the sense of frustration over the perceived irrelevance of the doctrine of the Trinity for practical Christian living. Several analytical comments need to be made, however.

1. It appears that Rahner's reaction is somewhat extreme. Thus, he says, if the economic Trinity and the immanent Trinity are not the same, "there would no longer be any connection between 'mission' and the intra-trinitarian life. . . . Our sonship in grace would in fact have absolutely nothing to do with the Son's sonship, since it might equally well be brought about without any modification by another incarnate person. . . . That which God is for us would tell us absolutely nothing about that which he is in himself, as triune."[42] But does this follow? If they are not the same, is there *no* connection between them, so that the difference is *absolute?* This seems not to have been established by Rahner.

2. It appears that both Rahner and LaCugna are working with understandings of religious language according to which there is

41. Wolfhart Pannenberg, *Systematic Theology* (Grand Rapids: Eerdmans, 1991), 1:306–7.
42. *The Trinity*, p. 30.

only equivocal or univocal meaning. The possibility of analogical meaning does not seem to be considered here.

3. Closely related to this is the nature or style of revelation. Calvin and others have argued that because of the vast difference between God and humans, when God reveals himself to human beings, there necessarily is an element of accommodation. He stoops down to the level of humans to reveal himself in ways that will be intelligible to them, like a nurse lisping to little children. This he does, says Calvin, lowering himself to represent himself not as he really is, but as we conceive of him.[43] This conception of the revelation as adapted to our understanding, or as anthropomorphic in nature, does not really seem to be a part of Rahner's view.

4. A particular conception of the modes of revelation seems to underlie this theology, namely, the view that revelation is largely restricted to divine acts. Thus, nothing could really be known about the persons of the Trinity, or about the fact of the Trinity itself, apart from the divine acts of the history of salvation. This works very well with the Gospels, and with some portions of the Epistles, insofar as they deal with the historical events. Yet it seems to overlook the other modalities of revelation that bear on this, such as divine speech, whether through dreams, visions, or concurrent inspiration.[44]

5. There is, in a sense, a lack of appreciation for what change or changes the incarnation may actually have effected in the Godhead. If one member of the Trinity took upon himself human form, that represented a radically different situation from what preceded the incarnation. Is it really possible to argue back from this situation to the prior relationships among those persons? Might it not be that this was a temporary and functional adjustment of the relationship, which was not representative of the relations before, or for that matter, after the earthly presence of the second person?

6. There is, in LaCugna's thought, a specific metaphysical dimension to the concept bearing on the understanding of salvation. From her perspective, perichoresis involves not only the

43. John Calvin, *Institutes of the Christian Religion,* I, xiii, 1; I, xvii, 13.

44. Bernard Ramm, *Special Revelation and the Word of God* (Grand Rapids: Eerdmans, 1961), pp. 53–69.

three persons of the Trinity in relationship to each other but also human persons in relationship to God. Thus, as she puts it, *"Trinitarian life is also our life."* She speaks of the "deified human being."[45] This, however, seems to confuse the relationship of salvation with ontology, so that we are not only related to God but joined with him metaphysically.

7. A number of the crucial steps in Rahner's argument seem to remain unproved, thus being assumptions rather than demonstrated premises. So, for example, he says that "the ways in which each person is a person are so different that they allow of only a *very loosely* analogical concept of person, as *equally* applicable to the three persons."[46] He also states that the conclusion that would follow from the principle of the interchangeability of the three persons, namely, that what God is for us would tell us absolutely nothing about himself as triune, "go[es] against the whole sense of Scripture." Apart from the problem already noted, namely the mistaking of a contrary for a contradictory, Rahner does not establish this by the use of even one Scripture reference. He simply says that "This should and could be shown in detail," yet he fails to supply even one such scriptural detail.[47] If the whole sense of Scripture is opposed to a concept, then the contradiction should be demonstrable at some specific point, especially when one says not only that it could, but also that it should, be done.

8. LaCugna is correct in her assessment that we are here dealing with a parallel in the doctrine of the Trinity to the Christology from above/Christology from below distinction and relationships. There is, however, a significant difference between the two doctrines. It is the contention that the whole second person of the Godhead became incarnate, thus coming within the sphere of human experience and of historical research. No part of him remained transcendent in that sense. The Trinity, however, is different, for it is not maintained that the Father ever became incarnate. Thus, his acting within human history is quite different from that of the Son, being much more analogous to such action of the Son prior to the incarnation. Unless one is prepared to say

45. LaCugna, *God for Us*, p. 228.
46. Rahner, *Trinity*, p. 29.
47. Ibid., p. 30.

that the entire Trinity became incarnate or that the Son is only the Father in a certain action, this parallel to Christology seems to break down. The former of these alternatives would be a somewhat novel doctrine. The latter, which LaCugna at times seems to approximate, would appear to be a type of modalism.

9. Bromiley has correctly seen that generation, thought of as an eternal occurrence, involves subordination of the Son to the Father. His attempt to separate eternal subordination and superiority from inferiority seems to be a verbal distinction to which no real distinction corresponds. A temporal, functional subordination without inferiority of essence seems possible, but not an eternal subordination. And to speak of the superiority of the Father to the Son while denying the inferiority of the Son to the Father must be contradictory, unless indication is given of different senses in which these are being used. Without further elaboration and argument, this appears a meaningless concept.

Is there a preferable alternative? I believe that there is, and that the way has been shown us by Warfield, Boff, and Pannenberg. There is a rather obvious sense in which we can say that the immanent Trinity and the economic Trinity are the same. That would be the metaphysical identity, whereby there are not two different Trinities. The epistemological identity is something quite different, however. While the economic Trinity is certainly part of the immanent Trinity epistemologically, it does not necessarily exhaust it.

I would propose that there are no references to the Father begetting the Son or the Father (and the Son) sending the Spirit that cannot be understood in terms of the temporal role assumed by the second and third persons of the Trinity, respectively. They do not indicate any intrinsic relationship among the three. Further, to speak of one of the persons as unoriginate and the others as either eternally begotten or proceeding from the Father is to introduce an element of causation or origination that must ultimately involve some type of subordination among them.

An alternative would be to say that the person of the Trinity who became incarnate and thus also took upon himself the responsibility of dying an atoning death did so voluntarily, in conjunction with the decision of the other two persons. He did this not because he lost a two to one vote within the Godhead. On these grounds, the will of the Father to which he so clearly was subject was at that point the will that the Father asserted on behalf of the Trinity, but it was the will in which the Son had participated, in the original decision. Similarly, the work of the Spirit—calling to remembrance the words of Jesus, directing persons' thinking toward him, and glorifying him—was the result of a decision in which the Spirit had participated.

If the Triune God from all eternity willed what was to come to pass, and did so with full knowledge of all of the consequences, then that willing was a truly informed decision-making process. The decision to create was a decision as well that sin would be allowed to occur, and that they (he) would provide salvation through one of them becoming incarnate. That decision presumably also included the decision as to which of them would be the one to carry out each of the respective functions. Even within the period of earthly ministry that constituted a functional subordination of the Son and the Spirit, however, there are some indications of a mutual submission. Thus, the Father, as Gruenler points out, glorifies the Son, has entrusted all judgment to the Son, hears the Son's requests, and carries out his bidding.[48] There is no permanent distinction of one from the other in terms of origination. While the Father may be the cause of the existence of the Son and the Spirit, they are also mutually the cause of his existence and the existence of one another. There is an eternal symmetry of all three persons.

---

48. Royce Gruenler, *The Trinity in the Gospel of John: A Thematic Commentary on the Fourth Gospel* (Grand Rapids: Baker, 1986), pp. x–xi. While Gruenler overstates the argument at some points and stretches the concept of "mutual deference," there is indication that the relationship is not totally asymmetrical.

14

Prayer, Worship, and the Triune God

We come now to an issue that is both doctrinal in the theoretical sense and practical. It is the question of worship of and prayer to the Triune God. In some ways it is difficult to state categorically which consideration is dominant, the practical or the theoretical. Does the question of the relative and appropriate place of the various members of the Trinity arise from the practice of believers, out of their piety and devotion, or does the question of to whom we should pray arise from our study of the doctrinal teachings? Catherine LaCugna has noted that the Arian controversy was one of long duration, lasting longer than that provoked by most heresies.[1] Wiles comments that people do not ordinarily feel this deeply about religious matters unless they are felt to bear upon practice.[2] At the root of this issue of the real nature and status of Jesus is the question of whether prayer and worship should be directed to him as to the Father.

The issue may be posed as follows: Should we pray to and worship the Father, the Son, and the Holy Spirit, individually or collectively? Or are prayer and worship to be directed to the Father, either primarily or even exclusively? In particular, this seems to center upon the issue of prayer. I am working here with an as-

1. Catherine LaCugna, *God for Us: The Trinity and Christian Life* (San Francisco: Harper, 1991), p. 111.
2. Maurice Wiles, *The Making of Christian Doctrine: A Study in the Principles of Early Doctrinal Development* (London: Cambridge University Press, 1967), p. 62.

sumption: that these two matters are linked. If we are to worship someone, we also ought appropriately to pray to that person, and vice versa. While this linkage may be refined and even challenged, it seems workable and will enable us to draw data from either area or either practice.

The "Father Only" View

There are roughly two major schools of thought regarding this issue. One, which we might term the "Father only" view, maintains that we are to direct prayers to the Father. This approach relies heavily on explicit statements, and especially, commands, found in Scripture. So it notes that we are nowhere in Scripture commanded to pray to the Son and to the Holy Spirit. Such commands are only found with respect to the Father. Further, when Jesus' disciples requested that he teach them to pray, he gave the model prayer generally referred to as "The Lord's Prayer." There Jesus instructed his disciples (and us) to pray: "Our Father. . . . " If this is the way we are to pray, then we have no justification for praying in any other manner (or to any other person). The assumption here is that we basically restrict the normative authority of the Bible to didactic or instructional passages. Where we have explicit commands, we must follow them. Where we lack such commands, we need not necessarily follow that practice. A second assumption or axiom is that there are certain proper works of each member of the Trinity. These ought not to be confused with one another. These would involve creation by the Father, redemption by the Son, sanctification by the Spirit. Answering prayer is evidently one of these works and is the proper domain and role of the Father. Consequently, prayer should be directed to him, rather than to the other members of the Trinity, who would have to "forward" it to the Father.

The "All Three" Approach

The other approach I would call the "all three" approach. This is the view that all three persons are to be worshiped, and that prayer, as appropriate, is to be directed to each person and to the Triune God, collectively. This school of thought tends to rest the practice on doctrine, inferring the nature of prayer from what it understands to be the nature of the Trinity and the relationships among the members. This position reasons that all three persons are divine and that they are equal in nature, although they may at times be subordinated. Consequently, if it is appropriate to pray to one member of the Trinity, it is appropriate to pray to each of them. This view also holds that there are divine works proper to each member of the Godhead. From this, however, it draws a conclusion opposite to that of the first group. We ought to pray to each person of the Trinity regarding that person's appropriate works. Thus, thankfulness for the redemption that we have received should be directed to the Son, who achieved that redemption for us. Prayer for sanctification should be directed to the Spirit, the one who sanctifies. And since the Trinity is a unity of the three persons, it is ordinarily the one Triune God to whom prayer should be directed.

Methodological Considerations

We must now ask ourselves how this issue is to be resolved, for certainly we have here conflicting views of what constitutes proper practice. If the criteria suggested by the Father-only view are followed, namely, guiding our actions strictly by the explicit commands (and prohibitions) of Scripture, then we end up with what appears to be an undue restriction of policy, one that we do not follow in all other areas of Christian practice. For certainly not all of God's intention for our conduct or even all of doctrine is explicitly stated in the Bible. If we restricted ourselves to that, then we would be severely limited in our ability to adapt our methodology of evangelism, for example, to changing situations in different times and places. Indeed, we would not have the doctrine of the Trinity at all. It may be that we here have a difference something like that between the more moderate and the more radical wings of the Reformation. The more radical reformers, such as the Anabaptists, resolved to retain from the practice of the Catholic Church only those things that were explicitly taught in Scripture. The less radical reformers, such as the Lutherans, felt justified in retaining anything not explicitly prohibited in Scripture.

The larger issue, however, relates to the authority of narrative passages, or of passages that indicate the practice of the New Testament believers. Are these practices of value, either in requiring or at least in authorizing or legitimizing our own practice as believers? We should, of course, be careful about uncritically universalizing or generalizing to all situations, at all times and places, that which was intended for a specific situation. We also need to look for God's evaluation of, or reaction to, these practices. Yet with these cautions in place, we need to look carefully at the practice of believers both within the Scripture and in the subsequent history of the church.

Cautions are in order regarding the methodology of the "all three" school, as well. For from the doctrinal tenet of the equal deity of each of the persons, we cannot deduce conclusions regarding worship and prayer without additional premises. It is apparent from passages such as Galatians 3:28 and 1 Corinthians 12:14–26 that believers are all equal in standing in the sight of God. It does not follow, however, that they all have the same role or function in the church, as Paul observes throughout 1 Corinthians 12. So it is possible that although the three persons are equal, the Father would receive prayer and even worship of the Trinity on behalf of the other two members. What must be determined is the status of any additional premise in addition to the minor premise, "The Father, Son, and Holy Spirit are all equally God."

The Practice of the Church: Worship of Jesus

Let us turn, then, to the practice of the church to see whether that can give us any guidance. We are not here attempting to derive doctrine from practice; we have engaged in that endeavor in another place.[3] Rather, our goal is practice, and for that the move from practice to practice is more direct, although not as direct as might seem to be the case. In determining whether this practice or this facet of a practice is to be retained, we seek to identify the underlying doctrinal basis.[4] Nonetheless, we are pri-

---

3. Millard J. Erickson, *The Word Became Flesh* (Grand Rapids: Baker, 1991), pp. 470–72.

4. For a discussion of this issue, see Millard J. Erickson, *Perspectives and Issues in Hermeneutics* (Grand Rapids: Baker, 1993), pp. 67–68.

marily moving from practice to practice, rather than from practice to doctrine or vice versa.

We may begin by noting that very early, even during the New
Testament times, Christians worshiped Jesus. Much quoted is
the early statement of the younger Pliny. Writing to Emperor
Trajan in A.D. 112, he reported that the Christians sang hymns to
their Lord "as God."[5] Examples of these hymns have been preserved for us in the New Testament. There is wide scholarly
agreement, for example, that Philippians 2:6–11 and Colossians
1:15–20 were not merely passages written by Paul, but were existing hymns used within the church that Paul incorporated into
his writings.[6] In Philippians 2:10–11 Paul quotes from Isaiah
45:23, where Yahweh declares his own uniqueness as Lord. In
other words, this was seen as a continuation of the Old Testament worship of Yahweh.

We have in the New Testament, furthermore, actual indications of the practice of worship of Jesus Christ. The Book of Revelation, which gives us more glimpses of worship than any other
New Testament book, shows us several examples of worship of
the Lord, in an eschatological setting. In 5:8–14 there is a pro-
gression of worshipers of the Lamb, expanding outward. First
the four living creatures and the twenty-four elders fall down before the Lamb (v. 8) in the traditional posture of worship. Then
they sing a hymn of praise to the Lamb (vv. 9–10). It is apparent
from what they sing regarding his worthiness to receive praise
because he was slain and by his blood has purchased men for
God from every tribe and language and people and nation that
this lamb is Jesus Christ. Next, in verse 12 a huge number of angels also sing to this lamb. Then, every creature "in heaven and
on earth and under the earth and on the sea, and all that is in
them" join in the song (v. 13); the four living creatures say
"Amen" and the elders fall down and worship.

A somewhat different picture is given in 7:9–12. Here is a great
multitude of people, from all nations, standing before the throne

---

5. Pliny's letter to Trajan, *Epistles* 10.96.

6. E.g., R. P. Martin, *Carmen Christi; Philippians 2:5–11 in Recent Interpretations and
in the Setting of Early Christian Worship* (Cambridge: Cambridge University Press, 1967);
Jack T. Sanders, *The New Testament Christological Hymns: Their Historical Religious
Background* (Cambridge: Cambridge University Press, 1971).

and in front of the Lamb, who is in the center of the throne. They cry out, "Salvation belongs to our God, who sits on the throne, and to the Lamb" (v. 10). Then they are explicitly said to fall down on their faces before the throne and worship (v. 11), saying, "Amen! Praise and glory and wisdom and thanks and honor and power and strength be to our God for ever and ever. Amen!" It could of course be argued that the worship is only to God, who sits on the throne, and not to the Lamb, who is in the center of the throne, but the context seems not to make this restriction. For one thing, these who so worship are wearing white robes, which they have washed clean in the blood of the Lamb (v. 14). The description of them relative to the Lamb in verses 15–17 seems to give him a status so closely linked with God as to be the worthy recipient of such praise and worship as well, as is also indicated by the Lamb's presence in the center of the throne. Further, these worshipers appear to be the same persons or at least comparable worshipers to those who in chapter 5 worship the Lamb. This identification is made even clearer in the final such reference in 22:3, which says, "The throne of God and of the Lamb will be in the city, and his servants will serve him." Note that the throne is now identified as the throne of God *and of the Lamb*, a designation also found in verse 1. John also says, "his servants will serve him," without giving indication, either explicitly or contextually, of the antecedent of "his" and "him." It is quite possible that the pronouns refer to both in one, just as the throne now is the throne of both.

One additional relevant text in Revelation comes at the very beginning of the book (1:5–6), where John, obviously referring to Christ ("his God and Father"), says, "to him be glory and power for ever and ever! Amen." This certainly appears to be an expression of worship. It is a bit different from the other passages we have cited, however, for it is not the words of others reported by John, but his own assertion at this point. And, whereas it could be argued with respect to those other passages that this is an appropriate practice for the future being described by John, here it is a practice engaged in by John at the time of his writing.

What of worship of Jesus Christ in the Gospels? Here it should be noted that although the title "Lord" was regularly applied to him, that does not necessarily automatically carry the connotation of deity and of worship. The Aramaic *mar,* and the Greek *kyrios,* could, in an appropriate context, simply speak of a human, with great respect. In the Gospels, however, it appears to mean more than that.[7] There are numerous instances in the Gospels of persons falling down before Jesus, worshiping him in gesture. They are reported to have bowed down or prostrated themselves before him. Instances are to be found in Matthew 2:2, 8, 11; 8:2; 9:18; 14:13; 15:35; 20:20; 28:9, 17; Mark 1:40; 5:6, 22; 10:17; 15:19 (ironically); Luke 5:12; 8:41; 17:16; 24:52; John 9:38; 11:32; 18:6. It should be noted that this does not necessarily mean formal worship, but at least, great respect.[8]

There are, however, some other, clearer instances of worship of Jesus in the Gospels. The most definite is Thomas's "My Lord and my God" in John 20:28. Less obvious is Peter's expression in Luke 5:8, "Go away from me, Lord; I am a sinful man!" This was the story of the miraculous catch of fish, obtained under unfavorable conditions (in daylight and in the deep part of the lake, after they had fished unsuccessfully all night). Peter's falling at Jesus' feet, his confession of his sinfulness, and his use of "Lord" suggest that he was aware of Jesus' deity and was paying homage to him.

There also is indication that the worship of the early church centered on Jesus. Baptism was a frequent part of that worship and was "into Christ" (Rom. 6:3; Gal. 3:27). The central act of the worship was the communion, or the Eucharist, depending on one's ecclesiastical tradition, and it is significant that it is "the Lord's Supper" (1 Cor. 11:20) or the "cup of the Lord" (v. 27; cf. 10:21). Indeed, the churches were called "the churches of Christ" (Rom. 16:16). Paul described Jesus as the head of the whole church (Eph. 1:22–23; 5:23) and its bridegroom (5:25–32).

Practice of the Church: Prayers to Jesus

Another aspect of the church's practice involves prayers to Christ. We have noted that there was no command by Christ or

7. Geoffrey Wainwright, *Doxology: The Praise of God in Worship, Doctrine and Life* (New York: Oxford University Press, 1980), pp. 46–47.

8. R. T. France, "The Worship of Jesus: a Neglected Factor in Christological Debate?" in *Christ the Lord,* ed. Harold H. Rowden (Downers Grove, Ill.: InterVarsity, 1982), pp. 26–27.

anyone else to people to pray to him. This is partly because Jesus was still present with these people, so that requests could be addressed directly to him. One does not ordinarily think of prayer as something to be made to someone who is physically present. Otherwise we could consider all of the requests directed to Jesus during his lifetime on earth to be prayers, especially if the person issuing the request thought of him as God. It is with respect to the risen and ascended Lord that there could be prayers. Here we find several interesting incidents.

The first of these is the stoning of Stephen. As the uproar was raised against Stephen, he looked up to heaven and saw the glory of God and Jesus standing at the right hand of God (Acts 7:56). Then, as he was being stoned, he "prayed," according to Luke, addressing two requests to the Lord: "Lord Jesus, receive my spirit" (v. 59); "Lord, do not hold this sin against them" (v. 60). Several observations about this incident are significant. Luke refers to it as a prayer, indicating that in Luke's mind there evidently was nothing improper about a prayer to Jesus. Possibly it was not as unusual or remarkable a practice in the early Christian community as we might otherwise conclude from the paucity of references to such a practice. Further, Stephen definitely and consciously identified the one to whom he was praying as Jesus. It may, of course, be argued that this was a mistaken act on Stephen's part, that the prayer should have been directed instead to the Father. Such an argument is at least plausible, but improbable, in view of the fact that Luke describes Stephen as "full of the Holy Spirit" (v. 55). That this Spirit, who empowered and guided the church so remarkably in this book and enabled Stephen to have such loving forgiveness toward his murderers, would have allowed Stephen to err in such an important matter seems rather improbable.

The next instance follows closely upon this one. Saul of Tarsus, who witnessed and consented to the murder of Stephen, was confronted by a bright light from heaven and fell to the ground (Acts 9:3–4). A voice spoke to him twice (vv. 4, 5b), the second time identifying himself as Jesus, and Saul spoke once to him (v. 5b). Then the Lord called to Ananias in a vision, and they had an extended conversation (vv. 10–16). The voice makes clear that he is the Lord, who has spoken to Saul (vv. 15–16), and Ananias not only speaks to him twice but subsequently indicates to Saul that it was the Lord Jesus who had spoken to him (v. 17). Both Saul's and Ananias's conversations with Jesus must be considered prayer, if prayer is conscious and intentional communication with God.

Another pertinent case is Paul's three-time repeated prayer for the removal of his "thorn in the flesh" in 2 Corinthians 12. He does not specifically and overtly identify the person to whom he prayed, other than "the Lord" (v. 8). Then that one prayed to responds, saying, "My grace is sufficient for you, for my power is made perfect in weakness" (v. 9a). Paul's comment is, "Therefore I will boast all the more gladly about my weaknesses, so that Christ's power may rest upon me. That is why, for Christ's sake, I delight in weaknesses, in insults, in hardships, in persecutions, in difficulties. For when I am weak, then I am strong" (vv. 9b–10). The connection between "my strength" and "Christ's power" and "for Christ's sake" strongly argues that this was, in Paul's mind, Christ to whom he was praying.

An example of a more widely used prayer is the *Maranatha*. An instance is found in 1 Corinthians 16:22: "If anyone does not love the Lord—a curse be on him. Come, O Lord!" That this Lord is Jesus seems clear from the two succeeding verses: "The grace of the Lord Jesus Christ be with you all. My love to all of you in Christ Jesus" (vv. 23–24). This was apparently a prayer prayed rather commonly in the church. An Aramaic expression was used with a Gentile church that otherwise would be unfamiliar with Aramaic; this suggests that it was in wide circulation and use, being virtually a formula.

One other expression that potentially bears on this issue is, "To the church of God in Corinth, to those sanctified in Christ Jesus and called to be holy, together with all those everywhere who call on the name of our Lord Jesus Christ—their Lord and ours" (1 Cor. 1:2). Is this not an indication of a widespread practice of praying to Jesus Christ? Some have denied that prayer is implied by an expression such as this. They say that this was simply the same as invoking the name of Caesar as support for one's request. It was not addressing Jesus when calling upon his name, but rather a matter of "praying in Jesus' name." Is this really so, however? It appeals to a Roman practice, rather than that of the

Jewish faith out of which this Christian belief had come. It seems more likely that this should be seen as a parallel to the Old Testament for worship and praise offered to God. Examples of this practice can be found in a large number of places. In Genesis 4:26 we read that "At that time men began to call on the name of the Lord." Abram built an altar and there "called on the name of the Lord" (Gen. 13:4). Similar expressions are found in Psalm 105:1; Jeremiah 10:25; and Joel 2:32.

One of the most significant instances of such expressions is found in Romans 10:13: "Everyone who calls on the name of the Lord will be saved," a quotation from Joel 2:32. That Paul is here referring to Jesus seems evident from verse 9, where he says that if one confesses with one's mouth, "Jesus is Lord," one will be saved. Calling on the Lord is evidently asking Jesus for salvation.

The reception of Christ as Savior and committing oneself to him as Lord is an act of prayer. Becoming a Christian is essentially a direct response to Christ. He says in Revelation 3:20, "Here I am! I stand at the door and knock. If anyone hears my voice and opens the door, I will go in and eat with him, and he with me." Persons do not become Christians by praying to the Father, asking him to apply the redeeming work of Christ to their lives. Rather, they come to the Father through the Son (John 14:6).

There also are Pauline benedictions, which while not in the strict sense prayers, are more than simply well-wishing. They are invoking the blessing of the Lord on his readers. One of these is in 2 Thessalonians 3:16: "Now may the Lord of peace himself give you peace at all times and in every way. The Lord be with all of you." Sometimes a benediction links the Father and the Son together: "Now may our God and Father himself and our Lord Jesus clear the way for us to come to you. May the Lord make your love increase and overflow for each other and for everyone else, just as ours does for you. May he strengthen your hearts so that you will be blameless and holy in the presence of our God and Father when our Lord Jesus comes with all his holy ones" (1 Thess. 3:11–13). Another example of a joint benediction is 2 Thessalonians 2:16: "May our Lord Jesus Christ himself and God our Father, who loved us and by his grace gave us eternal encouragement and good hope, encourage your hearts and strengthen you in every good deed and word." These benedictions come close to being prayers for these works of Christ in their lives.

Let us now summarize the matter of prayer to and worship of Jesus Christ. In the New Testament we have definite commands to pray to the Father. We also have the example of our Lord himself, as well as the model prayer that he gave his disciples and us. We do not have such commands with respect to prayer to Jesus. Jesus himself never commanded it, nor did Paul or any of the other New Testament writers. One can, however, understand Jesus' reluctance (or, in one sense, inability) to teach thus regarding himself. Much of his teaching was about the Father, although Harnack has exaggerated this dimension with his claim that Jesus' teaching was exclusively about the Father, not the Son. Jesus could hardly have given command to pray to him, at least within that contemporary setting. There were, however, invitations and commands that had something of that implication. One example was his statement, "Come to me, all you who are weary and burdened, and I will give you rest. Take my yoke upon you and learn from me, for I am gentle and humble in heart, and you will find rest for your souls. For my yoke is easy, and my burden is light" (Matt. 11:28–30). Such an invitation calls for a relationship and an interchange with Jesus that certainly seem to involve prayer, if it is to be continued and available after his departure from the earth.

It appears, then, that while this practice was not explicitly taught or commanded, it is at least implied. It should be noted that this is also the case with the doctrine of the Trinity itself. It is nowhere taught explicitly in Scripture, but is certainly implied. Thus, it can be inferred. If this is true of the doctrine, then it is not surprising if it is true of the accompanying practice as well.

The practice of believers had already come to include this within the New Testament period. Examples of prayer and worship are to be found within the New Testament, and a secular source from the early second century refers to the practice of Christians singing hymns to their Lord. Sometimes the argument from silence is used against the practice of prayer to Jesus Christ: If this is so important, then should it not be mentioned and commanded in the New Testament? The argument can, however, be turned on its head. If this is inappropriate, should not its practice be prohibited within the New Testament, where there are definite indications that it existed? Silence of the biblical writers would seem to be less compatible with improper than with proper practice.

Our conclusion, then, is that it is both appropriate and desirable to worship and pray to Jesus Christ. If the early church practiced it, then so should we. If we are called to a life of relationship and communion with and obedience to Jesus Christ, this surely must involve some sort of communication between us and the Lord. And what is this but prayer? If Christ is the head of the church, should not our relationship to him be expressed in some way, and is this not worship?

Worship of and Prayer to the Holy Spirit

When we come to the question of a relationship to the Holy Spirit, however, the problem is more involved and troublesome. We have very little material in the Scriptures to draw on in formulating our practice. That, in a sense, is not surprising, for there is really very little material about the Holy Spirit in general within Scripture, when compared with the treatments of the Father and the Son. There simply was less said about the Spirit, perhaps because his "era," as it were, was relatively late in coming, and perhaps in part because as the inspirer of the Scripture writers and thus derivatively of the Scriptures, the Holy Spirit directed attention primarily to the other two members of the Trinity.

One passage that some believe indicates worship of the Holy Spirit is Philippians 3:3. In the New International Version, this is translated: "For it is we who are the circumcision, we who worship by the Spirit of God, who glory in Christ Jesus, and who put no confidence in the flesh." The significant portion of the verse, for our purposes, is the second of the "who" clauses. In the Greek it reads, οἱ πνεύματι θεοῦ λατρεύοντες. There is an ambiguity here, centering on the word πνεύματι. This can be translated either "by the Spirit" or "the Spirit." If the latter, then we have "who worship the Spirit," and a clear case of Spirit-worship in the New Testament. The noun is in the dative (or locative or instrumental) case. It would therefore normally be translated "by (or "through") the Spirit." However, the verb λατρεύω takes the dative case with the direct object, so that on purely linguistic and grammatical grounds it could equally well be translated "worship the Spirit" as it could "worship by the Spirit." Augustine thought this passage was referring to worship of the Spirit, and his influence created something of a tradition.

The decision regarding the correct rendering must be made on syntactical grounds. Here the question concerns to what the clause "worship [by] the Spirit" is parallel. If it is a parallel to "glory in Christ Jesus," then "worship the Spirit" would be the preferred rendering. If, however, it is to be understood as parallel to "have no confidence in the flesh," that would favor the translation "worship by the Spirit." There is a neat symmetry between the clauses "who worship the Spirit" and "glory in Christ Jesus," but it should be noted that "glory in Christ Jesus" is not exactly parallel to "worship the Spirit."

Again we find difficulty untying the knot on the syntactical level. It would appear that the next source of insight will need to be the contextual issue. Here the fact that Paul seems throughout the section to be stressing not having confidence in the flesh favors the idea of worshiping by the Spirit, depending on him, rather than worshiping him. This is not, of course, conclusive, but it renders the translation, "who worship the Spirit" sufficiently unlikely that we cannot really rest such a significant practice on it.

The other text sometimes appealed to in support of the idea of worship of the Spirit is 1 Corinthians 6:19. A recent translation of this is "Honor God with your body." Here again, because of the identical form of the dative, instrumental, and locative cases, and the ambiguity of the preposition ἐν, the phrase can be translated either "with your body" or "in your body." Augustine, who knew only Latin, not Greek, rendered it, "Glorify the God in your body" (i.e., the Holy Spirit, whose temple the body is). The Latin with which Augustine worked allowed this translation, which in its fullness would have been, "Glorify the God (which is) in your body." The Greek, however, permits only the adverbial idea, "Glorify God in (or with) your body." Thus, this supposed text is seen to have been misunderstood.

The conclusion that follows is that in the New Testament we do not have either texts commanding or texts describing worship of or prayer to the Holy Spirit. Geoffrey Wainwright says, "So we may conclude that there is no case in which the Spirit figures as an object of worship in the New Testament writings."[9] Arthur Wainwright puts it equally strongly: "There is no evidence in the New Testament that the Spirit was worshipped or received prayer."[10] It appears, then that in the New Testament the Holy Spirit was not the recipient, but rather, the instrument, the enabler, of prayer. Prayer was done "in the Spirit," or "by the Spirit," rather than "to the Spirit."

If, then, we can find in the New Testament neither instruction nor example of worship of the Holy Spirit, we need to ask at what point such practice did enter the church. Leonard Hodgson has affirmed that there was no early practice of this: "Now it is true, so far as I know, there is extant no instance of hymns or prayers addressed to the Holy Spirit that is certainly earlier than the tenth century. It is also true that the standard form of Christian worship is worship offered by the Christian to the Father in union with the Son through the Spirit."[11] This seems, however, to be a bit of an overstatement. While rare during the first five centuries, there are indications of worship of the Spirit in conjunction with the Father and Son. There was a growing practice of prayer and worship of the Holy Spirit. Basil of Caesarea claims that in the third century Origen used a form of the Gloria in which the Spirit was placed on the same level with the Father and the Son.[12] There actually is evidence of such a practice earlier. In the apocryphal *Ascension of Isaiah*, both Christ and the Holy Spirit are objects of worship. This passage (9:16) occurs in a section termed "The Vision of Isaiah," which has been dated at the latest to the end of the second century, and may have been in circulation much earlier.[13] In the third-century *Acts of Thomas* there is a series of eight invocations made to the Holy Spirit.[14] Here definite requests are made, which must conclusively be understood as instances of prayer. So we have record of prayer to

9. Wainwright, *Doxology,* pp. 92–93.

10. Arthur W. Wainwright, *The Trinity in the New Testament* (London: SPCK, 1962), p. 228.

11. Leonard Hodgson, *The Doctrine of the Trinity* (New York: Scribners, 1944), p. 232.

12. *On the Holy Spirit* 73.

13. Wainwright, *Trinity in the New Testament,* p. 229.

14. *The Acts of Thomas* 27.

the Holy Spirit in the third and even the second centuries. Since, however, this evidence is in books not considered part of mainstream Christianity of the time, it cannot be used as evidence of generally accepted prayer and worship.

It appears that the growth of such practices was slow, but was stimulated by the presence of the Arian heresy. The creed drawn up at the Council of Nicea in 325 had been very brief regarding the Holy Spirit, saying simply "and [we believe] in the Holy Spirit." Beginning about 340 in Antioch, there were increased worship and prayer to the Holy Spirit. Actually Christians in Mesopotamia had worshiped thus for some time, since in the Syrian language the only conjunction is "and." Basil introduced an intentionally anti-Arian doxology: "to God the Father *with* the Son, *together with* the Holy Spirit." He was accused of being a revolutionary and an innovator. He wrote *On the Holy Spirit* in 375. He was hesitant to call the Holy Spirit God, since the New Testament does not do so. He used the idea of *homotimos* (same praise) of the Spirit, as the equivalent of *homoousios*. He maintained that it was permissible to worship the Spirit *together with* the Father and the Son, if not in isolation. He argued from the liturgy to the nature of the Spirit.

Basil contended that it was not orthodoxy with its trinitarianism that was guilty of ranking the Holy Spirit with the Father and the Son. Rather, it was Jesus Christ himself who had done so by giving the baptismal formula in the name of Father, Son, and Holy Spirit.[15] Athanasius had earlier made much of the formula, suggesting that if one did not accept the deity of the Holy Spirit, the work of baptism could not then have its full effect. Basil went on to contend that if baptism is into the name of the Father, the Son, and the Holy Spirit, and if the Spirit is but a creature, then one has not truly been initiated into the full Godhead.[16] Further, not only in the baptismal formula and the doxology, but in the hymn sung at the lighting of the lamps each evening there was evidence of the ancient practice, which was preserved in the words "We praise Father, Son, and God's Holy Spirit."[17] It was at the Council of Constantinople that the Holy Spirit really came

15. *On the Holy Spirit* 10.24.
16. Ibid., 29.75.
17. Ibid., 29.73.

into his own for the first time. Now the Spirit was declared to be *homoousios* with the Father and with the Son. At last full equality had been accorded the Spirit with the other persons of the Trinity.

What, now, shall we say regarding the proper practice for us to engage in regarding the Holy Spirit? We have noted that there was no evidence of the worship of and prayer to the Holy Spirit in the New Testament, nor in the earliest church. The practice began slowly and accelerated following Nicea. What should be noted here is that there was not explicit statement of the deity of the Holy Spirit within the pages of the New Testament, either. The belief and teaching were only implicit. Indeed, for much of the church during this period there appears to have been at least functionally a dyadic, rather than a fully triadic, faith. There is, however, an interesting parallel between the explicit formulation of the doctrine and the growth of the practice of trinitarian worship. The making explicit of the doctrine and the growth of the practice are intimately intertwined in ways that make it difficult at times to ascertain which is cause and which is effect. It does seem, however, that the increase in the practice of worshiping and praying to the Holy Spirit was a logical consequence of coming to belief in the deity of the Holy Spirit. Causal effect is of course difficult to establish, but coordinate development certainly argues for the probability of causal effect.

Practice as Inference from the Doctrine of the Holy Spirit

If this contention is correct, that the origin and growth of worship of the Holy Spirit paralleled and were derived from the development of the doctrinal belief regarding the Spirit, then there are two questions we need to resolve to determine our practice with respect to the Spirit as well: Was the church correct in its conclusion of the *homoousion* of the Spirit? Was the church correct in deriving its practice of worship of the Spirit from this belief? We will, for purposes of this discussion, assume the answer to the first question to be "yes." The treatment of the biblical materials supporting the doctrine of the Trinity will be considered to have resolved this issue as well. That leaves us to grapple with the latter question, whether prayer and worship follow from the doctrine of that Holy Spirit.

We need to note that the Holy Spirit is a person, with all the qualities of a person. He exercises a personal ministry in the lives of persons. He does the convicting or convincing of unbelievers—of sin, of righteousness, and of judgment (John 16:8–11). He regenerates or gives new life (John 3:5–8). He guides into truth (John 16:13). He inspired the Scripture writers to produce the books of the Bible as we have them. He sanctifies believers (Rom. 8:1–17). He empowers for service (Acts 1:8). We are not told that in any of these works he does what he does through the Father or the Son. These are direct ministries, involving a direct relationship.

As a person, the Spirit also should be capable of being related to personally. This we also find in the Scriptures. Ananias and Sapphira were told that they had lied to the Holy Spirit (Acts 5:3). Paul commanded his readers not to grieve the Holy Spirit (Eph. 4:30). Surely, however, only a person can be grieved or lied to.

Now if these things are true, that the Holy Spirit ministers directly and personally to us and we are able to relate directly and personally to him, then what is the nature of that relationship? Does it not involve communication of a direct and personal nature? And what is such communication, if it is not prayer? If we wish for someone else to be convicted of sin, if it is the Holy Spirit who does that, should not our prayer that such be done be directed either to the Triune God or to the Holy Spirit? Why would we pray for the Father to do that which is properly the work of the Spirit? If we desire to be filled with the Spirit, or to be more responsive to his sanctifying work, should not that be declared to him? If we wish to thank him for his work of regenerating us, or of guiding and illuminating us, should this not be expressed to him?

If we do not do that, if we instead direct our prayers exclusively to the Father, it would seem to be for one (or more) of six reasons. It may be that we do not really believe in the personal nature of the Holy Spirit. It may be that we have not really thought about the distinctive works of individual members of the Trinity. It may be that we believe that all prayer has to be received on behalf of the Trinity by the Father. It may be that we consider the works performed by the Father to be somehow more important than those of the Spirit. It may be that we consider all the works of the Trinity to be done primarily by the Father. It may be that we consider the works done by the Holy Spirit to be done under the direction or ultimate control of the Father. If, however, it is because of any of the last three or even four of these reasons, is this not an indication of belief in the subordination (real or essential subordination, not merely functional subordination) of the Holy Spirit and presumably also of the Son to the Father?

If the decision of the Council of Constantinople was correct, and if this involved not only the deity and personality but also the equality of the three persons of the Trinity, then are we not to engage in prayer to the Holy Spirit? Our failure to do so is a failure to carry through on the practical implications of our belief.

It seems, however, that worship is properly to be directed primarily to the Triune God, or all three persons collectively. Thus, most of our activity in worship will be worship of "God," rather than "Father," "Son," or "Holy Spirit." While we may in worship praise God for individual works or roles, and in that respect direct that element of our worship especially to that one person, we should not detach it from the worship of the three-in-one. The same applies to prayer. For the most part, we will pray to the Triune God. Even when we pray regarding one of the works that is the distinctive special responsibility of one of the three, and direct it to that person, we will retain the consciousness that the whole Trinity is involved in that work, and that it is one of those persons especially doing that work on behalf of the triunity of persons, or of the triunity doing that work through that one person. Our belief is in one Triune God, not in three gods, and we will want to be careful to preserve that distinctness in our belief and experience.

Conclusion

Practical Considerations and Future Prospects

In this conclusion, we aim to do several things. First, we will respond to the issue of the practicality of the doctrine of the Trinity, as raised by both Immanuel Kant and Karl Rahner, as well as the more recent popular objectors. We also, however, wish to look at the future of the doctrine of the Trinity. Having in an earlier portion of this work examined the way in which the doctrine of the Trinity was progressively assembled in its definitive form by theologians, or where it has come from, we want to attempt to anticipate where it might go from here. Finally, we want to raise the practical question of ways in which the doctrine, if it is really important to our Christian faith, might be preached and taught effectively.

The Practicality of the Doctrine of the Trinity

When we ask about whether something is practical, we must always ask what we mean by practical and for whom it is practical. In the 1960s it was popular to dismiss issues and viewpoints as "irrelevant," without asking, "irrelevant for whom?" I used to employ as an example, the expression "irrelevant as the anatomy of a penguin," until a biologist pointed out to me that the anatomy of a penguin is very relevant to a penguin. Thus, hidden within unqualified statements about relevance or irrelevance or practicality or impracticality are frequently tacitly assumed one's own viewpoint or perspective. The statement, "That's not practical," may mean nothing more nor less than, "That does not fit my tastes or preferences."

The statement "that is practical," or "that works," is therefore a relative statement. It really should be, "That is practical for . . . ," or "that works for . . ." Something may be very helpful in preparing someone to be a good thief, prostitute, or drug pusher. Whether it is good in some more absolute sense, however, depends on whether one endorses those activities or the values embodied in them. On a purely pragmatic basis, that higher value would have to be justified on other pragmatic grounds as to whether it contributes to a still higher value. It would seem probable, however, that such a pragmatic justification cannot be carried on indefinitely. At some point, it has to be supported by whether it contributes to a value established on some other basis.

Typically, Christian beliefs and practices are evaluated by whether and the degree to which they enable believers to fulfill Christian values, those revealed by God. Those values may be quite different than those that the general public would endorse. Yet they are in keeping with God's nature and plans. So, for example, many persons, some of them even non-Christians, quote Romans 8:28: "And we know that in all things God works for the good of those who love him, who have been called according to his purpose." They then, however, are angry and resentful when unpleasant and even seemingly disastrous things happen to them—illness, loss of a job, loss of a loved one, or the like. Note, however, that they are setting their own standards of the good, namely, what is pleasant and comfortable for them, and evaluating what God does by the extent to which it contributes to the realization of such goals in their lives. Yet, examined in context, we can ask what "the good" is. That is seen in verse 29: "For those God foreknew he also predestined to be conformed to the likeness of his Son." This, then, is the criterion of practicality: whether it contributes to the realization of this goal, the conforming of believers to the likeness of Christ, rather than whether it contributes to the success, happiness, comfort, or whatever, of such persons.

There is, however, a more basic question that can be posed regarding any idea. Does this have any sort of implications for some sort of conceivable behavior or action, or is it indifferent to action at all? When we pose this question, we must also make sure that we are stating the doctrine accurately and with sufficient detail so that it really is this idea being fairly evaluated. This is one aspect of the response to Kant's criticism of the Trinity, namely, his claim that it makes no difference for practical action whether one worships three gods or ten. It may well be that there is no material difference between the implications of these two different numbers. Yet we must ask whether this is the crucial aspect of the Trinity. The real facet that bears on this is the nature of the relationships among the members of the Trinity. In other words, does the idea of three persons, in the sense of three centers of consciousness that completely share their lives with one another, have any bearing on behavior of humans, either as individuals or in groups? Does this offer any pattern for living, and do these patterns contribute to any values recognized on other grounds?

Let us briefly summarize again the understanding of the Trinity we have developed in these pages. The Trinity is a communion of three persons, three centers of consciousness, who exist and always have existed in union with one another and in dependence on one another. Each is dependent for his life on each of the others. They share their lives, having such a close relationship that each is conscious of what the other is conscious of. They have never had any prior independent existence, and will not and cannot have any such now or in the future. Each is essential to the life of each of the others, and to the life of the Trinity. They are bound to one another in love, *agapē* love, which therefore unites them in the closest and most intimate of relationships. This unselfish, *agapē* love makes each more concerned for the other than for himself. There is therefore a mutual submission of each to each of the others and a mutual glorifying of one another. There is complete equality of the three. There has been, to be sure, temporary subordination of one member of the Trinity to the other, but this is functional rather than essential. At the same time, this unity and equality do not require identity of function. There are certain roles that distinctively belong primarily to one, although all participate in the function of each.

One of the first points from which our bridge of applicability of the doctrine to the practice is to be built is the image of God in which all humans have been created (Gen. 1:26–27). If this God in whose image humans have been made is triune, then it ought to be the case that the image in some way reflects this triunity. It was because of this that Augustine looked for a trinity within each human. That was done, to a large extent, however, within an essentially individualistic context, considering each human individually as the image. The understanding we have formulated and are advocating here calls for a somewhat large base for consideration of the implications of this triune image.

It should be noted that certain types of general social philosophies or philosophies of culture and society can be correlated to some extent with certain interpretations of the Trinity. For example, tritheism would correlate with individualism, for tritheism sees the Godhead as composed of three relatively independent persons. On the other hand, views of the Trinity that are more monarchical in nature would incline toward a sheer monotheism and thus would fit an understanding of social unit in which authority is more concentrated in a single individual central group, in other words, a more authoritarian or even totalitarian view of the group or of society. Thus, the type of trinitarian interpretation that is found more appealing will depend to some extent on the social orientation within which it is being considered. In Western society at the present time there tends to be a rather strong individualism, causing the more tritheistic view to seem more plausible. However, Eastern cultures, with a stronger group consciousness and even a patriarchal or in some cases a matriarchal organization of the family or the society, may find a monarchical view of the Trinity more natural. There may, on the other hand, be a negative reaction, so that for those still living within a society in which decision making is concentrated in the hands of a few, the appeal of a more communal view may be great.

What would be the effect of this communal understanding of the Trinity first on our understanding of the person, even the individual person? It would seem that a first implication would be to stress that true personhood involves social interaction, social relationships. To the extent that the individual reflects the image of the Triune God, that individual would not be solitary or independent, but would be related to other persons, and as we shall see in a moment, related in a particular way. Catherine LaCugna says, "The truth about both God and ourselves is that we were meant to exist as persons in communion in a common household, living as persons from and for others, not persons in isolation or withdrawal or self-centredness."[1] Leonardo Boff says much the same thing: "In the light of the Trinity, being a person in the image and likeness of the divine Persons means acting as a permanently active web of relationships."[2] Some have tried to find a concrete content in the social or communal personhood that constitutes the Trinity. Karl Barth, for example, saw the maleness-femaleness dichotomy as a reflection of the Trinity.[3] He read Genesis 1:27 as a three-strophe parallelism, so that "male and female he created them," was equivalent to "God created man in his own image," and "in the image of God he created him." Whether this is a correct interpretation of the passage, and whether this interpersonal communion must be reflected in relationships with persons of the opposite sex, it appears that this general point reflects the social and communal nature of God. Strong individualism is difficult to sustain on this basis.

Note, too, the nature of such relationships, if they are to reflect the nature of the intratrinitarian relationships. These relationships of Father and Son and Spirit must be understood as bound by *agapē*, self-sacrificial, giving love. There is mutual submission of each of the members of the Trinity to each of the others. Thus, the type of relationship that should characterize human persons, particularly believing Christians who have accepted the structure of intratrinitarian relationships as the pattern for their own relationships to others, would be one of unselfish love and submission to the other, seeking the welfare of the other over one's own. Humility, then, in the best senses of the word, will be one of the prized virtues. This, of course, goes contrary to much of contemporary society in the United States and many other similar societies with the emphasis on self-realization, self-gratification, self-fulfillment, machismo, and a certain assertiveness.

1. Catherine Mowry LaCugna, *God for Us: The Trinity and Christian Life* (San Francisco: HarperCollins, 1991), p. 383.
2. Leonardo Boff, *Trinity and Society* (Maryknoll, N.Y.: Orbis, 1988), p. 149.
3. Karl Barth, *Church Dogmatics* (Edinburgh: T. & T. Clark, 1958), vol. 1, part 1, 184–87.

But what of the implications of this for the most basic social structure, the family? Here it would seem that if the aim of the Christian is to emulate the pattern of relationships among the members of the Godhead, there will certainly not be quite the sort of patriarchalism that has sometimes characterized the family. Not just the welfare or the desires or pleasure of one member of the family, but that of all members will be paramount to the existence of the family. This is not to say that all will necessarily have an equal voice in determining the actions of the family. There is still the possibility and at least to some extent, the necessity, of something of the functional subordination that is found among members of the Trinity. One cannot necessarily derive a purely egalitarian family pattern from this characteristic of the internal relations of the Trinity alone.

When carried over into relationships with other believers, there will be definite implications as well. The model that Paul gives is that of Christ. He says, "Each of you should look not only to his own interests, but also to the interests of others. Your attitude should be the same as that of Christ Jesus" (Phil. 2:4). He then goes on to describe the fashion in which Jesus, although he was equal with God, did not regard that equality as something to be clung to, but emptied himself by taking on the form of a servant. This action, however, if we have correctly understood intratrinitarian dynamics, is representative of the mutual deference of each person of the Trinity to the others. Concern for others and their needs will therefore be a primary value and goal for us. The same servanthood that Jesus practiced toward the Father will be practiced by us toward each other. This was what lay behind Jesus' washing of the feet of the disciples, the desire to give them and us an example. Not insisting on one's own way, not insisting on receiving the credit and recognition for what is done, is an emulation of the nature of the Trinity. Indeed, Jesus said of those who desired such recognition, "they have received their reward in full" (Matt. 6:5).

This concern for and feeling the needs and sharing the life of others will change our attitude toward our possessions as well. It was an amazing characteristic of the early church that its membership sold their property and came and deposited the proceeds in a common fund or treasury. Luke says of them, "All the believers were one in heart and mind. No one claimed that any of his possessions was his own, but they shared everything they had" (Acts 4:32). They did not think in terms of helping someone else out of their own resources, but thought of the resources as being owned by the group. So there was not even any credit, for which one could perhaps feel some pride, in someone being helped. It was not, "This brother has a need, and I have the means to help him." Rather it was the case that, "We (the group) have a need, and we have the means to meet that need." There was a sense of joint ownership by the group of all that anyone within it had, and in this respect there was a resemblance to the openness, sharing, and communion of the members of the Trinity. Stewardship, of course, begins with the realization that everything that we hold actually belongs to God. In the case of the early church, that extended to the conception that this was even to be held by the group, not any of the individuals.

This should also be reflected within the organization of the church. While this may not dictate a particular form of church government, it is most easily fitted with a congregational form of government, where each communicant has a share in the power of determination of the group's actions. Whatever the form of government, however, no one will seek to dominate, to force his or her view and desires on the group. Each will be solicitous of the convictions of the others. There will be no coercion, no political bargaining, no seeking to restrict the power to a small group.

Jesus indicated that this was to be the pattern of leadership. He said that the leaders of the Gentiles "lord it over" those over whom they have been given authority. Instead, anyone who wants to be the leader should become the servant of all. It was particularly incongruous that these disciples should be arguing among themselves as to who was the greatest of all, when Jesus made himself subject to them, as he also had subjected himself to the Father.

This should also be present in the area of interchurch relationships. If there is a tritheistic understanding of the Trinity, or in other words, an understanding in which the three are relatively independent of one another, then one might expect that churches would also be independent of one another. Each might do its own ministry without any real regard for other congregations. Indeed, any form of cooperative endeavor, such as is appropriate either in the more formal relationship of denominations, or more informally in the mutual fellowship of fraternal congregations, would tend to be disregarded. There might well be competition between the ministries of neighboring or rival congregations. In fact, there might be disregard for the geographical sphere of ministry of another congregation, or the membership of another church. The only thing that would matter would be the "prospering" of the ministry of one's own church.

If, on the other hand, we have understood and are living by the pattern of the Trinity, then there will be a sense of the oneness of the entire body of Christ. Christ, after all, prayed that his followers would be one as he and the Father were one. Each would, in this pattern, be cognizant that in a sense, they and other believers and congregations are simply part of one great whole. When there was some disagreement over a matter of common concern and participation, one congregation would not pull away from another to go its own way or act independently. Not insisting on one's own way (1 Cor. 13:5), it would work in dialogue with others. It would not see all of its resources as its own (which, of course, according to our understanding of stewardship, is true, since even after being given to "the Lord's work," it belongs to him, not to his agencies). It would not seek to undercut the ministry of another church, or to proselytize from another congregation. It would be able to rejoice in the prospering of another congregation, just as greatly as in the prospering of its own ministry.

But what, however, of the implications of this for the larger structure of society? Here liberation theologians have made much of the communion of equals within the Trinity as a basis for society. Leonardo Boff notes that the communion within the Trinity has not simply remained within itself. It also has extended beyond itself to the creation. So, says Boff, "human beings cannot concentrate on their own interpersonal relations to the exclusion of a sense of their wider, trans-personal and structural relationships, with society and history."[4] So there must be involvement with the conflicts and processes of social change, seeking to establish new relationships, which are more participa-

4. Boff, *Trinity and Society*, p. 149.

tory and humanizing. Even the community must place itself within a greater whole.[5]

When measured against the ideal of trinitarian communion modern society shows considerable aberrations, in both of its principal current embodiments, capitalism and socialism. Boff says that capitalism involves the dictatorship of the property-owning classes, whose individualistic and business interests are always shored up by mechanisms of state control. This domination is the cause of most of the misery of the world's poor, especially in the third world. Together with this goes the imposition of one political model. Differences from the one right system are regarded as pathological deviations from the norm. On the other hand, societies based on socialism at least have grasped the right principle, of communion between all and involvement of all in the means of production. This social element is, however, put to work collectivistically, without going through the essential process of accepting differences between persons and communities. It must be seen as the imposition of the social element from above, through the party. This bureaucratic imposition fails to produce a society of equality within the bounds of respect for differences. Rather, it gives one of collectivization with elements of massification. It does not respect and preserve individual differences. It subsumes individuals into a homogenizing and egalitarian whole. Thus it too is not the ideal embodiment of the trinitarian model of communion. The sort of society that would emerge from inspiration by the trinitarian model would be one characterized by fellowship, equality of opportunity, and sharing.[6]

Whether we follow Boff's precise reasoning, there is a point to be observed here. If we believe that all humans and the human race collectively are made in the image of God and that God is trinitarian, then the relationships of communion that characterize that God should be present in the society as well. Christians, as responsible members of a given society and of the world community, will not be able to remain indifferent to the needs and concerns of those in other parts of our society or of the world. Most certainly, we would not be able to prosper personally or nationally through exploitation of others.

5. Ibid.
6. Ibid., pp. 150–51.

This concern does not dictate any one political or economic system, as even Boff concedes. It should, however, give us certain basic values that we will want to preserve in our selection of any such system. Just how this is implemented will depend to a large extent on our conviction regarding the relationship of the church and of Christianity in general to the structures of society, political and otherwise. Since the image of God is universal, being given to Adam, who was at that point the entire human race (Gen. 1:26–27), and is still present in humans after the fall (Gen. 9:6), our concern should extend beyond Christians to all persons. Whether Christian values can be used openly or only tacitly as our motivation, they should provide some impetus for us to work for the establishment of societal structures that take into account this fundamental communion dimension of the Trinity as the model for the relationships among the highest earthly creatures.

So far we have spoken primarily about the practical effect of the doctrine of the Trinity with respect to social relationships. We need to ask also about the implications of this understanding of the doctrine for our individual piety or devotion. The major effect may be in helping us understand that the three members of the Trinity do not act in isolation or independence of one another. Rather, all are involved in any given action by one of them. In practice, many Christians are either tritheist or Arian. Frequently, the Father, Son, and Holy Spirit are thought of somewhat separately, almost like three different and distinct persons. This understanding of communion and perichoresis tends to nullify that effect. And, because of understanding that the three persons are fully equal, any indications of subordination being related to the state of humiliation, we will treat the Son and the Spirit with all of the reverence and worship that we already accord to the Father.

For example, the atonement is sometimes pictured in legal terms in which the Father (the judge) finds the defendant (sinful humanity) guilty; then a third party (the Son) steps in and pays the penalty that has been imposed. There is, to all appearances, something improper about this arrangement, in which a judge administers a sentence to an innocent party. In fact, it almost appears as if this third party is made to submit to an externally imposed edict. When viewed from the perspective that we have been describing, however, this is seen quite differently. The analogy almost should be modified so that it is the judge who steps down from the bench and pays the fine or serves the sentence himself. The decision to offer a sacrifice and the administering and transferring of the judgment are not something done by independent and separate persons. The Son participates in the judgment decision as does the Father, and the Father undergoes the effects of that judgment as genuinely as does the Son.

There is a fresh understanding of the problem of evil as well. Because earlier theologians were rightfully desirous of avoiding the modalistic heresy, they sought to protect the doctrine from patripassianism, according to which the Father suffered. In so doing, however, God was made to appear aloof and indifferent to human need and suffering. Thus the problem of evil seemed to be aggravated by an understanding of God as uncaring because he was impervious to the suffering in his world. He simply was unable to experience these ills. The understanding of the Trinity that we have sketched, however, sees the Father participating in the pain of this world, because, as a result of the close relationship to the Son, he has also experienced vicariously the ills of human existence.

This should also give us a sense of closer relationship with all of the members of the Trinity than we might otherwise posses. We sometimes think of the Father as rather far removed from us, so that our primary relationship and experience is with either the Son or the Spirit, who dwell within us. If, however, we understand that each of the persons is at work in and through the work of each of the others, we will recognize that we are also related to the Father in being related to the Son or the Spirit. It is through them that his presence is mediated.

The Future of the Doctrine of the Trinity

Will the doctrine of the Trinity fade in importance or will it continue to be regarded as crucial? If the latter, will it be held in such a way as to have influence and implication for the practical living of life, as well as for the official doctrinal statements of the church? If it is widely held, what form of understanding will it take?

To a large extent, the answers to these questions depend on the extent to which other, larger factors prevail. One of these will be the future of interreligious dialogue. There will be increasing penetration of societies such as the United States, where Christianity has been dominant, by other religions. This will be both through immigration and through missionary endeavor. The affinity of "new age" type thinking to much Eastern thought will also be a factor. In these dialogues, the doctrine of the Trinity and its accompanying doctrine, the incarnation, will be crucial factors, for they separate Christianity from strictly monotheistic religions, such as Judaism and Islam, on the one hand, and from polytheistic or pantheistic religions, such as Hinduism and Buddhism, on the other. If increasing numbers of Christians become pluralistic in their outlook, the doctrine of the Trinity will have to be abandoned, ignored, or greatly modified. If inclusivism increases, it will mean that belief in the uniquely Christian doctrines will be seen as less important. One may come to be related to the Triune God of Christianity, with less necessity of conscious belief in that doctrinal understanding of God. At the time of this writing, pluralism and inclusivism seem to be increasing. At some point, there will certainly be a reversal of that trend, but it does not yet seem to be emerging. In addition, given the mood of the times, in which tolerance of diversity is politically correct, even those who see significant differences between Christianity and other religions and believe they cannot be assimilated to one another, will be hesitant to express such opinions. Until that time comes, there will be a popular tendency to mute the expression of the doctrine of the Trinity.

At the same time, the rise of theological interest in the doctrine seems to show no sign of declining. This is in part probably stimulated by the encroachments of non-Christian and non-trinitarian religions. It becomes increasingly important to understand just what is meant by the doctrine if Christianity is to engage in dialogue with other religions. Thus, the direct effects of the efforts of those in the areas of world religions may have the indirect effect, among theologians, of heightening the concern for and articulation of the doctrine of the Trinity.

Certain other forces are at work, tending to minimize the necessity of doctrine in general. One example is the kind of church growth movement we discussed in the introductory chapter, which is more oriented to meeting of human felt needs than on abstract hairsplitting regarding doctrine. We can probably expect a decline in preaching and teaching about the Trinity and other similar doctrines in the churches that have accepted this theory.

At the same time that these forces are at work, tending to minimize the place of the doctrine of the Trinity, other forces will tend to give it greater prominence. For example, the rise of third world Christianity will also be reflected in theology being developed by those segments of the church. In general, those societies are less individualistic and more group conscious than the more individualistic Western church. Consequently, it will probably be the case that a sense of the oneness of the group will make thinking of the three members of the Trinity more natural. Indeed, this may tend to place the emphasis more strongly on the oneness rather than the threeness of the Trinity. In addition, the emphasis on "high touch," which in American society is tending to complement "high tech,"[7] should help create an atmosphere more conducive to the social conception of the Trinity. Moreover, the encounter with other world religions, while in some cases tending to blunt the doctrine of the Trinity, will also have the effect in some circles of bringing about a more clearly and firmly enunciated statement of this doctrine. There also are indications of a protest against the pragmatism of ministry that minimizes doctrine in favor of numerical success.[8] This should also encourage serious doctrinal reflection and belief.

At this point, it appears unlikely that a great deal more will be contributed to construction of the doctrine of the Trinity from biblical studies, where probably most of the relevant biblical passages have been well examined. What is more likely, however, is that more progress will be made in understanding the conceptual factors in the doctrine of triunity. More work such as *Philosophy and the Christian Faith*,[9] *Logic and the Nature of God*,[10] and

7. John Naisbitt, *Megatrends: Ten New Directions Transforming Our Lives* (New York: Warner, 1982), pp. 39–53.

8. E.g., *No God But God: Breaking with the Idols of Our Age*, ed. Os Guinness and John Seel (Chicago: Moody, 1992).

9. Thomas Morris, ed., *Philosophy and the Christian Faith* (Notre Dame, Ind.: University of Notre Dame Press, 1988).

10. Stephen T. Davis, *Logic and the Nature of God* (Grand Rapids: Eerdmans, 1983).

Trinity, Incarnation, and Atonement[11] will help refine our trinitarian doctrine. The growing number of philosophers giving serious attention to philosophical issues related to Christian theology provide a valuable resource for theology. This is evidenced by the rapid growth in membership of the Society of Christian Philosophers, which now numbers over one thousand internationally.

Teaching and Preaching the Doctrine of the Trinity

But what shall be done by way of teaching this important doctrine to Christian believers and would-be believers? If this indeed is a core belief of Christianity, it is of great importance. It appears as if the teaching of this doctrine has not been given adequate attention in the past. It has been part of the official doctrinal standards of many Christian groups and has been taught through the catechism, but may otherwise have been one of those beliefs that were simply left relatively unexplained. Given the types of considerations we observed in the opening chapter, it will be important to explain and emphasize this more fully.

With respect to preaching and public worship, we might well begin by making certain that Trinity Sunday is observed each year in our churches. Perhaps because of a fear of being associated with liturgy, many evangelical churches make little of the church calendar, other than Christmas and Easter (usually referred to that way, rather than Advent and Lent). Indeed, in many churches Mother's Day (and possibly even Father's Day), Memorial Day, Independence Day, Labor Day, and Thanksgiving Day receive more attention and are more regularly observed than are Pentecost Sunday and Ascension Sunday, as well as Trinity Sunday. The point is not whether the service on that specific day is geared to the understanding of the Trinity, but whether there is a regular means by which attention is required to be directed to the doctrine of the Trinity. Observing Trinity Sunday would have the benefit of projecting a sense of identification with the broader Christian church. There would be a sermon on the Trin-

---

11. Ronald Feenstra and Cornelius Plantinga, Jr., eds., *Trinity, Incarnation, and Atonement: Philosophical and Theological Essays* (Notre Dame, Ind.: University of Notre Dame Press, 1989).

ity preached in the context of a service planned to highlight the trinitarian character of Christian faith. The songs sung and the Scripture selected would contribute to the emphasis upon the Trinity.

There should be other times as well when the Trinity is emphasized. In our preaching, there are numerous places where it is possible to point out the significance of the doctrine. For example, when speaking of the birth of Jesus, the role of the Father in sending the Son and the Spirit in bringing about the virginal conception needs to be included. In discussing the death of Christ, the trinitarian dimension of the atonement could well be enunciated. Songs should be selected in such a way that the faith of the believer is not directed one-sidedly to one member of the Trinity in relative disregard of the other persons.

We definitely need to show the practical significance of the doctrine. For example, prayer is often done with little thought given to the person or persons to whom directed. Some Christian "specialists" address their prayers almost exclusively to the Father or to the Son. The dynamics of this can be better explicated. This also involves creating an appreciation for the role of each person of the Trinity in each of the significant experiences of the Christian life. The doctrine of salvation should be enriched by a study of the relative place of each person, and by understanding, for example, the suffering of the Father in the life and death of the Son.

People today are very oriented to the visual, and have a relatively short attention span. Because of this various dramatic techniques may be desirable to seek to convey the concepts involved. For example, one pastor presented a three-point sermon; in each point he presented the work of a different member of the Trinity, in first-person form. After each five-minute presentation, the congregation sang a different stanza of "Praise Ye the Triune God." A separate song, focused on a different person of the Trinity, could have been substituted for this. Then the conclusion emphasized the unity and the unified action of the three.

Another pastor gave a sermon in two parts. In one part, three chairs were placed on the platform, facing each other. The pastor then moved from one chair to another, presenting the respective roles and perspectives of each of the persons of the Godhead, with respect to the atoning death of Christ. In the other half of the message, separated from the first by music, three men appeared, wearing one large white robe that covered their entire bodies from neck to floor, and with three openings through which the three heads protruded. They engaged in discussion with one another regarding the incarnation, and decided together on the roles each would take. By linking these two parts of the message and these two images together, this pastor sought to emphasize both the oneness and the threeness, and to deal with the tendency, in our "unofficial theology," of being either modalistic unitarians or tritheists, or possibly, of alternating between them. In general, however, the imagery of personal relationships is not only more effective in helping the members of the audience understand the doctrine, but is also doubtless closer to the actual nature of the triunity than are illustrations drawn from the physical realm, such as ice, liquid water and steam, or an egg with yolk, white, and shell.

Modeling can be done as well. The way in which the person leading the congregation in corporate prayer addresses prayer to the Godhead is important. After one service in which I had attempted to offer thanksgiving in the prayer to each of the persons of the Trinity for what each had done respectively in the work of salvation, I had one parishioner come up to me following the service and say, "You prayed to just about everyone in that prayer. I've never heard anyone pray that way before." I almost asked why no one had prayed that way before, or why that seemed odd. It perhaps indicates that in practice we may, in our prayers, be practical Arians.

The educational program of the church can be utilized for teaching this important doctrine. This will, especially on the adult level, require some rethinking of the purpose and major subjects to be dealt with in the educational endeavor. Recently, much of this, whether in books or viewing and discussing of videos, has tended to center on matters of personal and social concern, such as child-rearing or self-esteem. There will need to be a swing back to greater emphasis on doctrinal beliefs, rather than on merely "felt needs." There can, however, be a demonstration that these doctrines have definite implications for the so-called practical areas. For example, creation and redemption by the Triune God are a powerful basis for self-esteem, issuing from an understanding of the worth of the believer in the sight of God.

It is with respect to younger persons, however, that the greatest potential exists. While it is difficult for young people to grasp the complexities of trinitarian doctrine, care can be exercised to avoid conveying misleading ideas, such as just "loving Jesus" or contrasting Jesus too strongly with "God." And more can be done to upgrade the level of the illustrations used to teach young people. Analogies drawn from the realm of human psychology may not only be more adequate as expressions of the nature of the Trinity, but may also be more easily understood and identified with by young persons.

Finally, we may help inculcate the doctrine of the Trinity and demonstrate its relevance by employing it as an underlying motivation for some of the practical dimensions of the Christian life. For example, the relationships of love, mutual submission, and honoring of one another, which characterize the persons of the Trinity, can be invoked when we exhort believers regarding their love for one another, or mutual concern and respect and support of one congregation or segment of society by another.

Scripture Index

Genesis

1:2   236, 277
1:26   167, 168
1:26–27   332, 338
1:27   168, 280, 333
2:24   174, 231
3:22   169
4:26   320
9:6   338
11:7   169
13:4   320
16:7, 9, 11   171
18:1   169
18: 2, 3, 4, 10, 13, 14, 16,
    17, 18, 19, 22   170
18:14   213
21:17   171
22:1, 11, 15, 16   172
22:11   171
22:15   53
24:7, 40   171
27:33–37   163
31:11   171
31:11–33   171
32:24–30   171
48:15–16   171

Exodus

3   209
3:2   171
3:2–6   172
3:4   171
3:6   61
3:14   209, 218
4:17   172
6:2   210

14:19   172
20:3   61, 173

Numbers

20:26   171
21:4–5   164
23:20–26   171
32:33–33:17   171
63:9   171

Deuteronomy

6   34
6:4   79, 174, 231
6:4–5   173
18:15   56
32:11–12   279
32:18   279

Joshua

5:13–6:2   171
7:5   164

Judges

2:1–5   171, 172
6:11–24   172
6:11–40   171
6:34   165–166
13:2–23   172
14:6, 19   166
15:14   166

1 Samuel

10:10   166
2 Samuel
19:14   165

2 Kings

2:29   164

Job

18:17–19   164
26:13   236
33:4   236

Psalms

2:7   53, 103, 305
17:8   279
26:2   163
33:6   43
33:6   47
36:7   279
57:1   279
91:1, 4   279
96:5   235
96:10   53
102:26–27   213
104:30   236
105:1   320
110:1   53
139:2–10   219
147:5   219

Proverbs

4:3   173
8:22–26   109
8:22–31   44, 77, 78, 81
8:23   306
15:3   219

Isaiah

6:3   97
6:8   170

Subject Index